# NORTH CAROLINA LAND GRANTS
### RECORDED IN
# GREENE COUNTY, TENNESSEE

Compiled by Goldene Fillers Burgner

*SOUTHERN HISTORICAL PRESS*
*%The Rev. S. Emmett Lucas, Jr.*
*P. O. Box 738*
*Easley, South Carolina   29640*

*ISBN   0-89308-204-X*

*Library of Congress Card Catalog Number:   81-50450*

# LAND GRANTS

In 1783 the State of North Carolina decided Washington District which extended as the present State of Tennessee to the Mississippi River. A line was surveyed beginning at William Williams' place on Horse Creek to the Mouth of Big Limestone, to Chimney Top Mountain to the mouth of Cloud's Creek on Holston River. All land south and west of this line was Greene County, North Carolina.

There was the l nd and the water, few trails and settlers were coming fast. Land was being taken fast for homes and farms, and large tracts for speculation. Surveying was inadequate, property lines overlapped but by 1800, after much despute and re-surveying, correct lines were established.

These grants do put the settlers in the general section which can be shown by the map of rivers.

I hope you enjoy this.

Goldene Fillers Burgner

vol.1 State of NC   1 - 46

BK I B        47- 93    ( State of Tn. Entries)
                 Small Entries

BK II  State of Franklin   9 3 - 9 6

BK III  NC Grants      96 -   146

BK IV              ?

BK V                        146- 160

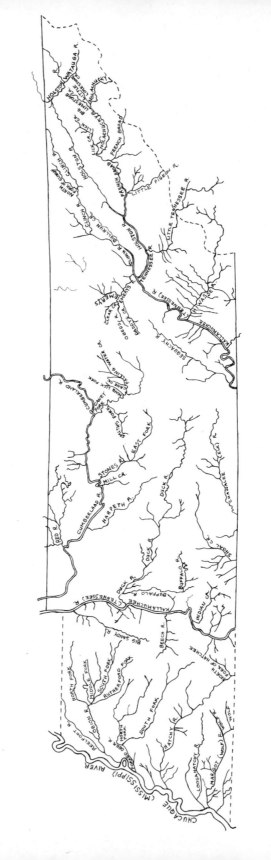

Greene (now Tennessee) was formed in 1783 from Washington (now Tennessee). Washington County was formed in 1777 from the District of Washington. It was roughly the territory west of Wilkes County, North Carolina, between Wilkes and the Virginia line, which had been allowed three representatives in the General Assembly of North Carolina in 1776.

Sullivan (now Tennessee) was formed in 1779 from Washington County. Part of Washington (Tennessee) was annexed to Wilkes County, North Carolina, in 1792.

This book contains approximately 2,000 land grants recorded in Greene County, Tennessee. Some of these grants were made by the U.S. Government to pay off debts to officers and soldiers who served in the Revolutionary War; some of the grants was  land owned and sold by Lord Granville; while other grants were issued by the states of North Carolina and Tennessee to encourage settlement in the new state of Tennessee. All grants had to be registered by the claimant in order for his grant to be legal. Not only do we see grants issued by the states as described above, but these also contain deeds between persons for which some obligation had been undertaken. The land grants in Tennessee issued by the federal government to officers and soldiers in the Continental Line had to be entered in the county within 12 months, while these grants recorded in Greene County like later deeds had to be registered, but there was no proscribed period from the date of issue to the date of registration.

## TENNESSEE

TENNESSEE.
AT THE BEGINNING OF
1790
Showing Approximate County Divisions
within Present State Boundaries

No. 1     Page 1
State of North Carolina to General N. Greene in accord with an act for
relief of officers and soldiers in the Continental line, a tract of
25,000 acres in Greene County, on south side of Duck River.  Sealed by
Alexander Martin, Esq., our governor, captain-general, and commander-
in-chief at Danbury, March 1, 1785, J. Glasgow, secretary by his excel-
lency's command.
Commissioner's office at French Lick - above surveyed by Daniel Smith.


No. 3     Page 2
North Carolina Military grant to David Wilson 2,000 acres in Greene
County in middle district of western lands on Cany Spring Creek on
north side of Duck River.  Sealed by Alexander Martin at Newbern,
November 19, 1784.
Surveyed by David Wilson February 28, 1784.  Witnesses: Joseph Kerr,
Ebenezer Alexander, R. Teakley.


No. 367     Page 3
For 50 shillings per 100 acres, to William Ritchey 150 acres in Washington County on east side of Lick Creek near the warpath.  Sealed by
Alexander Martin at Hillsborough October 13, 1783.  Surveyed January 13,
1782.


No. 385     Page 4
For 50 shillings per 100 acres, to Isaac Odle 300 acres in Washington
County on branch of Lick Creek adjoining John Tye, John Newman, Joseph
Henderson, Joseph Hacker.  Sealed by Alexander Martin at Hillsboro
October 13, 1783.  Recorded by M. Phillips, sec.


No. 429     Page 5
For 50 shillings per 100 acres, to William Ritchey 200 acres in Washington County on west side of Lick Creek near the war road.  Sealed by
Alexander Martin at Hillsboro October 13, 1783.  Surveyed February 13,
1782 by James Stuart.


No. 638     Page 6
For 50 shillings per 100 acres to Richard Condrey 100 acres in Washington
County on the Christians War Road between George Martin and Garrett Vin-
cent.  Sealed by Alexander Martin at Newbern, November 10, 1784.


No. 516     Page 7
For 50 shillings per 100 acres, to John Houser 200 acres in Washington
County on branches of Lick Creek between Benjamin Pibourne and John
Howard.  Sealed by Alexander Martin November 10, 1784.


No. 368     Page 8
For 50 shillings per 100 acres, to William Berry 25 acres in Washington
County on the mill fork of Big Limestone on the west side of Daniel
Kennedy.  Sealed by Alexander Martin at Hillsboro October 15, 1783.


No. 401     Page 8
For 50 shillings per 100 acres, to William Berry 150 acres in Washington
County on head of Sinking Creek between John Morrels and Asahel Rawlings.
Sealed by Alex. Martin at Hillsboro October 13, 1783.

No. 464    Page 9
For 50 shillings per 100 acres, to William Berry 150 acres in Washington
County at head of Sinking Creek between John Morrel and Asahel Rawlings
Sealed by Alex. Martin at Hillsboro October 13, 1783.


No. 654    Page 10
For 50 shillings per 100 acres, to William Prewitt 150 acres in Washington County on Lick Creek including said Prewitt's improvement. Sealed
by Alex Martin at Newbern November 10, 1784.


No. 491    Page 11
For 50 shillings per 100 acres, to Asahel Rawlings 121 1/4 acres in
Washington County on Lick Creek between Archibald Sloan and the Walnut
Valley, and land of William Ritchey, south of Sloan. Sealed at Newbern
November 10, 1784.


No. 565    Page 12
For 50 shillings per 100 acres, to Asahel Rawlings 30 acres in Washing-
ton County adjacent to the south side of Sloan. Sealed at Newbern,
November 10, 1784.


No. 355    Page 13
For 50 shillings per 100 acres, to Daniel Rawlings 200 acres in Washington County on west side of Lick Creek and a creek called Plumb Creek, on
each side of the War Path. Sealed at Hillsboro, October 13, 1783.


No. 356    Page 13
For 50 shillings per 100 acres, to Andrew Reed 100 acres in Washington
County on Cedar Fork of Lick Creek including a large fall on said fork.
Sealed at Hillsboro, October 13, 1783.


No. 103    Page 14
For 2 pounds per 100 acres, to Henry Conway 600 acres in Greene County
on north side of Nolichuckey River, bounded by Ray, Leeper. Sealed by
Richard Caswell at Kinston, November 1, 1786.


No. 122    Page 15
For 10 pounds per 100 acres, to William Conway 600 acres in Greene County
on north side of Nolichuckey River at the nob below the mouth of Lick
Creek. Sealed at Kinston, November 1, 1786.


No. 88    Page 16
For 2 pounds per 100 acres, to Garret Fitzgerald 600 acres in Greene
County on north side of the French Broad River beginning at the mouth
of a gut on the bank of the river on David Hayley's line, and Acquila
Lane's line. Sealed by Richard Caswell.


No. 42    Page 17
For 10 pounds per 100 acres, to Garret Fitzgerald 300 acres in Greene
County on north side of French Broad River. Sealed by Richard Caswell,
November 1, 1786.


No. 142    Page 18
For 10 pounds per 100 acres, to Garret Fitzgerald 150 acres in Greene
County on south side of Nolichuckey River. Sealed by Richard Caswell
at Kinston, November 1, 1786.


No. 105    Page 19
For 10 pounds per 100 acres, to William McGaughey 100 acres in Greene

County. Sealed at Kinston, November 1, 1786.


No. 22     Page 19
For 10 pounds per 100 acres, to James Hubbart 1000 acres in Greene County
on north side of Tennessee River a half mile below Shelby's encamping
ground when going to Chickamauga town. Sealed at Kinston, November 1,
1786.


No. 97     Page 20
For 10 pounds per 100 acres, to James Hubbart 600 acres in Greene County
on an island in French Broad River known as Hubbert's Island, bounded by
Wilcock. Sealed by Richard Caswell at Kinston, November 1, 1786.


No. 47     Page 21
For 2 pounds per 100 acres, to James Hubbert and William Terrel Lewis
600 acres in Greene County on north side of French Broad River, including mouth of Copelings Creek, bounded by James Randall. Sealed by
Richard Caswell at Kinston, November 1, 1786.


No. 94     Page 22
For 2 pounds per 100 acres to John Smith 500 acres in Greene County on
Robertson's Creek on south side of Holston River known by name of the
Grapy Springs. Sealed by Richard Caswell at Kinston, November 1, 1786.


No. 85     Page 22
For 10 pounds per 100 acres, to John Smith 300 acres in Greene County on
north side of Nolichuckey River on a fork of Bent Creek called the White
Horn, bounded by Abraham Chapman. Sealed by Richard Caswell at Kinston,
November 1, 1786.


No. 111     Page 23
For 10 pounds per 100 acres, to James Hubbard 400 acres in Greene County
on north side of French Broad River, bounded by Silas George. Sealed by
Richard Caswell at Kinston, November 1, 1786.


No. 100     Page 24
For 10 pounds per 100 acres, to James Hubbert 400 acres in Greene County
on north side of French Broad River. Sealed by Richard Caswell at
Kinston, November 1, 1786. Recorded by G. W. Sheppard, sec.


No. 29     Page 25
For 10 pounds per 100 acres, to James Walker 200 acres in Greene County
on north side of French Broad River bounded by Williams, Tate. Sealed
by Richard Caswell at Kinston, November 1, 1786. Recorded by C. Mark-
land, Jr., sec.


No. 66     Page 25
For 10 pounds per 100 acres, to William Rainy 300 acres in Greene County
on north side of the French Broad River. Sealed by Richard Caswell at
Kinston, November 1, 1786.


No. 70     Page 26
For 10 pounds per 100 acres, to James Houston 200 acres in Greene County
on north side of Nolichuckey River on Richland Creek, on east side of
Creek, bounded by Andrew McPheron, Henry Farnsworth. Sealed by Richard
Caswell at Kinston, November 1, 1786.


No. 84     Page 27
For 10 pounds per 100 acres, to Joseph Lusk 200 acres in Greene County

bounded by Solomon Ree, Joseph Gist. Sealed by Richard Caswell at
Kinston November 1, 1786.


No. 61      Page 28
For 10 pounds per 100 acres, to William Reed 100 acres in Greene County
on waters of Little Chuckey, bounded by Samuel Nance, Charles Lowery.
Sealed by Richard Caswell at Kinston, November 1, 1786.


No. 477     Page 29
For 10 pounds per 100 acres, to Aron Lewis 146 acres in Washington County
on east end of the Cedar Spring survey which belongs to said Lewis,
bounded by Charles Hay. Sealed by Alexander Martin at Newbern, November
10, 1784.


No. 508     Page 29
For 50 shillings per 100 acres, to Aron Lewis 100 acres in Washington
County on both sides of Lick Creek, joining James English's upper survey.
Sealed by Alex. Martin at Newbern, November 10, 1784.


No. 476     Page 30
For 50 shillings per 100 acres, to Aron Lewis 100 acres in Washington
County on both sides of Limestone Fork of Lick Creek, bounded by James
English's middle survey, crosses Big Spring branch. Sealed by Alexander
Martin at Newbern, November 10, 1784.


No. 473     Page 31
For 50 shillings per 100 acres, to Aron Lewis 200 acres in Washington
County adjoining former survey. Sealed by Alex. Martin at Newbern,
November 10, 1784.


No. 479     Page 31
For 50 shillings per 100 acres, to Aron Lewis 150 acres in Washington
County on north side of Limestone Fork of Lick Creek, joining James
English. Sealed by Alexander Martin at Newbern, November 10, 1784.


No. 28      Page 31
For 50 shillings per 100 acres, to Robert Kerr 300 acres in Greene County
joining spring boundary with Robert Hood, Andrew McFeron, James Lusk,
Davis Copeland. Sealed by Richard Caswell at Kinston, November 1, 1787.


No. 136     Page 33
For 10 pounds per 100 acres, to Hugh McClung 800 acres in Greene County
on north side of Tennessee River beginning at upper end of the forth
large bottom on the said Tennessee River below the mouth of Highwassa
(sic) River. Sealed by Richard Caswell at Kinston, November 1, 1786.


No. 60      Page 34
For 10 pounds per 100 acres to Annaniaz McCoy 500 acres in Greene County
on north side of Tennessee River. Sealed by Richard Caswell at Kinston,
November 1, 1786.


No. 86      Page 34
For 10 pounds per 100 acres, to Annanias McCoy 500 acres in Greene County
on north side of Tennessee River adjoining former survey. Sealed by
Richard Caswell at Kinston, November 1, 1786.


No. 54      Page 35
For 50 shillings per 100 acres, to Joseph Hixon 100 acres in Greene
County. Sealed by Richard Caswell at Kinston, November 1, 1786.

No. 119     Page 36
For 10 pounds per 100 acres, to John Hackett 253 acres in Greene County
on north side of Tennessee River being the second small bottom below
McClung's 800 acre entry.  Sealed by Richard Caswell at Kinston,
November 1, 1786.


No. 16     Page 37
For 10 pounds per 100 acres, to Silas George 150 acres in Greene County
on north side of French Broad River bounding James Hubbert.  Sealed by
Richard Caswell at Kinston, November 1, 1786.


No. 659     Page 37
For 50 shillings per 100 acres, to Henry Earnest 600 acres in Washington
County on south side of Nolichuckey River, bounded by Alexander Erwin.
Sealed by Alexander Martin at Newbern, November 10, 1784.


No. 106     Page 38
For 10 pounds per 100 acres, to James Hays 30 acres in Greene County on
Limestone Fork of Lick Creek, bounded by James English.  Sealed by
Richard Caswell at Kinston, November 1, 1786.


No. 618     Page 39
For 50 shillings per 100 acres, to Hugh Beard (Baird) 150 acres in
Washington County bounded by Emanuel Sedusky, crossing Horse Creek, and
joining William English.  Sealed by Alexander Martin at Kinston, November
1, 1786.


No. 124     Page 39
For 10 pounds per 100 acres, to Samuel Nance 250 acres in Greene County
on Little Chuckey, bounded by Frank Hamilton, Solomon Reed, Robert Lowery,
Reaves.  Sealed by Richard Caswell in Kinston, November 1, 1786.


No. 128     Page 40
For 10 pounds per 100 acres, to Alexander Kelley 500 acres in Greene
County on south side of Nolichuckey River, joining John Trimble, a wagon
road, John Chamberlain.  Sealed by Richard Caswell at Kinston, November
1, 1786.


No. 166     Page 41
For 50 shillings per 100 acres, to Henry Earnest 45 acres in Washington
County on north side of Nolichuckey River beginning at the river to a
mulberry in a small cane brake, thence south to a beach on the bank of
the river.  Sealed by Alexander Martin at Fairfield, October 24, 1782.


No. 25     Page 41
For 50 shillings per 100 acres, to James Delaney 100 acres in Washington
County on Holley's Creek, a branch of Nolichuckey River.  Sealed by
Alexander Martin at Fairfield, October 23, 1782.


No. 235     Page 42
For 50 shillings per 100 acres, to Alexander McFarlin 300 acres in
Washington County at the big spring on north side of Sinking Creek, and
adjoining Crow and Graham.  Sealed by Alexander Martin at Fairfield,
October 24, 1782.


No. 136     Page 43
For 50 shillings per 100 acres, to James Delaney 100 acres in Washington
County on Sider (Seder) Branch.  Sealed by Alexander Martin at Fairfield,
October 24, 1782.

No. 379　　　Page 43
For 50 shillings per 100 acres, to Francis Hues 300 acres in Washington
County on Camp Creek, joining Robert Culwell, Isaac Taylor, east side of
Camp Creek, Samuel Begham's spring, Nance, Nolichuckey River.


No. 351　　　Page 44
For 50 shillings per 100 acres, to Charles Hayz (sic) 200 acres in
Washington County on both sides Lick Creek at mouth of Raccoon Branch.
Sealed by Alexander Martin at Hillsboro, October 13, 1783.


No. 391　　　Page 45
For 50 shillings per 100 acres, to William Bigham 600 acres in Washing-
ton County on north side of Nolichuckey River, bounded by Thomas
Gillispie, to north side of Middle Creek, Hues's line, Gillispie.
Sealed by Alexander Martin at Hillsboro, October 13, 1783.


No. 386　　　Page 45
For 50 shillings per 100 acres, to William Whitesides 148 acres in
Washington County on branch of Lick Creek, joining Nathan Tracy.
Sealed by Alexander Martin at Hillsboro, October 13, 1783.


No. 156　　　Page 46
For 50 shillings per 100 acres, to David Campbell 200 acres in Washing-
ton County at head of Story's (Stone's?) Creek, joining David Rankin.
Sealed by Alexander Martin at Hillsboro, October 13, 1783.


No. 424　　　Page 47
For 50 shillings per 100 acres, to David Campbell 200 acres in Washing-
ton County on Reedy Fork of Sinking Creek, joining Anthony Moore, John
Delaney. Sealed by Alexander Martin at Hillsboro, October 13, 1783.


No. 91　　　Page 47
For 10 pounds per 100 acres, to David Taylor 200 acres in Greene County
on north side of Nolichuckey River, including saltpeter spring nearly
opposite the lower end of the island. Sealed by Caswell, November 1,
1786.


No. 109　　　Page 48
For 2 pounds per 100 acres, to Francis Alexander Ramsay 200 acres in
Greene County upon water of the Holston River including the swan pawn
(sic). Sealed by Caswell, November 1, 1786.


No. 110　　　Page 48
For 10 pounds per 100 acres, to Francis Alexander Ramsay 300 acres in
Greene County joining 200 acres including the swan pawn. Sealed by
Caswell, November 1, 1786.


No. 19　　　Page 49
For 10 pounds per 100 acres, to Francis Alexander Ramsay 400 acres in
Greene County on Conner's Mill Creek, where said creek rises after it
sinks. Sealed by Caswell, November 1, 1786.


No. 36　　　Page 49
For 2 pounds per 100 acres, to Francis Alexander Ramsay 200 acres in
Greene County in Conner's Mill Valley, joining Ananias McCoy, Josiah
Martin. Sealed by Caswell, November 1, 1786.


No. 71　　　Page 50
For 50 shillings per 100 acres, to Francis Alexander Ramsay 300 acres

in Greene County on Dumplin Creek, joining Thomas Gillespie. Sealed by Caswell, November 1, 1786.

No. 77        Page 51
For 10 pounds per 100 acres, to George Gilespy 50 acres in Greene County on McCartney's Branch, joining McCartney. Sealed by Caswell, November 1, 1786.

No. 45        Page 51
For 50 shillings per 100 acres, to Thomas Gilespie 200 acres in Greene County on Nolichuckey River, opposite mouth of Camp Creek, on Bucking-ham's line. Sealed by Caswell, November 1, 1786.

No. 48        Page 51
For 10 pounds per 100 acres, to George Gilespie 200 acres in Greene County on north side of Lick Creek, by Samuel Bowman, to Little Gap Creek, to Lick Creek. Sealed by Caswell, November 1, 1786.

No. 20        Page 52
For 10 pounds per 100 acres, to George Gilespy 200 acres in Greene County on north side of Nolichuckey River, joining former survey opposite mouth of Camp Creek. Sealed by Caswell, November 1, 1786.

No. 125        Page 53
For 10 pounds per 100 acres, to Jeremiah Jack 300 acres in Greene County on south side of Nolichuckey River, along line with Henry Willie called Craven Lands, Jamey Johnston, and a barren flat on east side of Plumb Branch. Sealed by Caswell, November 1, 1786.

No. 170        Page 54
For 10 pounds per 100 acres, to Thomas Gilespie in Washington County, 150 acres. Sealed by Caswell, November 1, 1786.

No. 138        Page 54
For 10 pounds per 100 acres, to James Ashmore 300 acres in Greene County on both sides of Lick Creek, joinind by Hezekiah Ashmore, James Steven-son. Sealed by Caswell, November 1, 1786.

No. 62        Page 55
For 2 pounds per 100 acres, to William Reed 100 acres in Greene County on waters of Little Chuckey, by Samuel Nance, Charles Lowry. Sealed by Caswell, November 1, 1786.

No. 21        Page 56
For 10 pounds per 100 acres, to William Nielson 300 acres in Greene County at lower end of a cane bottom running up a creek called Oven Creek, by Mathew Pates. Sealed by Caswell, November 1, 1786.

No. 56        Page 56
For 10 pounds per 100 acres, to William Nielson in Greene County, 640 acres on south side of Nolichuckey River. Sealed by Caswell, November 1, 1786.

No. 10        Page 57
For 10 pounds per 100 acres, to Alexander Outlaw 5000 acres in Greene County on north side of Tennessee River by Isaac Taylor, "under a cleft of rock on the lower end of a large cane brake, to a stake above the fork of the Tennessee and Holston Rivers." Sealed by Caswell, November 1, 1786.

No. 7        Page 58
For 10 pounds per 100 acres, to Alexander Outlaw 640 acres in Greene
County on north side of Nolichuckey River at Christians old camps,
including 4 small islands in said river.  Sealed by Caswell, July 15,
1786.


No. 6        Page 58
For 10 pounds per 100 acres, to Alexander Outlaw 140 acres in Greene
County on south side of Nolichuckey River.  Sealed by Caswell, July 15,
1786.


No. 15       Page 59
For 2 pounds per 100 acres, to Alexander Outlaw 400 acres in Greene
County on both sides of Bent Creek, "by tree marked by James Gailey Reed,
including Reed's former improvement and Galey's Place where he now lives
for a compliment. . . by John Howard, Henry Spears.  Sealed by Caswell,
November 1, 1786.


No. 9        Page 60
For 10 pounds per 100 acres, to Alexander Outlaw 640 acres in Greene
County on north side of Nolichuckey River including mouth of Bent Creek,
by David Campbell, Evans, Holoway.  Sealed by Caswell, November 1, 1786.


No. 4        Page 60
For 10 pounds per 100 acres, to Martin Canswell, 630 acres in Greene
County on north side of Nolichuckey River, by David Campbell, Alexander
Outlaw, John Hill.  Sealed by Caswell, July 15, 1786.


No. 8        Page 61
For 10 pounds per 100 acres, to John Hermitage 640 acres in Greene County
on north side of Nolichuckey River joining Martin Caswell, below the mouth
of Flat Creek.  Sealed by Caswell, July 15, 1786.


No. 44       Page 62
For 10 pounds per 100 acres, to Alexander Outlaw 640 acres in Greene
County on Holston River at upper side of a rocky ridge on south side of
the river, to a stake on an island in said river, by David Campbell's
line.  Sealed by Caswell, November 1, 1786.


No. 116      Page 62
For 10 pounds per 100 acres, to David Kerr 150 acres in Greene County on
north side of Nolichuckey River, joining John Ramsay, Henry Conway, including part of an island in the river.  Sealed by Caswell, November 1,
1786.


No. 89       Page 63
For 10 pounds per 100 acres, to James Ashmore 300 acres in Greene County
on Lick Creek near the mouth of the creek, joined by Hezekiah Ashmore,
William Tipton.  Sealed by Caswell, November 1, 1786.


No. 12       Page 63
For 10 pounds per 100 acres, to Charles Hodges 450 acres in Greene County
on Bent Creek "upon a ridge above the war path", joining Alexander Outlaw.
Sealed by Caswell, November 1, 1786.


No. 80       Page 64
For 10 pounds per 100 acres, to James Hill 400 acres in Greene County on
north side of Nolichuckey River, by Gideon Richey, "to a long beach on
the river bank."  Sealed by Caswell, November 1, 1786.

No. 117      Page 65
For 10 pounds per 100 acres, to James Hill 78 acres in Greene County on an island in Nolichuckey River near mouth of said river. Sealed by Caswell, November 1, 1786.


No. 25      Page 65
For 10 pounds per 100 acres, to Andrew Henderson 236 1/2 acres in Greene County on north side of French Broad River. Sealed by Caswell, November 1, 1786.


No. 93      Page 66
For 10 pounds per 100 acres, to Richard Woods 150 acres in Greene County on Cedar Creek branch of Holston River by McCamish, Copeland. Sealed by Caswell, November 1, 1786.


No. 51      Page 67
For 10 pounds per 100 acres, to Thomas Joniken 200 acres in Greene County on north side of Nolichuckey River by James Hill. Sealed by Caswell, November 1, 1786.


No. 58      Page 67
For 10 pounds per 100 acres, to Thomas Jonaken 640 acres in Greene County on Nolichuckey River, "above the mouth of a small hollow". Sealed by Caswell, November 1, 1786.


No. 87      Page 68
For 10 pounds per 100 acres, to Thomas Joniken 1000 acres in Greene County on south side of Holston River, the Shimney Rock bottom, joining Webster. Sealed by Caswell, November 1, 1786.


No. 39      Page 69
For 10 pounds per 100 acres, to Elijah Witt 200 acres in Greene County on branch of Long Creek, joining John Patterson. Sealed by Caswell, November 1, 1786.


No. 99      Page 69
For 10 pounds per 100 acres, to Elijah Witt 200 acres in Greene County on north side of Nolichuckey River on Long Creek, and both sides of said creek, beginning at a white oak at the lower end of the bottom below the war ford on the east side of the creek", . . . . then crossing the wagon road. Sealed by Caswell, November 1, 1786.


No. 74      Page 70
For 10 pounds per 100 acres, to Aquilla Lane 240 acres in Greene County on the north side of the French Broad River, joining "Garrett Fitzgerald opposite to the ten islands in said river", and joining Robert Lamb. Sealed by Caswell, November 1, 1786.


No. 84      Page 71
For 10 pounds per 100 acres, to Joseph Lusk 200 acres in Greene County by Solomon Reed and Joseph Gist. Sealed by Caswell, November 1, 1786.


No. 135      Page 71
For 10 pounds per 100 acres, to Henry Farnsworth 655 acres in Greene County upon "Richland Creek, beginning at a beach and 2 small dogwoods on the south side of the creek, then on along James Houston's line, crossing the creek . . . to 2 post oaks in a large barren, then south along James Gibson's line, crossing a small branch, to 2 post oaks on the spur of a nob, then south along Graham's and McCahan's line . . . to a black oak on top of a ridge, then north to the beginning." Sealed

by Caswell, November 1, 1786.

No. 118    Page 72
For 10 pounds per 100 acres, to Caleb Witt 100 acres in Greene County on a branch of Long Creek, joining Thomas Cannon, John Lyne, George Eager. Sealed by Caswell, November 1, 1786.

No. 133    Page 73
For 10 pounds per 100 acres, to Joseph Dunham 500 acres in Greene County on north side of Nolichuckey River by John Stone. Sealed by Caswell, November 1, 1786.

No. 79    Page 73
For 10 pounds per 100 acres, to Jeremiah Chamberlain 1000 acres in Greene County on north side of Holston River on Flat Creek, by a spur of House Mountain. Sealed by Caswell, November 1, 1786.

No. 82    Page 74
For 10 pounds per 100 acres, to Jeremiah Chamberlain 400 acres in Greene County joining Copeland, Johnston. Sealed by Caswell, November 1, 1786.

No. 61    Page 75
For 10 pounds per 100 acres, to Joseph Witt 160 acres in Greene County on French Broad River. Sealed by Caswell, November 1, 1786.

No. 81    Page 75
For 10 pounds per 100 acres, to Nenian Chamberlain 500 acres in Greene County on north side of Holston River on east fork of Flat Creek. Sealed by Caswell, November, 1786.

No. 98    Page 76
For 10 pounds per 100 acres, to John Chamberlain 150 acres in Greene County joined by John Trimble, Kelley, John McKinney. Sealed by Caswell, November 1, 1786.

No. 35    Page 77
For 10 pounds per 100 acres, to Andrew Chamberlain 3750 acres in Greene County on north side of Holston River on Richland Creek, west along Thomas Jonagon, thense along spurs of Clinch Mountain, north to Garrett Fitzgerald's line, then north to foot of the mountain, then along spurs of Clinch Mountain north, then east to the Dividing Ridge, thence along foot of Dividing Ridge between waters of Holston River and Richland Creek south. Sealed by Caswell, November 1, 1786.

No. 38    Page 78
For 10 pounds per 100 acres, to John Woods 1820 acres in Greene County on north side of Holston River by Archibald Sloans. Sealed by Caswell, November 1, 1786.

No. 112    Page 78
For 10 pounds per 100 acres, to John Balch 200 acres in Greene County on north side of French Broad River. Sealed by Caswell, November 1, 1786.

No. 120    Page 79
For 10 pounds per 100 acres, to Amos Balch 400 acres in Greene County on Long Creek joined by John Fenton, Andrew McDhinen. Sealed by Caswell, November 1, 1786.

No. 42      Page 80
For 10 pounds per 100 acres, to Garrett Fitzgerald 300 acres in Greene
County on north side of French Broad River. Sealed by Caswell, November
1, 1786.


No. 88      Page 80
For 10 pounds per 100 acres, to Garrett Fitzgerald 600 acres in Greene
County on north side of French Broad River joining David Hayley and
Acquilla Land. Sealed by Caswell, November 1, 1786.


No. 453     Page 81
For 10 pounds per 100 acres, to John McAdow 95 acres in Washington County
on Dry Valley. Sealed by Alexander Martin at Hillsboro, October 13, 1783.


No. 132     Page 81
For 10 pounds per 100 acres, to John Murfy 640 acres in Greene County on
both sides of Lick Creek at mouth of Wolf Creek, "by a white oak branded
E.C.", and joining William Hodges. Sealed by Caswell, November 1, 1786.


No. 27      Page 82
For 10 pounds per 100 acres, to Isaac Taylor 600 acres in Greene County
on south side of the Holston River below the mouth of Beaver Dam Creek.
Sealed by Caswell, November 1, 1786.


No. 53      Page 83
For 10 pounds per 100 acres, to Isaac Taylor 100 acres in Greene County
on south side of Clear Creek, joined by Bigham, Nicholas Neal. Sealed
by Caswell, November 1, 1786.


No. 55      Page 83
For 10 pounds per 100 acres, to Isaac Taylor 200 acres in Greene County
on a branch of the French Broad River, joining James Gibson. Sealed by
Caswell, November 1, 1786.


No. 75      Page 84
For 10 pounds per 100 acres, to Isaac Taylor 200 acres in Greene County
on the north side of Tennessee River. Sealed by Caswell, November 1,
1786.


No. 113     Page 84
For 10 pounds per 100 acres, to Isaac Taylor 4000 acres in Greene County
"on the north side of Tennessee River including the Pleasant Garden", to
Swift Creek, to Turkey Creek, "including the folks of Swift Creek and
Turkey Creek." Sealed by Caswell, November 1, 1786.


No. 108     Page 85
For 10 pounds per 100 acres, to Andrew Kerr 5000 acres in Greene County
on north side of Tennessee River on Swift Creek, joined by Joseph Harden.
Sealed by Caswell, November 1, 1786.


No. 23      Page 85
For 10 pounds per 100 acres, to Thomas Gilespie 200 acres in Greene
County on Dumplin Creek, joined by William Henry. Sealed by Caswell,
November 1, 1786.


No. 13      Page 86
For 10 pounds per 100 acres, to David Steward and Adam Wilson 420 acres
in Greene County on north side of Holston River between head of German
Creek and Doon Valley, joined by Thomas Henderson, William Daterson.

Sealed by Caswell, November 1, 1786.

No. 52      Page 86
For 10 pounds per 100 acres, to David Steward 400 acres in Greene County
on north side of the Tennessee River. Sealed by Caswell, November 1,
1786.

No. 59      Page 87
For 10 pounds per 100 acres, to David Steward 400 acres in Greene County
on north side of Tennessee River. Sealed by Caswell, November 1, 1786.

No. 33      Page 88
For 10 pounds per 100 acres to Samuel Dunwoody 300 acres in Greene County
on Delaney Creek, joined by Benjamin Delaney. Sealed by Caswell, November
1, 1786.

No. 31      Page 88
For 10 pounds per 100 acres, to Nicholas Neal 200 acres in Greene County
on Clear Creek, joined by Isaac Taylor, Baskin. Sealed by Caswell,
November 1, 1786.

No. 64      Page 89
For 10 pounds per 100 acres, to Abraham Swaggerty 200 acres in Greene
County on Clear Creek waters of the French Broad River below James Cosby,
and joined by John Parrot. Sealed by Caswell, November 1, 1786.

No. 129      Page 89
For 10 pounds per 100 acres, to Abraham Swaggerty 300 acres in Greene
County on Clear Creek by McConnell. Sealed by Caswell, November 1, 1786.

No. 127      Page 90
For 10 pounds per 100 acres, to Frederick Swagerty 400 acres in Greene
County on Clear Creek on northeast side of the French Broad River,
joining Swagerty's upper survey, and Abraham Swagerty. Sealed by
Caswell, November 1, 1786.

No. 139      Page 90
For 10 pounds per 100 acres, to Frederick Swagerty 200 acres in Greene
County on a bank of the French Broad River, joined by Walker, Anderson.
Sealed by Caswell, November 1, 1786.

No. 142      Page 91
For 10 pounds per 100 acres, to Garrett Fitzgerald 150 acres in Greene
County on north side of Nolichuckey River. Sealed by Caswell, November
1, 1786.

No. 37      Page 92
For 50 shillings per 100 acres, to John Crow 150 acres in Greene County
on Licking Creek, by Nicholas Hayes. Sealed by Caswell, November 1, 1786.

No. 101      Page 92
For 50 shillings per 100 acres, to John Crowe 300 acres in Greene County
on both sides of Sinking Creek. Sealed by Caswell, November 1, 1786.

No. 231      Page 93
For 10 pounds per 100 acres, to William Johnston 150 acres in Greene
County on Moss Creek. Sealed by Caswell, September 20, 1787.

No. 153     Page 93
For 10 pounds per 100 acres, to William Robertson 478 acres in Greene
County on the north side of the Holston River on Big Creek above
Christopher Taylor's land.  Sealed by Caswell, September 20, 1787.


No. 178     Page 94
For 10 pounds per 100 acres, to Shaderick Inman 200 acres in Greene
County on north side of Nolichuckey River by John Heritage.  Sealed
by Caswell, September 20, 1787.


No. 40     Page 95
For 10 pounds per 100 acres, to Anthony Moore 100 acres in Greene County
on head of Stoney Creek, a stake near foot of Bear Nob.  Sealed by Caswell, November 1, 1787.


No. 200     Page 95
For 10 pounds per 100 acres, to Robert Hood 175 acres in Greene County.
Sealed by Caswell, September 20, 1787.


No. 68     Page 96
For 50 shillings per 100 acres, to Major Temple 240 acres in Greene
County on a branch of Richland Creek joined by Whittenberger.  Sealed
by Caswell, November 1, 1786.


No. 50     Page 96
For 10 pounds per 100 acres, to William Wilcockson 150 acres in Greene
County on the waters of Dumplen Creek.  Sealed by Caswell, November 1,
1786.


No. 119     Page 97
For 10 pounds per 100 acres, to John Hackett 255 acres in Greene County
on north side of Tennessee River "being the second small bottom below
McClung's 800 acre entry."  Sealed by Caswell, November 1, 1786.


No. 60     Page 98
For 10 pounds per 100 acres, to Ananias McCoy 500 acres in Greene County
on north side of Tennessee River.  Sealed by Caswell, November 1, 1786.


No. 86     Page 98
For 10 pounds per 100 acres, to Ananias McCoy 500 acres in Greene County
on north side of Tennessee River adjoining other survey.  Sealed by
Caswell, November 1, 1786.


No. 136     Page 99
For 10 pounds per 100 acres, to Hugh McClung 800 acres in Greene County
on north side of Tennessee River "beginning at the upper end of the
fourth large bottom on the Tennessee River below the mouth of Highwassee
(sic) River".  Sealed by Caswell, November 1, 1786.


No. 659     Page 100
For 50 shillings per 100 acres, to Henry Arnest (Earnest) 600 acres in
Washington County on south side of Nolichuckey River, joined by Alexander
Ervin.  Sealed by Alexander Martin at Newbern, November 10, 1784.


No. 466     Page 101
For 50 shillings per 100 acres, to John Delaney 400 acres in Washington
County on Sinking Creek, joined by Jacob Smiley.  Sealed by Alexander
Martin at Hillsboro, October 13, 1783.

No. 72       Page 101
For 10 pounds per 100 acres, to Robert Armstrong 300 acres in Greene
County on south side of Nolichuckey River joined by Robert McFarlin.
Sealed by Caswell, November 1, 1786.


No. 644      Page 102
For 50 shillings per 100 acres, to Thomas West 85 acres in Washington
County joining James Rodgers and Owen Owens. Sealed by Alexander Martin
at Newbern, November 10, 1784.


No. 606      Page 103
For 50 shillings per 100 acres, to Absalom Hayworth 150 acres in Washington County on west side of Moore's land, joining Moore, McAdow. Sealed
by Alexander Martin at Newbern, November 10, 1784.


No. 543      Page 103
For 50 shillings per 100 acres, to Samuel Moore 150 acres in Washington
County near head of Little Sinking Creek, on south side of McCartney Nob
towards Brown's Creek, joining Moore's other survey, John Gilliham.
Sealed by Alexander Martin at Newbern, November 10, 1784.


No. 90       Page 104
For 10 pounds per 100 acres, to Amos Bird 400 acres in Greene County on
north side of Nolichuckey River, joined by William White. Sealed by
Caswell, November 1, 1786.


No. ___      Page 105
Military grant to David Wilson, 2000 acres in Greene County in the
middle district of the western lands on Cany Spring Creek on north side
of Duck River. Sealed by Alexander Martin at Newbern, November 19, 1784.


No. 145      Page 106
For 10 pounds per 100 acres, to Harwood Jones 2500 acres in Greene County
on Mossy Creek a branch of Holston River "near Lost Creek Path", joined
by William Johnston, Big Spring Branch, James Willis. Sealed by Caswell,
April 23, 1787.


No. 96       Page 107
For 10 pounds per 100 acres, to Hezekiah Balch 250 acres in Greene County
on branch of Richland Creek, by McRay, Major Temple. R.D., 11/1/1786.


No. 170      Page 107
For 50 shillings per 100 acres, to Joseph Eaton 200 acres in Greene
County on Miry Branch by Thomas Mitchel, Roberts, Charles Dotson.
R.C. 11/1/1786.


No. 63       Page 108
For 10 pounds per 100 acres, to James Allison 222 acres in Greene County
"on Dumplin Creek, the waters of the north side of the French Broad
River, beginning above the mouth of Cedar Branch, running down the creek
and including a beaver dam." Sealed by Richard Caswell, September 20,
1787.


No. 252      Page 109
For 10 pounds per 100 acres, to Joseph Eaten 200 acres in Greene County
on north side of the Holston River below the Sulphur Spring Branch, by
Chamberlain. Sealed by Richard Caswell, September 20, 1787.

No. 110    Page 110
For 50 shillings per 100 acres, to Joseph Eaten 200 acres in Greene
County on the Miry Branch by Thomas Mitchell, Roberts. Sealed by
Richard Caswell, September 20, 1787.


Numbers 63 and 252 are duplicated on page 111 of the Deed Book.


No. 191    Page 110
For 10 pounds per 100 acres, to Joseph McRandall 130 acres in Greene
County on north side of Nolichuckey River by Ebinezar Byram, Joseph Gest,
Joseph Lusk. Sealed by Richard Caswell, September 20, 1787.


No. 111    Page 110
For 10 pounds per 100 acres, to Jeremian Chamberlain 640 acres in Greene
County on north side of Holston River, by Joseph Eaten, below mouth of
Sulphur Spring Branch, above mouth of Spring Creek. Richard Caswell,
September 20, 1787.


No. 24    Page 111
For 10 pounds per 100 acres, to Thomas Gilespie 100 acres in Greene
County on Dumplin Creek. Richard Caswell, November 1, 1786.


No. 260    Page ____
For 10 pounds per 100 acres, to Thomas Ray 150 acres in Greene County on
Little Chuckey by Andrew Leeper, Conway, Boid. Richard Caswell, September
20, 1787.


No. 22    Page 112
For 10 pounds per 100 acres, to James Hubbert 1000 acres in Greene County
"on north side of the Tennessee River, a half mile below Shelby's encamping ground when going to Chickamoga Town". Richard Caswell, November
1, 1786.


No. 47    Page 112
For 10 pounds per 100 acres, to James Hubbert 600 acres in Greene County
on north side of the French Broad River, including mouth of Copeling's
Creek, and by James Randall. Richard Caswell, November 1, 1786.


No. 97    Page 115
For 10 pounds per 100 acres, to James Hubbert 600 acres in Greene County
on an island in the French Broad River, known by the name of Hubbert's
Island, joining Wilcockson. Richard Caswell, November 1, 1786.


No. 111    Page 115
For 10 pounds per 100 acres, to James Hubbert 400 acres in Greene County
on north side of the French Broad River by Silas George. Richard Caswell, November 1, 1786.


No. 66    Page 116
For 10 pounds per 100 acres, to William Rainy 300 acres in Greene County
on north side of the French Broad River. Richard Caswell, November 1,
1786.


No. 29    Page 117
For 10 pounds per 100 acres, to James Walker 200 acres in Greene County
north side of French Broad River by William Tate. Richard Caswell,
November 1, 1786.


15

No. 177     Page 118
For 10 pounds per 100 acres, to Thomas Flippen 200 acres in Greene County on north side of Holston River. Richard Caswell, September 20, 1787.

No. 187     Page 119
For 10 pounds per 100 acres, to Thomas Flippen 200 acres in Greene County on north side of the Holston River opposite the mouth of McCartney's Branch. Richard Caswell, September 20, 1787.

No. 249     Page 119
For 10 pounds per 100 acres, to Thomas West 300 acres in Greene County on south side of Holston River at the mouth of Falling Branch. Richard Caswell, September 20, 1787.

No. 43     Page 120
For 10 pounds per 100 acres, to William Ansley 640 acres in Greene County on Price's Creek, including both sides of the War Path. Richard Caswell, November 1, 1786.

No. 114     Page 121
For 10 pounds per 100 acres, to William Ansley 640 acres in Greene County on north side of the Nolichuckey River on Lick Creek, by Charles Hodge. Richard Caswell, November 1, 1786.

No. 67     Page 122
For 10 pounds per 100 acres, to John Trimble 500 acres in Greene County on south side of Nolichuckey River, by Adam Sherrell, Alexander Kelley, John Chamberlain. Richard Caswell, November 1, 1786.

No. 123     Page 123
For 10 pounds per 100 acres, to Alexander Kelley 500 acres in Greene County on south side of Nolichuckey River by John Trimble, the wagon road, and John Chamberlain. Richard Caswell, November 1, 1786.

No. 207     Page 123
For 10 pounds per 100 acres, to James Conner 1000 acres in Greene County on north side of Clinch River opposite the mouth of Buffalo Creek. Richard Caswell, September 20, 1787.

No. 156     Page 124
For 10 pounds per 100 acres, to John Hackett 800 acres in Greene County on north side of Clinch River by Stokely Donnelson's thousand acre survey. Richard Caswell, September 20, 1787.

No. 157     Page 125
For 10 pounds per 100 acres, to John Hackett 640 acres in Greene County "in Cumberland Valley on Clear Creek known by the name of the White Walnut Bottom between the Muscle Shoals men's tract and the Cumberland Mountain." Richard Caswell, September 20, 1787.

No. 166     Page 125
For 10 pounds per 100 acres, to John Hackett 600 acres in Greene County on north side of Tennessee River on Mill Creek . . . to a stake on the river bank opposite to some Indian houses. Richard Caswell, September 20, 1787.

No. 204     Page 126
For 10 pounds per 100 acres, to John Hackett 214 acres in Greene County on north side of Holston River on east side of Little Sinking Creek.

Richard Caswell, September 20, 1787.

No. 208    Page 127
For 10 pounds per 100 acres, to Stokely Donnelson 1000 acres in Greene County on north side of Tennessee River, "on Neal's Fork of Deep River beginning and cornering on a hickory on the left hand of the Muscle Shoals men's tract." Richard Caswell, September 20, 1787.

No. 209    Page 128
For 10 pounds per 100 acres, to Stokely Donnelson 5000 acres in Greene County in Pleasant Garden Valley on north side of Tennessee River by Cosby, Hackett. Richard Caswell, September 20, 1787.

No. 210    Page 128
For 10 pounds per 100 acres, to Stokely Donnelson 1000 acres in Greene County on north side of Tennessee River in Cumberland Valley on east fork of Richland Creek, joined by Donnelson's 640 acre survey. Richard Caswell, September 20, 1787.

No. 212    Page 129
For 10 pounds per 100 acres, to Stokely Donnelson 1000 acres in Greene County on north side of Tennessee River in Cumberland Valley on Richland Creek by the Muscle Shoals Men's path, and by Gest. Richard Caswell, September 20, 1787.

No. 215    Page 130
For 50 shillings per 100 acres, to Stokely Donelson 400 acres in Greene County "in a small valley on the south side of Cumberland Valley on an east branch of Piney River, by Donelson's 400 acre survey. Richard Caswell, September 20, 1787.

No. 216    Page 131
For 10 pounds per 100 acres, to Stokely Donelson 200 acres in Greene County in Cumberland Valley on west fork of Richland Creek, by his 250 acre survey. Richard Caswell, September 20, 1787.

No. 219    Page 132
For 10 pounds per 100 acres, to Stokely Donelson 400 acres in Greene County in a small valley on the south side of Cumberland Valley on an east fork or branch of Piney River. Richard Caswell, September 20, 1787.

No. 220    Page 133
For 10 pounds per 100 acres, to Stokely Donnelson 1000 acres in Greene County on north side of Tennessee River in Cumberland Valley on north side of Muscle Shoals men's tract. Richard Caswell, September 20, 1787.

No. 221    Page 133
For 50 shillings per 100 acres, to Stokely Donnelson 640 acres in Greene County on north side of Tennessee River in Cumberland Valley at forks of Richland Creek, by his 250 acre survey, his 1000 acre survey and his 250 acre survey. Richard Caswell, September 20, 1787.

No. 222    Page 135
For 50 shillings per 100 acres, to Stokely Donnelson 600 acres in Greene County on north side Tennessee River in Cumberland Valley "on north side of the trace to Chickamoga." Richard Caswell, September 20, 1787.

No. 223    Page 135
For 50 shillings per 100 acres, to Stokely Donnelson 600 acres in Greene

County on north side of Tennessee River in Cumberland Valley on Camp Creek, beginning below the Boiling Spring on each side of the spring branch, by his 500 acre survey. Richard Caswell, September 20, 1787.

No. 213     Page 136
For 50 shillings per 100 acres, to Abraham Utter 300 acres in Greene County on north side Clinch River known by name of Pleasant Garden. Richard Caswell, September 20, 1787.

No. 225     Page 137
For 50 shillings per 100 acres, to Amos Bird 500 acres in Greene County on north side Tennessee River above mouth of Richland Creek, by Hackett and Donnelson's 2000 acre survey. Richard Caswell, September 20, 1787.

No. 243     Page 138
For 50 shillings per 100 acres, to James Woods Lackey 300 acres in Greene County on head of Firs Creek that empties in below the mouth of Holston River on north side of said Tennessee River. Richard Caswell, September 20, 1787.

No. 154     Page 139
For 10 pounds per 100 acres, to William Black 640 acres in Greene County on north side Tennessee River in Cumberland Valley, on east fork of Richland Creek, by his 1000 acre survey on north side of Muscle Shoal men's trace, by Joshua Guest's 1000 acre survey, and Donelson. Richard Caswell, September 20, 1787.

No. 227     Page 139
For 10 pounds per 100 acres, to William Black 640 acres in Greene County on north side Clinch River, the "next bottom below Hackett and Donnelson's survey", by Abraham Swagerty. Richard Caswell, September 20, 1787.

No. 175     Page 140
For 10 pounds per 100 acres, to James White 800 acres in Greene County on north side of Clinch River known by name of White Rock Place. Richard Caswell, September 20, 1787.

No. 218     Page 140
For 10 pounds per 100 acres, to James Cosby and Samuel Givens 2000 acres in Greene County on north side of Tennessee River in Pleasant Valley Garden, by Donnelson survey (2000 acres) and Donelson's 5000 acre survey. Richard Caswell, September 20, 1787.

No. 17     Page 142
For 10 pounds per 100 acres, to David Campbell 270 acres in Greene County on Flat Creek, by John Heritage. Richard Caswell, November 1, 1786.

No. 248     Page 142
For 10 pounds per 100 acres, To John Bags 100 acres in Greene County on east side of Little Chuckey. Richard Caswell, September 20, 1787.

No. 230     Page 143
For 10 pounds per 100 acres, to Samuel Sample 150 acres in Greene County on south side of Holston River, by William Doneal. Richard Caswell, September 20, 1787.

No. 272     Page 144
For 10 pounds per 100 acres, to Samuel Samples 200 acres in Greene County on south side of Holston River, on east fork of Spring Creek. Richard

Caswell, September 20, 1787.

No. 179        Page 145
For 10 pounds per 100 acres, to William Doak 300 acres in Greene County
on north side of Holston River to the south side of Houth Mountain below
the mouth of Rossberry Creek by Brandon.  Richard Caswell, September 20,
1787.

No. 198        Page 145
For 50 shillings per 100 acres, to William Doak 300 acres in Greene
County south of the Holston River, crossing Doak's Branch.  Richard
Caswell, September 20, 1787.

No. 357        Page ___
For 50 shillings per 100 acres, to Nathaniel Tracy 150 acres in Washing-
ton County on a branch of Lick Creek, joining Samuel Lyle.  Alexander
Martin at Nollsboro, October 13, 1783.

No. 247        Page 147
For 10 pounds per 100 acres, to Claudias Bailey 100 acres in Greene County
on branch of Lick Creek.  Richard Caswell, September 20, 1787.

No. 250        Page 148
For 10 pounds per 100 acres, to Claudias Bailey 300 acres in Greene
County on Lick Creek, joining Joseph Randles, Thomas Bayles.  September
20, 1787.

No. 269        Page 148
For 50 shillings per 100 acres, to Claudias Bailey 200 acres in Greene
County on south branch of Lick Creek, by Joseph Runnald.  Richard
Caswell, 1787.

No. 237        Page 149
For 10 pounds per 100 acres, to Michael Woods 200 acres in Greene County
south of Nolichuckey River, by McDonel's line, to Meadow Creek.  Richard
Caswell, September 20, 1787.

No. 244        Page 150
For 10 pounds per 100 acres, to Michael Woods 200 acres in Greene County
on south side of Nolichuckey River on Cove Creek, by Frethias Wall.
Richard Caswell, September 20, 1787.

No. 232        Page 151
For 10 pounds per 100 acres, to Andrew Leeper 250 acres in Greene County
on north side of Nolichuckey River by William Caliar, the Poplar Beach,
and Thomas Ray.  Richard Caswell, September 20, 1787.

No. 233        Page 152
For 50 shillings per 100 acres, to Benjamin Jameson 100 acres in Greene
County on Holley's Creek, by John McCroskey, Nathaniel McClure, Henry
Farnsworth.  Richard Caswell, September 20, 1787.

No. 218        Page 153
For 50 shillings per 100 acres, to Henry Farnsworth 224 acres in Greene
County joining Benjamin Jameson's land that "lies upon the waters that
Burnt Cabbin place is upon."  Richard Caswell, September 20, 1787.

No. 189       Page 153
For 10 pounds per 100 acres, to Joseph Bogel 236 acres in Greene County
on Little Chuckey at the mouth of Delaney's Creek, by Gamil.  Richard
Caswell, September 20, 1787.


No. 271       Page 154
For 10 pounds per 100 acres, to John Corbet 200 acres in Greene County on
Blue Spring Branch, by William Wilson.  Richard Caswell, September 20,
1787.


No. 579       Page 155
For 50 shillings per 100 acres, to Thomas Bailey 320 acres in Greene
County on Little Gap Creek, including part of the watery branch, by
Thomas Ishma.  Samuel Johnston, governor, at Edenton, September 1,
1788.


No. 408       Page 156
For 50 shillings per 100 acres, to Mather Parrimore 200 acres in Washington County "on the north fork of Lick Creek, the Indian Camp, the second
fork above Thomas Williams's entry called Bluff Creek between Bay's
Mountain and the War Path including the old Indian Camp and the watery
branch."  Alexander Martin at Hillsboro, October 13, 1783.


No. 34
For 10 pounds per 100 acres, to John Sevier and Richard Caswell 37 1/2
acres in Greene County "including the island in the French Broad River
that the War Path leads through."  Richard Caswell, November 1, 1786.


No. 103
For 10 pounds per 100 acres, to Henry Conway 600 acres in Greene County
on north side of Nolichuckey River.  Richard Caswell, November 1, 1786.


No. 30        Page 158
For 10 pounds per 100 acres, to Alexander McMullin 500 acres in Greene
County on south side of Holston River "above the head of the Deep Spring."
Richard Caswell, November 1, 1786.


No. 417       Page 158
For 10 pounds per 100 acres, to Joseph Gest 200 acres in Greene County by
McRunnel, McCall, Benjamin Gisse and Kidwell.  Richard Caswell, September
20, 1787.


No. 560       Page 159
For 10 pounds per 100 acres, to Hugh Bryson 200 acres in Greene County on
Richland Creek, near the mouth of the Cedar Branch, by William Goforth,
Samuel Fishback, Benjamin Ray.  Richard Caswell, September 20, 1787.


No. 92        Page 160
For 10 pounds per 100 acres, to John Corbet 100 acres in Greene County.
Richard Caswell, November 1, 1786.


No. 343       Page 161
For 10 pounds per 100 acres, to William Goforth 300 acres in Greene
County on Richland Creek, from the mouth of Cedar Branch, by Fishback,
"to a box oak in the Barrens", and by Hugh Brison.  Richard Caswell,
September 20, 1787.


No. 302       Page 162
For 10 pounds per 100 acres, to Thomas Galbreath 640 acres in Greene

20

County on Little Chuckey, by Nicholas Davis. Richard Caswell, September 20, 1787.


No. 202     Page 163
For 10 pounds per 100 acres, to James McGill 260 acres in Greene County on Sinking Creek, by Johnathan Evans on east side of Sinking Creek. Richard Caswell, September 20, 1787.


No. 532     Page 164
For 10 pounds per 100 acres, to Thomas Graham 200 acres in Greene County by Samuel Moore, James McKehon and Henry Farnsworth. Richard Caswell, September 20, 1787.


No. 530     Page 165
For 10 pounds per 100 acres, to Benjamin Ray 320 acres in Greene County on Richland Creek, by John Bennett, "to a box oak on the bank of a branch thence south to a hickory tree near a large rocky spring, south with the line with Jacob Fishback, to Hugh Brison, to the line of Hezekiah Balch." Richard Caswell, September 20, 1787.


No. 286     Page 166
For 10 pounds per 100 acres, to James Galbreath 200 acres in Greene County on south side of Holston River. Richard Caswell, September 20, 1787.


No. 363     Page 167
For 10 pounds per 100 acres, to James Galbreath 31 1/4 acres in Greene County by Robert Parris, David Campbell and David Rankin. Richard Caswell, September 20, 1787.


No. 429     Page 168
For 10 pounds per 100 acres, to James Galbreath 50 acres in Greene County on a branch of Nolachucky River on Reedy Fork of Sinking Creek, adjoining Campbell, Robert Parus. Richard Caswell, September 20, 1787.


No. 442     Page 169
For 10 pounds per 100 acres, to James McCamish 800 acres in Greene County on south side of Holston River, on head of Fall Creek. Richard Caswell, September 20, 1787.


No. 469     Page 170
For 10 pounds per 100 acres, to William Galbreath 200 acres in Greene County - Cub Creek on waters of Holston River adjoining Cox. Richard Caswell, September 20, 1787.


No. 375     Page 171
For 50 shillings per 100 acres, to Richard Martin 300 acres on waters of Clinch River. Richard Caswell, September 20, 1787.


No. 283     Page 172
For 50 shillings per 100 acres, to James Delany 200 acres on Delany's Creek adjoining Samuel Dunwoody. Richard Caswell, September 20, 1787.


No. 647     Page 172
For 10 pounds per 100 acres, to James Richardson 640 acres on south side Nolachucky River adjoining William Burney. Samuel Johnston, July 11, 1788.

No. 385     Page 173
For 10 pounds per 100 acres, to George Doherty 38 acres in Greene County, island in French Broad River opposite mouth of Little Pigeon River. Richard Caswell, September 20, 1787.


No. 620     Page 178
For 10 pounds per 100 acres, to William Lenoir and William Sevier 3500 acres in Greene County north side of Tennessee and Holston Rivers, corner to Isaac Taylor up Tennessee and Holston Rivers including mouth of Muddy Creek. Samuel Johnston at Edenton, 23 August 1788.


No. 560     Page 175
For 10 pounds per 100 acres, to James Conner 500 acres in Greene County south of Clinch River above Island Ford. Sealed by Samuel Johnston, 23 August 1788.


No. 624     Page 176
For 10 pounds per 100 acres, to James Conner 500 acres in Greene County south of Clinch River including mouth of Conners Mill Shoal Creek. Registered 21 November 1788.


No. 572     Page 177
For 10 pounds per 100 acres, to John Hackett 225 acres in Greene County in Cumberland Valley, on west fork of Richland Creek north of Tennessee River, adjoining 500 acre tract. Registered 21 November 1788.


No. 576     Page 178
For 10 pounds per 100 acres, to John Hacket 500 acres in Greene County north side of Clinch River opposite Gallohers 600 acre survey. Samuel Johnston at Edenton, 2 August 1788.


No. 587     Page 179
For 10 pounds per 100 acres, to John Hacket 600 acres in Greene County north side of Holston River in Meadow Creek Valley adjoining James Anderson. Samuel Johnston at Edenton, 23 August 1788.


No. 593     Page 180
For 10 pounds per 100 acres, to John Hacket 640 acres north side of Holston River on Little Sinking Creek. Samuel Johnston at Edenton, 3 August 1788.


No. 595     Page 181
For 10 pounds per 100 acres, to John Hacket 250 acres in Greene County on south side of Clinch River, known by name of Indian Bottom, above James Robinsons Tract - up Clinch River. Samuel Johnston at Edenton, 23 August 1788.


No. ___     Page 182
For 10 pounds per 100 acres, to John Hackett 500 acres in Greene County north side of Holston River, first bottom below mouth of Little River, adjoining David McKee. Samuel Johnston at Edenton, 23 August 1788.


No. 621     Page 183
For 10 pounds per 100 acres, to John Hackett 500 acres in Greene County south side of Clinch River on head of spring of Conners Mill Creek, adjoining Francis Alexander Ramsey's survey, Abraham Swaggerty. 23 August 1788.


No. 618     Page 184
For 10 pounds per 100 acres, to John Hackett 2000 acres in Greene County

on north side of Tennessee River adjoining Bird and Donelson's 1000 acre
survey, in Pleasant Garden Valley.  23 August 1788.


No. 644     Page 185
For 10 pounds per 100 acres - to John Hackett 100 acres in Greene County
north side of French Broad River.  Samuel Johnston at Edenton, 23 August
1788.


No. 167     Page 186
For 10 pounds per 100 acres - to Andrew Miller 300 acres in Greene County
on south side of Nolichuckey River, on both sides of Cove Creek adjoining
Samuel Wilson.  20 September 1787.


No. 168     Page 187
For 10 pounds per 100 acres - to John Meadow 300 acres in Greene County
on south side of Holston River on Mossy Creek.  Richard Caswell at
Kinston, 20 September 1787.


No. 446     Page 187
For 10 pounds per 100 acres - to James Gibson 200 acres in Greene County
on head branch of Pigeon Creek.  Richard Caswell at Kinston, 20 September
1787.


No. 104     Page 188
For 10 pounds per 100 acres - to James Gibson 200 acres in Greene County
on head branch of Pigeon Creek.  Richard Caswell at Kinston, 20 September
1787.


No. 104     Page 188
For 10 pounds per 100 acres - to John Tool 100 acres in Greene County
near Joseph Tromells - 3/4 mile from Joseph Fowler.  1 November 1789.


No. 332     Page 189
For 10 pounds per 100 acres - to John Tool 29 1/2 acres in Greene County
on Browns Creek, adjoining Thomas Brown.  Richard Caswell, 20 September
1787.


No. 574     Page 190
For 10 pounds per 100 acres - to John Tool 600 acres in Greene County on
north side of Holston River, including Luckey Island.  Samuel Johnston at
Edenton, 3 August 1788.


No. 576     Page 191
For 10 pounds per 100 acres - to John Tool 400 acres in Greene County on
north side of Holston River adjoining Alexander Campbell.  Samuel Johnston at Edenton, 23 August 1788.


No. ___     Page 192
For 50 shillings per 100 acres - to Benjamin McCeeslon 200 acres in Greene
County on Long Creek adjoining Samuel McGeaness.  Samuel Johnston at
Fayelle, 29 November 1788.


No. 263     Page 192
For 10 pounds per 100 acres - to David Eagleton 500 acres in Greene County
on Little Chucky adjoining Joseph Wilson.  Richard Caswell at Kinston, 20
September 1787.

No. 418      Page 193
For 10 pounds per 100 acres – to John Hitchcock 125 acres in Greene
County on north side of Chucky River on Little Chucky adjoining
Egerton. Richard Caswell at Kinston, 20 September 1787.


No. 420      Page 194
For 10 pounds per 100 acres – to John Hitchcock 82 acres in Greene County.
Richard Caswell, 20 September 1787.


No. 304      Page 195
For 50 shillings per 100 acres – to Austin Brumley 100 acres in Greene
County on a branch of Nolichucky River. Richard Caswell, 20 September
1787.


No. ___      Page 196
For 50 shillings per 100 acres – to Austin Brumley 100 acres – 200 acres
in Greene County on north side Nolachucky River adjoining Henry Earnest
corner, continuing down river. 11 July 1788.


No. ___      Page 196
For 10 pounds per 100 acres – to John Kelley 100 acres in Greene County
on south side of Nolachucky River in bent of said river, above mouth of
Cove Creek going north. Samuel Johnston at Fairfield, 10 July 1788.


No. 623      Page 197
For 10 pounds per 100 acres – to Stokely Donelson 600 acres in Greene
County on south side of Clinch River above the first bluff above the
Island, above the mouth of Bufflar Creek opposite Donelson's 600 acre
survey. Samuel Johnston at Edenton, 3 August 1788.


No. 625      Page 198
For 10 pounds per 100 acres – to Stokely Donelson 640 acres in Greene
County on north side of Clinch River in Bent opposite mouth of Beaver
Creek, corner to McKay's survey. Samuel Johnston at Edenton, 23 August
1788.


No. 306      Page 199
For 10 pounds per 100 acres – to Joseph Wilson 300 acres in Greene County
on Little Chucky. Richard Caswell at Kinston, 20 September 1787.


No. 333      Page 200
For 10 pounds per 100 acres – to Henry Haggard 300 acres in Greene County
on branch of Lyles Creek. Richard Caswell at Kinston, 20 September 1787.


No. 334      Page 200
For 10 pounds per 100 acres – to James Randolph 600 acres in Greene
County on north side of French Broad River. Richard Caswell, 20 Sep-
tember 1787.


No. 15      Page 201
For 10 pounds per 100 acres – to Thomas English 400 acres in Hawkins
County on south side of Holston River below the mouth of McCartney's
Branch down river. Samuel Johnston at Edenton, 23 August 1788.


No. 608      Page 202
For 10 pounds per 100 acres – to Thomas English 100 acres in Greene
County on east side of McCartney's Branch. Samuel Johnston at Edenton,
23 August 1788.

No. 573    Page 203
For 10 pounds per 100 acres - to William Bryon 500 acres in Greene County
on south side French Broad River including an island of 120 acres, adjoining David Lisle up river to John McSpaddens. Samuel Johnston at
Edenton, 23 August 1788.


No. 643    Page 203
For 10 pounds per 100 acres - to David Walker 100 acres in Greene County
on north side of Holston River on East Branch of Third Creek. Samuel
Johnston at Edenton, 23 August 1788.


No. 323    Page 204
For 10 pounds per 100 acres - to William Walker 272 acres in Greene
County on south side of French Broad River. Richard Caswell, 20
September 1787.


No. 629    Page 205
For 10 pounds per 100 acres - to John McSpadon 300 acres in Greene County
on north side of French Broad River, corner to William Bryon, Archibald
McSpaddon. Samuel Johnston, 23 August 1788.


No. 626    Page 206
For 10 pounds per 100 acres - to Archibald McSpadden 100 acres in Greene
County on north side of French Broad River, corner to John McSpadon, up
river. Samuel Johnston, 23 August 1788.


No. 571    Page 207
For 10 pounds per 100 acres - to Ananias McCoy 400 acres in Greene County
on south side of Clinch River on Tenants Creek. Samuel Johnston, 3
August 1788.


No. 583    Page 207
For 10 pounds per 100 acres - to Ananias McCoy 200 acres in Greene County
on north side of Clinch River. Samuel Johnston, 23 August 1788.


No. 586    Page 208
For 10 pounds per 100 acres - to Ananias McCoy 640 acres in Greene County
on north side of Tennessee River on Caneys Creek, a west fork of Whites
Creek. Samuel Johnston, 23 August 1788.


No. 600    Page 209
For 10 pounds per 100 acres - to Ananias McCoy 640 acres in Greene County
on north side of Clinch River in the Bent opposite mouth of Beavers Creek,
adjoining Donelson. Samuel Johnston, 23 August 1788.


No. 452    Page 210
For 10 pounds per 100 acres - to John Delaney 100 acres in Greene County
on Sinking Creek adjoining his own land. Richard Caswell, 20 September
1787.


No. 115    Page 211
For 10 pounds per 100 acres - to David Craig 300 acres in Greene County
on north side of French Broad River. Richard Caswell, 1 November 1786.


No. 482    Page 211
For 10 pounds per 100 acres - to Alexander Moore 400 acres in Greene
County on Meadow Creek adjoining Samuel Sherrill, Junr. Richard Cas-
well, 20 September 1787.

25

No. 172        Page 212
For 10 pounds per 100 acres - to David Stewart 200 acres in Greene County on north side of Tennessee River on second creek below mouth of Clinch River, known by name of Stewarts Creek. Richard Caswell, 20 September 1787.

No. 176        Page 213
For 10 pounds per 100 acres - to David Stewart and John Hill 368 acres in Greene County on south side of French Broad River adjoining John Wards, William Job. Richard Caswell, 20 September 1787.

No. 192        Page 214
For 50 shillings per 100 acres - to David Stewart 300 acres in Greene County on north side of Holston River, bounded by Clinch Mountain, on north side of Richland Creek, adjoining James McDonal. Richard Caswell, 20 September 1787.

No. 228        Page 214
For 10 pounds per 100 acres - to David Steward 200 acres in Greene County on waters of Russell Creek and Powels River under River Ridge, adjoining John Horton. Richard Caswell at Kinston, 20 September 1787.

No. 240        Page 215
For 50 shillings per 100 acres - to David Stewart and Jonathan Douglas 640 acres in Greene County on south side of Holston River at the head of McCartney's Branch. Richard Caswell at Kinston, 20 September 1787.

No. 254        Page 216
For 10 pounds per 100 acres - to David Stewart and William Cocke 400 acres in Greene County on waters of Clinch River on War Creek, including a limestone spring near Bunches Path. Richard Caswell, 20 September 1787.

No. 256        Page 217
For 50 shillings per 100 acres - to David Stewart 300 acres in Greene County on south side Powels River on the Cedar Branch of Russells Creek, including a large Buffalo Lick, adjoining Dunham (Lanhams ?). Richard Caswell at Kinston, 20 September 1787.

No. ___        Page 219
For 10 pounds per 100 acres - to Jeremiah Meek 400 acres in Greene County on Lick Creek adjoining Isaac Bullard. Richard Caswell at Kinston, 20 September 1787.

No. ___        Page 219
For 10 pounds per 100 acres - to David Stewart 470 acres in Greene County on Russells Creek, waters of Powels River, adjoining Horner. Richard Caswell at Kinston, 20 September 1787.

No. 262        Page 220
For 50 shillings per 100 acres - to David Stuart 500 acres in Greene County on north side of Tennessee River adjoining Thomas King. Richard Caswell at Kinston, 20 September 1787.

No. 650        Page 221
For 10 pounds per 100 acres - to David Stuart 250 acres in Greene County on north side of French Broad River, adjoining Thomas Stockton and James Hubbarts. Samuel Johnson at Fairfield, 11 July 1788.

No. 196      Page 222
For 50 shillings per 100 acres - to Thomas Love 300 acres in Greene
County on south side of Nolachucky River where Love now lives, adjoining
Robert Armstrong.  Richard Caswell at Kinston, 20 September 1787.


No. ___      Page 222
For 10 pounds per 100 acres - to Joseph Hough 200 acres in Greene County
on east side of French Broad River adjoining Joseph Williams.  Richard
Caswell at Kinston, 20 September 1787.


No. ___      Page 223
For 10 pounds per 100 acres - to William McBroom 100 acres in Greene
County on Burnt Cabin Spring.  Richard Caswell at Kinston, 20 September
1787.


No. 416      Page 224
For 10 pounds per 100 acres - to William McBroom 100 acres in Greene
County near Blue Spring adjoining Joseph Notion.  Richard Caswell at
Kinston, 20 September 1787.


No. 282      Page 225
For 10 pounds per 100 acres - to Mathew Pate 72 acres in Greene County on
north side of Nolachucky River.  Richard Caswell at Kinston, 20 September
1787.


No. 383      Page 225
For 50 shillings per 100 acres - to Mathew Pate ___ acres in Greene
County on north side of Nolachucky River.  Richard Caswell at Kinston,
20 September 1787.


No. 390      Page 226
For 10 pounds per 100 acres - to Mathew Pate 200 acres in Greene County
on north side of Nolachucky River opposite Beech Bottom.  Richard Caswell at Kinston, 20 September 1787.


No. 602      Page 227
For 50 shillings per 100 acres - to Jacob Smencer 100 acres in Greene
County on Holley's Creek, waters of Nolachucky River.  Samuel Johnston
at Edenton.


No. 303      Page 228
For 10 pounds per 100 acres - to Andrew Coffman 200 acres in Greene
County west side of Lick Creek adjoining Wyat.  Richard Caswell at
Kinston, 20 September 1787.


No. 698      Page 228
For 50 shillings per 100 acres - to Philip Hale 100 acres in Greene
County on north side of Nolachucky River.  Samuel Johnston at Fair-
field, 11 July 1788.


No. 800      Page 229
For 50 shillings per 100 acres - to James Huston 640 acres in Greene
County on north side French Broad River, Rocky Path to a Cove Spring
south side of Copeland Path.  Samuel Johnston at Fayetteville, 19
November 1788.


No. 461      Page 230
For 10 pounds per 100 acres - to Moses Shanks 500 acres in Greene County
on waters of Lick Creek, called Punshan Gap Creek.  Richard Caswell at

Kinston, 20 September 1787.


No. 615      Page 231
For 10 pounds per 100 acres – to Robert Armstrong 400 acres in Greene
County on south side of Holston River. Samuel Johnston at Edenton, 23
August 1788.


No. 396      Page 232
For 50 shillings per 100 acres – to Joseph Ray 150 acres in Greene County
on head of McCartney's Creek Branch, adjoining John Crockett. Richard
Caswell at Kinston, 20 September 1787.


No. 380      Page 233
For 10 pounds per 100 acres – to David Prewit 115 acres in Greene County
on Little Chucky adjoining Thomas Galbreath. Richard Caswell at Kinston,
20 September 1787.


No. 477      Page 233
For 10 pounds per 100 acres – to George Samples 160 acres in Greene
County on waters of Little Chucky adjoining David Prewit, Gamble.
Richard Caswell, 20 September 1787.


No. 724      Page 234
For 10 pounds per 100 acres – to John Keeny 671 acres in Greene County on
French Broad River, including a large island opposite Robert Lamb's
plantation. Samuel Johnston at Fairfield, 11 July 1788.


No. 277      Page 235
For 10 pounds per 100 acres – to George Doherty 400 acres in Greene
County on south side of Nolachucky River, bounded by Jack's line,
McNeal. Richard Caswell at Kinston, 20 September 1787.


No. 307      Page 236
For 10 pounds per 100 acres – to George Doughterty 300 acres in Greene
County. Richard Caswell at Kinston, 20 September 1787.


No. 360      Page 237
For 10 pounds per 100 acres – to George Doherty 100 acres in Greene
County. Richard Caswell at Kinston, 20 September 1787.


No. 522      Page 238
For 10 pounds per 100 acres – to George Doherty 100 acres in Greene
County on north side of Nolachucky River below mouth of Fowlers Branch,
to a point of small island. Richard Caswell at Kinston, 20 September
1787.


No. 716      Page 238
For 10 pounds per 100 acres – to Samuel Reed 400 acres in Greene County
on south side of Nolachucky River on Big Creek, including John Cozby's
improvement. Samuel Johnston at Fairfield, 11 July 1788.


No. 596      Page 239
For 10 pounds per 100 acres – to Thomas Gilespy 200 acres in Greene
County on north side of Clinch River below mouth of Buffalo Creek,
adjoining McCoy survey. Samuel Johnston at Edenton, 3 August 1788.

No. 619    Page 240
For 10 pounds per 100 acres - to Thomas Gillespy 300 acres in Greene
County on south side of Clinch River. Samuel Johnston at Edenton, 23
August 1788.


No. 370    Page 241
For 50 shillings per 100 acres - to Hugh Cavanaugh 100 acres in Greene
County on Dunhams Branch adjoining Samuel Bigham and James Whitesides.
Richard Caswell at Kinston, 20 September 1787.


No. 511    Page 242
For 50 shillings per 100 acres - to Hugh Cavanaugh 100 acres in Greene
County on Dunhams Branch adjoining Anthony Moore. Richard Caswell at
Kinston, 20 September 1787.


No. 500    Page 243
For 10 pounds per 100 acres - to David Copeland 300 acres in Greene County
on south side of Holston River on head spring of Fall Creek, adjoining
Dawson Cheek's line, Russell's line. Richard Caswell at Kinston, 20
September 1787.


No. 293    Page 243
For 10 pounds per 100 acres - to John Gilespy 450 acres in Greene County
on Lick Creek, adjoining Thomas Witchaker? Richard Caswell at Kinston,
20 September 1787.


No. 348    Page 244
For 10 pounds per 100 acres - To James Gilespy 150 acres in Greene County
on Lick Creek, adjoining John Gilespy. Richard Caswell at Kinston, 20
September 1787.


No. 631    Page 245
For 10 pounds per 100 acres - to John McGirt 100 acres in Greene County
on French Broad River where he now lives, adjoining Robert Mansfield
Balch's survey. Samuel Johnston at Edenton, 23 August 1788.


No. 1 or 4?  Page 246
For 10 pounds per 100 acres - to Alexander Outlaw and William Lewis 5000
acres in Greene County on north side of Tennessee River. Richard Caswell
at Kinston, 20 September 1787.


No. 342    Page 247
For 10 pounds per 100 acres - to Bryent Bryan 400 acres in Greene County
on both sides of Lick Creek, adjoining David Coffman, David Reed, John
Murpheas, Andrew Coffman. Richard Caswell at Kinston, 20 September
1787.


No. 122    Page 248
For 10 pounds per 100 acres - to William Conway 600 acres in Greene
County on north side of Nolachucky River, at Nob below mouth of Lick
Creek. Richard Caswell at Kinston, 1 November 1786.


No. 601    Page 249
For 50 shillings per 100 acres - to Thomas Beardon 400 acres in Greene
County on Long Creek where he now lives. Samuel Johnston, 23 August
1788.

No. 492      Page 250
For 10 pounds per 100 acres - to Joseph Stuart 400 acres in Greene County
on White Horn, a branch of Bent Creek on Nolachucky River, adjoining
James Roddy entry at mouth of Whitehorn Creek, adjoining John Buller to
foot of Bays Mountain, adjoining Nicholas Smith.  Richard Caswell at
Kinston, 20 September 1787.


No. 151      Page 250
For 10 pounds per 100 acres - to Adam Meek 488 acres in Greene County in
valley between Sinking Creek and Bevere Creek, known as Cany or Sinking
Branch.  Richard Caswell at Kinston, 23 April 1786.


No. 143      Page 251
For 10 pounds per 100 acres - to Adam Meek 600 acres in Greene County on
south side of Holston River on First Creek above Richland Creek, adjoining Joseph McCullough.  Richard Caswell at Kinston, 23 April 1787.


No. 463      Page 252
For 10 pounds per 100 acres - to John Moore 100 acres in Greene County on
south side of Nolachucky River, including Horse Shoe Bent of said river.
Richard Caswell at Kinston, 20 September 1787.


No. 152      Page 253
For 10 pounds per 100 acres - to Adam Meek 200 acres in Greene County on
south side of Holston River, known as Sherrels Place, lying near dividing
ridge between Holston River and French Broad River.  Richard Caswell at
Kinston, 23 April 1787.


No. 347      Page 254
For 10 pounds per 100 acres - to Abraham Carter 275 acres in Greene
County on Lick Creek and Dry Fork, adjoining Joseph Bullard, Daniel
Carter, John Carter.  Richard Caswell at Kinston, 23 April 1787.


No. 147      Page 255
For 10 pounds per 100 acres - to Adam Meek 200 acres in Greene County on
south side of Holston River, adjoining William Johnston's old survey of
150 acres.  Richard Caswell at Kinston, 23 April 1787.


No. 807      Page 256
For 10 pounds per 100 acres - to George Edgere 300 acres in Greene County
on north side of Nolachucky River on Sinking Fork of Lick Creek.  Samuel
Johnston at Gayelle, 30 November 1788.


No. 148      Page 256
For 10 pounds per 100 acres - to Adam Meek and David Stewart 200 acres in
Greene County on south side of Holston River on Dry Fork of Swettens
Creek, adjoining Edward Biggs.  Richard Caswell at Kinston, 23 April
1787.


No. 346      Page 257
For 10 pounds per 100 acres - to John Carter Junr. 250 acres in Greene
County on Lick Creek and Dry Fork, including his improvement, adjoining
Ephraim Carter, George Wagoner.  Richard Caswell at Kinston, 20 September
1787.


No. 369      Page 258
For 10 pounds per 100 acres - to John Spurgeon 100 acres in Greene County
on south side of Nolachucky River.  Richard Caswell at Kinston, 20
September 1787.

No. 483    Page 259
For 10 pounds per 100 acres – to David Linsey 640 acres in Greene County on Plumb Creek and Churn Camp Creek, adjoining James Mitchel. Richard Caswell at Kinston, 20 September 1787.


No. 391    Page 260
For 10 pounds per 100 acres – to Drury Hodges 300 acres in Greene County on Lick Creek, adjoining William Hodges. Richard Caswell at Kinston, 20 September 1787.


No. 450    Page 261
For 10 pounds per 100 acres – to Robert King 300 acres in Greene County on south side of Nolachucky River, down river. Richard Caswell at Kinston, 12 September 1787.


No. 455    Page 262
For 10 pounds per 100 acres – to John Howard Senr. 200 acres in Greene County on a branch of Long Fork, adjoining James English, Gideon Morris. Richard Caswell at Kinston, 20 September 1787.


No. 453    Page 262
For 10 pounds per 100 acres – to John Watson 100 acres in Greene County, adjoining Edward Claim, Trotter McBride. Richard Caswell at Kinston, 20 September 1787.


No. 540    Page 263
For 10 pounds per 100 acres – to William Hodges 300 acres in Greene County on both sides of Lick Creek, chiefly on east side adjoining Amos Hodges and John Murphey, Drury Hodges. Richard Caswell at Kinston, 20 September 1787.


No. 434    Page 264
For 10 pounds per 100 acres – to David Lindsay 400 acres in Greene County on Lick Creek and Plumb Creek. Richard Caswell at Kinston, 20 September 1787.


No. 278    Page 265
For 10 pounds per 100 acres – to David Coffman 200 acres in Greene County on south side of Lick Creek shere he now lives, below Buffalo Ford, adjoining Bryant Bryon. Richard Caswell, 20 September 1787.


No. 368    Page 266
For 10 pounds per 100 acres – to David Reed 200 acres in Greene County on waters of Little Chuckey. Richard Caswell at Kinston, 20 September 1787.


No. 120    Page 267
For 10 pounds per 100 acres – to James Roddy 400 acres in Greene County on Bent Creek at Hains Branch, adjoining Jesse Hoskins. Richard Caswell, 1 November 1786.


No. 656    Page 268
For 10 pounds per 100 acres – to Isaac Taylor 200 acres in Greene County on north side of Holston River on west fork of Flat Creek. Samuel Johnston at Edenton.


No. 401    Page 268
For 10 pounds per 100 acres – to Isaac Davis 125 acres in Greene County on branches of Little Gap Creek, beginning at a tree marked $\mathcal{D}$ . Richard Caswell at Kinston, 20 September 1787.

31

No. 603        Page 269
For 10 pounds per 100 acres - to Isaac Taylor 250 acres in Greene County
on Dumplin Creek, including Beaver Dam. Samuel Johnston at Edenton, 23
August 1788.


No. 662        Page 270
For 10 pounds per 100 acres - to William Colier 130 acres in Greene
County on north side of Nolachuckey River adjoining land he bought of
John Byrd and William Hogan. Samuel Johnston at Fairfield, 11 July 1788.


No. 354        Page 271
For 10 pounds per 100 acres - to Isaac Johnston 100 acres in Greene
County on south bank of the Horse Stamp Fork, waters of Lick Creek,
including Grahams Cane Brake. Alexander Martin at Hillsboro, 13
October 1783.


No. 431        Page 272
For 10 pounds per 100 acres - to John Beard 400 acres in Greene County
on north side of French Broad River and Deep Creek, adjoining Edward
Higgens. Richard Caswell at Kinston, 20 September 1787.


No. 529        Page 272
For 10 pounds per 100 acres - to William Wyat 520 acres in Greene County
on Lick Creek, adjoining Andrew Coffman. Richard Caswell at Kinston, 20
September 1787.


No. 413        Page 273
For 10 pounds per 100 acres - to Henry Reynolds 300 acres in Greene
County on both sides of Camp Creek, beginning on west of Morass Top of
Piney Ridge, adjoining McMurtrey. Richard Caswell at Kinston, 20
September 1787.


No. 184        Page 274
For 10 pounds per 100 acres - to Acquilla Lane 400 acres in Greene County
on Bent Creek, adjoining William Russell, James Roddy. Richard Caswell
at Kinston, 20 September 1787.


No. 185        Page 275
For 10 pounds per 100 acres - to Acquilla Lane 270 acres in Greene County
on north side of Nolichucky River, adjoining Jesse Rounds. Richard Caswell, 20 September 1787.


No. 285        Page 276
For 50 shillings per 100 acres - to John Morris 100 acres in Greene
County adjoining James Hawkins, John Addles, James Milligan. Richard
Caswell, 20 September 1787.


No. 396        Page 277
For 10 pounds per 100 acres - to Isaac Johnston 100 acres in Washington
County. Alexander Martin at Hillsbro, 13 October 1783.


No. 279        Page 278
For 10 pounds per 100 acres - to Jonathan Hicks 300 acres in Greene
County on north side of Nolichucky River on Batts Branch. Richard
Caswell at Kinston, 20 September 1787.


No. 298        Page 278
For 10 pounds per 100 acres - to Daniel Carter 400 acres in Greene County

32

on both sides of Lick Creek including his improvements, adjoining Joseph
Bullard, Abraham Carter, George Waggoner. Richard Caswell at Hillsbro,
20 September 1787.


No. 721      Page 279
For 50 shillings per 100 acres - to Christopher Lotspeach 122 acres in
Greene County on south side of Chuckey River, adjoining Robert Oneal,
Benjamin Williams, where Williams now lives. Samuel Johnston, 11 July
1788.


No. 300      Page 280
For 10 pounds per 100 acres - to John Parrett 640 acres in Greene County
on Clear Creek, waters of French Broad River, adjoining Abraham Swaggerty.
Richard Caswell at Kinston, 20 September 1787.


No. 639      Page 281
For 10 pounds per 100 acres - to Edward George 400 acres in Greene County
on north side of French Broad River, adjoining James Hobbert, crossing
Sinking Spring Branch. Samuel Johnston at Edinton, 23 August 1788.


No. 589      Page 282
For 10 pounds per 100 acres - to Abraham Swaggerty 600 acres in Greene
County on north side of Clinch River, 2nd bottom above mouth of Beaver
Dam Creek, up Clinch River. Samuel Johnston at Edinton, 23 August 1787.


No. 634      Page 283
For 10 pounds per 100 acres - to Abraham Swagerty 640 acres in Greene
County on south side of Clinch River. Samuel Johnston at Edinton, 3
August 1788.


No. 633      Page 284
For 10 pounds per 100 acres - to Abraham Swaggerty 1000 acres in Greene
County on north side of Clinch River, on mouth of Poplar Creek, on Big
Creek. Richard Caswell at Edinton, 23 August 1788.


No. 610      Page 285
For 10 pounds per 100 acres - to Thomas Galiher 600 acres in Greene County
on south side of Clinch River, first bottom below mouth of Conner Mill
Shoal Creek. Samuel Johnston at Edinton, 23 August 1788.


No. 687      Page 285
For 50 shillings per 100 acres - to Mathias Wilhoit 200 acres in Greene
County on Cumpling Creek, adjoining Alexander. Samuel Johnston at Fair-
field, 11 July 1788.


No. 663      Page 286
For 10 pounds per 100 acres - to Spencer Rece 347 acres in Greene County
on south side of Nolichucky River on Clay Lick Creek. Samuel Johnston at
Fairfield, 11 July 1788.


No. 667      Page 287
For 10 pounds per 100 acres - to Mathias Hoover 150 acres in Greene
County on south side of Nolichucky River, adjoining Philip Sherrill,
Joseph Doherty. Samuel Johnston at Fairfield, 11 July 1788.


No. 750      Page 288
For 10 pounds per 100 acres - to Joseph Kyler 200 acres in Greene County
on south side of Nolichucky River and northeast of Cove Creek, adjoining

Charles Robertson, John Cunningham, James Johnston. Samuel Johnston at Fairfield, 11 July 1788.


No. 344      Page 289
For 10 pounds per 100 acres - to Andrew McFerron 400 acres in Greene County on Long Creek, adjoining John Blackburn, Thomas Beardon and Amos Back (Buck?). Richard Caswell at Kinston, 20 September 1787.


No. 501      Page 290
For 10 pounds per 100 acres - to Thomas Johnston 200 acres in Washington County on waters of Lick Creek, adjoining Shadrack Morris, John Tyre and Hughes. Alexander Martin at Newbern, 10 November 1784.


No. 299      Page 291
For 10 pounds per 100 acres - to Edward Write 200 acres in Greene County on Pigeon Creek, adjoining Dunham. Richard Caswell, 20 September 1787.


No. 730      Page 292
For 10 pounds per 100 acres - to John McCrosky 100 acres in Greene County on north side Chuckey River. Samuel Johnston, 11 July 1788.


No. 734      Page 293
For 10 pounds per 100 acres - to John McCrosky 200 acres in Greene County on east side of Brown's line, west side of Holley's Creek, adjoining Samples. Samuel Johnston at Fairfield, 11 July 1788.


No. 606      Page 294
For 10 pounds per 100 acres - to John Sherril 250 acres in Greene County on Dry Fork of Cany Branch, adjoining Alexander Holley. Samuel Johnston, 3 August 1788.


No. 514      Page 295
For 10 pounds per 100 acres - to Robert Biggs 300 acres in Greene County on Sinking Fork of Long Creek. Richard Caswell, 20 September 1787.


No. 146      Page 295
For 10 pounds per 100 acres - to John Sevier and Richard Caswell ___ acres on north side of Tennessee River, known as Hatch Berry Bottom, adjoining Isaac Taylor. Richard Caswell, 3 April 1787.


No. 375      Page 296
For 10 pounds per 100 acres - to John Keney ___ acres in Greene County near Nolichucky River, adjoining Harmon King. Richard Caswell, 20 September 1787.


No. 505      Page 297
For 50 shillings per 100 acres - to Edward Roberts 300 acres in Greene County on Cedar Branch, adjoining Joseph Eaten, Roberts. Richard Caswell at Kinston, 20 September 1787.


No. 238      Page 298
For 10 pounds per 100 acres - to James Moore 130 acres in Greene County on north side of Holston River. Richard Caswell, 20 September 1787.


No. 169      Page 299
For 10 pounds per 100 acres - to James Moore 200 acres in Greene County below mouth of Mossy Creek, north side Holston River. Richard Caswell, 20 September 1787.

No. 521     Page 300
For 50 shillings per 100 acres - to Philip Babb 100 acres in Greene
County on south branch of Lick Creek, adjoining Charles Arrington,
William Stockton.  Richard Caswell, 20 September 1787.


No. 282     Page 301
For 10 pounds per 100 acres - to James Fulgam 90 acres in Washington
County on north side of Nolichucky River, adjoining William Storey.
Alexander Martin at Fairfield, 21 October 1782.


No. 357     Page 302
For 10 pounds per 100 acres - to William Willock 187 acres in Greene
County on north side Chucky River, head of Medow Creek.  Richard Cas-
well at Kinston, 20 September 1787.


No. 686     Page 302
For 10 pounds per 100 acres - to William Lewis 500 acres in Greene County
on Alexanders Creek, waters of Nolichucky River, containing William
Hodges claim and most of Swan Pon Creek.  Samuel Johnson at Fairfield,
11 July 1788.


No. 744     Page 303
For 10 pounds per 100 acres - to Benjamin Gooden and Joel Lewis 600 acres
in Greene County on a draught of Lick Creek that emties in against Snod-
dies Camp, adjoining James Mehan.  Samuel Johnson at Fairfield, 11 July
1788.


No. 697     Page 304
For 10 pounds per 100 acres - to Henry Speere 200 acres in Greene County
on Bent Creek, waters of Nolichucky River, including Zenas Baldwins improvements.  Samuel Johnson at Fairfield, 11 July 1788.


No. 755     Page 305
For 10 pounds per 100 acres - to Samuel Wilson 150 acres in Greene County
on south side of Nolichucky River and Cove Creek, adjoining Andrew Miller.
Samuel Johnston at Fairfield, 11 July 1788.


No. 743     Page 306
For 10 pounds per 100 acres - to Samuel Wilson 300 acres in Greene County
on south side of Nolichucky River near Cove Creek.  Samuel Johnson at
Fairfield, 11 July 1788.


No. 517     Page 307
For 10 pounds per 100 acres - to Joseph Carter 250 acres in Greene County
on Grassy Creek, a branch of Lick Creek.  Richard Caswell at Kinston, 12
September 1787.


No. 239     Page 308
For 10 pounds per 100 acres - to George Russell 300 acres in Greene
County on head of Fall Creek.  Richard Caswell at Kinston, 20 September
1787.


No. 274     Page 308
For 10 pounds per 100 acres - to George Russell 600 acres in Greene
County on Fall Creek, adjoining Donelson.  Richard Caswell at Kinston,
20 September 1787.


No. 599     Page 308
For 10 pounds per 100 acres - to Joseph Bullard 100 acres in Greene

35

County on south side of Holston River.  Samuel Johnston at Edenton, 23 August 1788.


No. 598      Page 310
For 10 pounds per 100 acres - to Joseph Bullard 400 acres in Greene County on south side of Holston River, head of Lost Creek.  Samuel Johnston at Edinton, 23 August 1788.


No. 611      Page 311
For 10 pounds per 100 acres - to Joseph Bullard 200 acres in Greene County at the head of Loss Creek, adjoining Bullard's 400 acre tract. Samuel Johnston at Edinton, 23 August 1788.


No. 592      Page 312
For 10 pounds per 100 acres - to Joseph Bullard 250 acres in Greene County on waters of Loss Creek.  Samuel Johnston at Edinton, 23 August 1788.


No. 588      Page 315
For 50 shillings per 100 acres - to Joseph Bullard 100 acres in Greene County on Little Sinking Creek, adjoining Robert Campble, Bullard, Reaves.  Samuel Johnston at Edenton, 23 August 1788.


No. 558      Page 314
For 10 pounds per 100 acres - to Joseph Bullard 600 acres in Greene County on Sinking Creek, adjoining Levy Carter, Jones, Daniel Carter. Richard Caswell at Kinston, 20 September 1787.


No. 475      Page 315
For 10 pounds per 100 acres - to Thomas Christian and Joshoa English 200 acres in Greene County on Clay Creek, a branch of French Broad River, adjoining Francis Bowen.  Richard Caswell at Kinston, 20 September 1787.


No. 188      Page 316
For 10 pounds per 100 acres - to Knise Johnston 200 acres in Greene County on north side of Holston River on Flat Creek.  Richard Caswell at Kinston, 20 September 1787.


No. 720      Page 316
For 10 pounds per 100 acres - to Hugh Weir 200 acres in Greene County on north side of Nolichucky River, adjoining John Russell.  Samuel Johnston at Fairfield, 11 July 1788.


No. 381      Page 317
For 10 pounds per 100 acres - To John Oliphant 50 acres in Greene County on McCartney's Creek, adjoining Tom Gillespie, Gabriel McCoal.  Richard Caswell at Kinston, 20 September 1787.


No. 245      Page 318
For 10 pounds per 100 acres - to Alexander McMillen 200 acres in Greene County on south side of Holston River at mouth of a branch.  Richard Caswell at Kinston, 20 September 1787.


No. 544      Page 319
For 10 pounds per 100 acres - to William Moore 300 acres in Greene County on Meadow Creek, to dry fork of Meadow Creek, to watery ford of Meadow Creek, adjoining Crow, Patterson.  Richard Caswell at Kinston, 20 September 1787.

No. 337     Page 320
For 10 pounds per 100 acres - to Benjamin Goodin 400 acres in Greene
County on Roaring Fork of Lick Creek including his own improvement,
adjoining John Carter.  Richard Caswell at Kinston, 20 September 1787.


No. 754     Page 321
For 10 pounds per 100 acres - to Benjamin Gooden 600 acres in Greene
County on the watery fork of Bent Creek above Blue Spring, adjoining
Capt. Roddy, Horton.  Samuel Johnston at Fairfield, 11 July 1788.


No. 183     Page 322
For 10 pounds per 100 acres - to Thomas Stockton 400 acres in Greene
County on north side of French Broad River.  Richard Caswell at Kinston,
1 November 1786.


No. 308     Page 322
For 10 pounds per 100 acres - to John Casteel 311 1/4 acres in Greene
County on Puncheon Camp Creek, adjoining Philip Varnel.  Richard Cas-
well at Kinston, 20 September 1787.


No. 650     Page 323
For 10 pounds per 100 acres - to Michael Box 150 acres in Greene County
on south side of Nolichucky River on Camp Creek, both sides of Camp Creek,
adjoining Thomas Davis, Lewis Morgan, David Reynolds.  Samuel Johnston at
Fairfield, 11 July 1788.


No. 242     Page 324
For 10 pounds per 100 acres - to John Mahan 300 acres in Greene County
on both sides of Lick Creek, adjoining George Hallmark, John Privince.
Richard Caswell at Kinston, 20 September 1787.


No. 563     Page 325
For 10 pounds per 100 acres - to Henry Dungham 200 acres on Pigeon Creek,
adjoining George Haworth, Joseph Keney, Ballenger.  Richard Caswell at
Kinston, 20 September 1787.


No. 506     Page 326
For 10 pounds per 100 acres - to Thomas Davis 200 acres in Greene County
on south side of Nolichucky River on Camp Creek, adjoining Davis and
Lewis Morgan.  Richard Caswell at Kinston, 20 September 1787.


No. 301     Page 327
For 10 pounds per 100 acres - to John Wier 200 acres in Greene County on
north side of Nolichucky River, known as Long Cane Break, including an
island in river and improvement he now lives on.  Richard Caswell at
Kinston, 20 September 1787.


No. 409     Page 328
For 50 shillings per 100 acres - to Marshal Lovelady 100 acres in Greene
County on Cedar Branch, adjoining Barnet Brumley.  Richard Caswell at
Kinston, 20 September 1787.


No. 374     Page 329
For 10 pounds per 100 acres - to William Clerk (Cocke?) 180 acres in
Greene County on River Ridge about 3/4 miles from French Broad River,
opposite John Gentry's cabbin.  Richard Caswell at Kinston, 20 September
1787.

No. 487      Page 329
For 10 pounds per 100 acres - to Thomas Stockton 100 acres in Greene
County on north side of French Broad River, nearly opposite mouth of
Little Pigeon River, known as Indian Old Fields, adjoining Stockton.
Richard Caswell at Kinston, 20 September 1787.


No. 548      Page 330
For 10 pounds per 100 acres - to Jacob Johnston 200 acres in Greene
County on north side of Nolichucky River, adjoining Joseph Damren
(Dunham?). Richard Caswell at Kinston, 20 September 1787.


No. 424      Page 331
For 10 pounds per 100 acres - to Hosea Stout 100 acres in Greene County
on south side of Nolichucky River on Lick Creek, adjoining Abraham White,
Abel Richardson. Richard Caswell at Kinston, 20 September 1787.


No. 645      Page 332
For 10 pounds per 100 acres - to James Robertson 200 acres in Greene
County on Cedar Branch. Samuel Johnston at Fairfield, 11 July 1788.


No. 605      Page 333
For 10 pounds per 100 acres - to James Robertson 150 acres in Greene
County on south side of Clinch River. Samuel Johnston at Edinton.


No. 610      Page 334
For 50 shillings per 100 acres - to Samuel Moore 100 acres in Washington
County on Little Sinking Creek. Alexander Martin at Newbern, 10 November
1784.


No. 649      Page 334
For 10 pounds per 100 acres - to Henry Conway 300 acres in Greene County
on north side of French Broad River opposite Gaser Dagy's. Samuel Johnston at Fairfield, 11 July 1788.


No. 476      Page 335
For 10 pounds per 100 acres - to Gideon Morris 400 acres in Greene County
on a branch of Holston River, known as Jlaven? Camp, adjoining Harmon Cox
at fork of Zuetters? Creek. Richard Caswell at Kinston, 20 September
1787.


No. 538      Page 336
For 10 pounds per 100 acres - to Adam Sherrill 300 acres in Greene County
on south side of Nolichucky River against the seven islands, adjoining
John Trimble. Richard Caswell at Kinston, 20 September 1787.


No. 329      Page 337
For 10 pounds per 100 acres - to James Bolinger 95 acres in Greene County
on Pigeon Creek, adjoining Henry Dunham, Joseph Keeney, John Reese,
Andrew Bogle. Richard Caswell at Kinston, 20 September 1787.


No. 162      Page 338
For 50 shillings per 100 acres - to James Grayham 29 1/4 acres in Greene
County on north side of Nolichucky River including mouth of Horse Creek,
adjoining Oneal south side Horse Creek. Richard Caswell at Kinston, 20
September 1787.


No. 524      Page 339
For 50 shillings per 100 acres - to Ephraim Cox 400 acres in Greene
County, adjoining John Patterson, bank of Nolichucky River in the

Barrons.  Richard Caswell at Kinston, 20 September 1787.


No. 435      Page 340
For 10 pounds per 100 acres - to James Bradley 400 acres in Greene County
on south side of Holston River, beginning mouth of Sinking Creek.  Richard
Caswell at Kinston, 20 September 1787.


No. 705      Page 341
For 50 shillings per 100 acres - to Edward Box 60 acres in Washington
County.  Richard Caswell at Kinston, 11 October 1786.


No. 530      Page 342
For 10 pounds per 100 acres - to John Russell 300 acres in Greene County
on north side of Nolichucky River, adjoining Hugh Wear, John Steal.
Richard Caswell at Kinston, 20 September 1787.


No. 443      Page 343
For 50 shillings per 100 acres - to William Moore 100 acres in Greene
County on Holley's Creek of Nolichucky River, adjoining Alexander Wilson,
Andrew Martin, William Henderson.  Richard Caswell at Kinston, 20 Sep-
tember 1787.


No. 566      Page 343
For 10 pounds per 100 acres - to Mathias Wall 317 acres in Greene County
on Cove Creek, adjoining Charles Robertson, James Crag.  Richard Caswell
at Kinston, 20 September 1787.


No. 710      Page 344
For 10 pounds per 100 acres - to William Job 500 acres in Greene County
on French Broad River, adjoining John Wards and said Job.  Samuel Johnston at Fairfield, 11 July 1788.


No. 732      Page 345
For 10 pounds per 100 acres - to Jason Isbel 100 acres in Greene County
on south side of French Broad River, the mouth of Big Pigeon.  Samuel
Johnston at Fairfield, 11 July 1788.


No. 468      Page 346
For 10 pounds per 100 acres - to Corben Lane 150 acres in Greene County
adjoining James McCartney.  Richard Caswell at Kinston, 20 September
1786.


No. 295      Page 347
For 10 pounds per 100 acres - to Benjamin Goodin 230 acres in Greene
County on both sides of Big Gap Creek, beginning above Bluff of Bays
Mountain, adjoining Joseph Harden.  Richard Caswell at Kinston, 20
September 1787.


No. 486      Page 348
For 10 pounds per 100 acres - to Thomas Goodin 300 acres in Greene County
on Lick Creek opposite mouth of Lick Run, adjoining Isaac Bullard.
Richard Caswell at Kinston, 20 September 1787.


No. 366      Page 349
For 10 pounds per 100 acres - to James Pierce 129 acres in Greene County
on south side of Nolichucky River.  Richard Caswell at Kinston, 20 September 1787.

No. 441     Page 349
For 10 pounds per 100 acres - to Asahel Rawlings 268 acres in Washington County on north side of Nolichucky River. Hillsboro, 13 October 1783.


No. 748     Page 350
For 10 pounds per 100 acres - to Job Sims 574 acres in Greene County on Lick Creek, adjoining Morris Mitchell. Samuel Johnston at Fairfield, 11 July 1788.


No. 685     Page 351
For 10 pounds per 100 acres - to Benjamin Douglass 200 acres in Greene County in valley between Clinch Mountain and the Copper Ridge, adjoining David Stewart. Samuel Johnston at Fairfield, 11 July 1788.


No. 427     Page 352
For 50 shillings per 100 acres - to Michael Rawlings 200 acres in Washington County on Cain Creek above Asahel Rawlings entry. Alexander Martin at Hillsboro, 13 October 1783.


No. 424     Page 353
For 10 pounds per 100 acres - to Nathaniel Rawlings 300 acres in Washington County on Carricks Branch of Lick Creek, including large Clay Lick in War Path above John Carricks improvement on Carricks Branch. Alexander Martin, 13 October 1783.


No. 377.1     Page 354
For 50 shillings per 100 acres - to Asahel Rawlings 200 acres in Washington County on Cain Creek. Alexander Martin, 13 October 1783.


No. 757     Page 355
For 10 pounds per 100 acres - to Garrett Fitzgerald 300 acres in Greene County on Richland Creek, to Buffalo Hide Creek. Samuel Johnston at Fairfield, 11 July 1788.


No. 356     Page 355
For 10 pounds per 100 acres - to Garrett Fitzgerald 400 acres in Greene County on north side of Holston River, below Mathew Sparks improvement. Samuel Johnston at Fairfield, 11 July 1788.


No. 355     Page 356
For 10 pounds per 100 acres - to John King Fitzgerald 400 acres in Greene County on a branch of French Broad River. Samuel Johnston at Fairfield, 11 July 1788.


No. 355.1     Page 357
For 50 shillings per 100 acres - to Daniel Rawlings 200 acres in Washington County on west side of Lick Creek, on a creek called Plumb Creek, on each side of War Path. Alexander Martin at Hillsboro, 13 October 1783.


No. 725     Page 358
For 10 pounds per 100 acres - to Thomas Lee 120 acres in Greene County at head of Flat Creek, including a Limestone Spring. Samuel Johnston at Fairfield, 11 July 1788.


No. 442     Page 358
For 50 shillings per 100 acres - to Nathaniel Rawlings 200 acres in Washington County on south fork of Cane Creek, on each side of War Path. Alexander Martin at Hillsboro, 13 October 1783.

No. 559     Page 359
For 10 pounds per 100 acres - to Peter Fine 200 acres in Greene County on
north side of French Broad River above mouth of Clear Creek, my improvement and an island, below waggon road on bank of river. Richard Caswell
at Kinston, 20 September 1787.


No. 549     Page 360
For 50 shillings per 100 acres - to Robert Caldwell 300 acres in Greene
County on south side of Nolichucky River at mouth of Camp Creek, big
stake, Old Indian Boundary Line. Richard Caswell at Kinston, 20 September 1787.


No. 454     Page 361
For 10 pounds per 100 acres - to William Morrow 170 acres in Greene
County on south side of Nolichucky River, adjoining Francis Hues,
William Haile, including island in river and plantation Benjamin
Williams lives on. Richard Caswell at Kinston, 20 September 1787.


No. 474     Page 362
For 10 pounds per 100 acres - to Isaac Bullard 640 acres in Greene County
on Lick Creek, adjoining Joseph Jones, Jeremiah Meeks, Jonathan Denlow.
Richard Caswell at Kinston, 20 September 1787.


No. 412     Page 363
For 50 shillings per 100 acres - to Aaron Rawlings 200 acres in Washington County on south side of Carricks Branch, waters of Lick Creek, including Clay Lick. Alexander Martin at Hillsboro, 13 October 1783.


No. 430     Page 363
For 50 shillings per 100 acres - to John Rawlings 200 acres in Washington
County on Lick Creek, on branch above Nathaniel Rawlings, including Clay
Lick. Alexander Martin at Hillsboro, 13 October 1783.


No. 397     Page 364
For 10 pounds per 100 acres - to Nicholas Smith 335 acres in Greene
County on the White Horn, a fork of Bent Creek, adjoining James Roddy.
Richard Caswell at Kinston, 20 September 1787.


No. 466     Page 365
For 10 pounds per 100 acres - to James Goodin 200 acres in Greene County
on both sides of Lick Creek, including his improvement, adjoining Thomas
Goodin, Isaac Bullard, Caleb Carter. Richard Caswell at Kinston, 20
September 1787.


No. 437.1     Page 366
For 10 pounds per 100 acres - to Benjamin Goodin 220 acres in Greene
County on head of Swan Pond Creek. Richard Caswell at Hillsboro, 20
September 1787.


No. 354     Page 366
For 10 pounds per 100 acres - to Brittain Smith Junr. 500 acres in Greene
County on south side of Holston River, including spring on Bomans Branch
of Bent Creek. Richard Caswell at Kinston, 20 September 1787.


No. 410     Page 367
For 10 pounds per 100 acres - to John Latherdale 200 acres in Greene
County on north side of Nolachucky River. Richard Caswell at Kinston,
20 September 1787.

41

No. 388      Page 368
For 10 pounds per 100 acres - to Joseph Tipton 400 acres in Greene County
on Lick Creek, adjoining Thomas Isbel. Richard Caswell at Kinston, 20
September 1787.


No. 384      Page 369
For 10 pounds per 100 acres - to John Richardson 240 acres in Greene
County on Grassy Branch of Lick Creek, adjoining Armstrong, Frank
Hamilton. Richard Caswell at Kinston, 20 September 1787.


No. 433      Page 370
For 10 pounds per 100 acres - to John Finn 150 acres in Greene County on
Lick Creek, on John Prices Branch, adjoining Thomas Standfield. Richard
Caswell at Kinston, 20 September 1787.


No. 542      Page 371
For 10 pounds per 100 acres - to Thomas Lusk 400 acres in Greene County
on north side of French Broad River at the mouth of Sinking Cain?, adjoining George Sherrill. Richard Caswell at Kinston, 20 September 1787.


No. 95      Page 372
For 10 pounds per 100 acres - to John Walker 250 acres in Greene County
on bank of French Broad River. Richard Caswell at Kinston, 1 November
1786.


No. 736      Page 372
For 10 pounds per 100 acres - to Frederick Whittenbarger 300 acres in
Greene County on north side of Nolichucky River, his own improvement on
river bank. Richard Caswell at Fairfield, 11 July 1788.


No. 326      Page 373
For 10 pounds per 100 acres - to Thomas Fowler 150 acres in Greene County
on Clay Creek. Richard Caswell at Kinston, 20 September 1787.


No. 718      Page 374
For 10 pounds per 100 acres - to Philip Hatter 100 acres in Greene County
on south side of Nolichucky River. Samuel Johnston at Fairfield, 11 July
1788.


No. 494      Page 375
For 10 pounds per 100 acres - to John Bradshaw 200 acres in Greene County
on head of Dumplin Creek, adjoining Richard Rankens, Meek. Richard Caswell at Kinston, 20 September 1787.


No. 523      Page 376
For 10 pounds per 100 acres - to George Erven 1040 acres in Greene County
on north side of Holston River. Richard Caswell at Kinston, 20 September
1787.


No. 339      Page 377
For 10 pounds per 100 acres - to Robert Seypart 600 acres in Greene
County on State Stone Creek between French Broad River and Nolichucky
River, 2 miles above mouth of said creek, including his improvements.
Richard Caswell at Kinston, 20 September 1787.


No. 340      Page 378
For 10 pounds per 100 acres - to Joseph McMurtrey 300 acres in Greene
County on both sides Camp Creek to bank of Laurel Spring Branch. Richard
Caswell at Kinston, 20 September 1787.

No. 821     Page 378
For 50 shillings per 100 acres - to Adam Starnes 300 acres in Greene
County. Samuel Johnston, 27 November 1789.


No. 750     Page 379
For 10 pounds per 100 acres - to Joseph Kyler 200 acres in Greene County
on south side of Nolichucky River, adjoining John Cunningham, Charles
Robertson, James Johnston, north side of Cove Creek. Samuel Johnston at
Fairfield, 11 July 1788.


No. 820     Page 380
For 50 shillings per 100 acres - to James Lowe 100 acres in Greene County
on north side of Nolichucky River on waters of Sinking Creek. Samuel
Johnston at Fayetteville, 27 November 1789.


No. 808     Page 381
For 50 shillings per 100 acres - to Ephraim Dunlap 600 acres in Greene
County on north side of Tennessee River, West Fork of Whites Creek.
Samuel Johnston at Edinton, 11 May 1789.


No. 528     Page 382
For 10 pounds per 100 acres - to William Morrow 327 acres in Greene
County on Richland Creek, adjoining Russell. Richard Caswell at Kin-
ston, 20 September 1787.


No. 501     Page 383
For 10 pounds per 100 acres - to Joel Matthews 200 acres in Greene County
on south side of Nolichucky River on Flag Branch, adjoining John Lee,
James Potter. Richard Caswell at Kinston, 20 September 1787.


No. 571     Page 384
For 10 pounds per 100 acres - to John Dey Armond 300 acres in Washington
County on south side of Nolichuckey River on Camp Creek. Alexander
Martin at Newbern, 10 November 1784.


No. 584     Page 384
For 10 pounds per 100 acres - to Samuel Dunwoody 200 acres in Greene
County on south side of Little Chucky above the head of the Spring Fork,
including the Sinking Spring, adjoining himself, William Davidson,
Garret Caudon. Samuel Johnston at Edinton, 3 August 1780.


No. 543     Page 385
For 10 pounds per 100 acres - to William English 640 acres in Greene
County on Horse Creek, adjoining John Beard. Richard Caswell at Kin-
ston, 20 September 1787.


No. 337     Page 386
For 10 pounds per 100 acres - to James Henderson 200 acres in Greene
County on south side of Nolichucky River near the bank. Richard Cas-
well at Kinston, 20 September 1787.


No. 664     Page 387
For 10 pounds per 100 acres - to David Brown 200 acres in Greene County
on Cane Branch between Clear Creek and Long Creek, adjoining George
Hopkins, William Boilstone. Samuel Johnston at Fairfield, 11 July 1788.


No. 430     Page 388
For 10 pounds per 100 acres - to Jacob Tipton 200 acres in Greene County,
adjoining Thomas Goodin. Richard Caswell at Kinston, 20 September 1787.

No. 439     Page 389
For 10 pounds per 100 acres – to Benjamin Anderson 600 acres in Greene County on Roaring Fork of Lick Creek. Richard Caswell at Kinston, 20 September 1787.


No. 822     Page 390
For 10 pounds per 100 acres – to Ananias McCoy 300 acres in Greene County on north side of Clinch River, adjoining Galliher's 600 acre tract, Hackett's 500 acre tract. Samuel Johnston at Edinton, 11 August 1789.


No. 28     Page 391
For 50 shillings per 100 acres – to Robert Kerr 300 acres in Greene County beginning at a spring a condition with Robert Hood, adjoining Andrew McFerron, James Lusk, David Copeland. Richard Caswell at Kinston, 1 November 1786.


No. 318     Page 392
For 10 pounds per 100 acres – to Robert Orr 273 acres in Greene County on south side of Nolichucky River, down in grant says Robert Kerr. Richard Caswell at Kinston, 20 September 1787.


No. 564     Page 392
For 10 pounds per 100 acres – To John Lee 220 acres in Greene County on south side of Nolichucky River on Flag Branch, beginning at Pine tree, Sherrills Road, corner to Joel Matthews. Richard Caswell at Kinston, 20 September 1787.


No. 632     Page 393
For 10 pounds per 100 acres – to William Black 300 acres in Greene County on north side Clear Creek. Samuel Johnston at Edinton, 23 August 1788.


No. 618     Page 394
For 50 shillings per 100 acres – to Hugh Beard 150 acres in Washington County, adjoining Sedusky, passing over Horse Creek, William English. Alexander Martin at New Bern, 10 November 1784.


No. 185     Page 395
For 50 shillings per 100 acres – to Caleb Hunter 93 acres in Washington County on Mill Creek, waters of Big Limestone, including Ferral McGopes improvement, adjoining Edwards. Alexander Martin at Fairfield, 24 October 1782.


No. 474     Page 396
For 50 shillings per 100 acres – to Thomas Brandon 400 acres in Washington County on Roaring Fork of Lick Creek, adjoining William Dono, Joseph Kuykendoll. Alexander Martin at Newbern, 10 November 1782.


No. 355     Page 397
For 10 pounds per 100 acres – to Thomas Gooden 150 acres in Greene County on a Draught of Lick Creek, including improvement made by John Cane. Richard Caswell at Kinston, 20 September 1787.


No. 488     Page 398
For 10 pounds per 100 acres – to Benjamin Crowe 300 acres in Greene County on south side of Nolichucky River on both sides of Meadow Creek, to watery fork of Meadow Creek. Richard Caswell at Kinston, 20 September 1787.

No. 813          Page 399
For 50 shillings per 100 acres - to James Paul 250 acres in Washington
County on west bank of Little River, north side of Crooked Creek.
Alexander Martin at Kinston, 20 September 1790.


No. 412          Page 400
For 10 pounds per 100 acres - to Robert Crockett 100 acres in Greene
County on waters of Lick Creek. Richard Caswell at Kinston, 20 Sep-
tember 1787.


No. 512          Page 401
For 50 shillings per 100 acres - to Michael Border 250 acres in Greene
County on south side of Nolichucky River, adjoining Thomas Gilespie.
Richard Caswell at Kinston, 20 September 1787.


No. 537          Page 402
For 10 pounds per 100 acres - to Acquilla Sherril 300 acres in Greene
County on Cove Creek, south side of Nolichucky River. Richard Caswell
at Kinston, 20 September 1787.


No. 821          Page 403
For 50 shillings per 100 acres - to Adam Starnes 300 acres in Greene
County. Samuel Johnston at Fayetteville, 27 November 1789.


No. 1066         Page 404
For 50 shillings per 100 acres - to James Rogers 200 acres in Washington
County on north side of Nolachucky River on Deals Branch of Lick Creek.
Alexander Martin at Dunbery, 11 May 1792.


No. 1247         Page 405
For 50 shillings per 100 acres - to Barnett Brumley 200 acres in Greene
County on south side of Nolachucky River, adjoining Shaderick McNew,
James Johnston. Alexander Martin at Newbern, 27 November 1792.


No. 1003         Page 406
For 50 shillings per 100 acres - to Moses Moore 200 acres in Washington
County on waters of Big Limestone, called Browns Creek, adjoining J.
Gilliam, Thomas Brown, including Moses Moore Junr. improvement.
Alexander Martin at Newbern, 27 November 1792.


No. 1234         Page 407
For 50 shillings per 100 acres - to George Smith 250 acres in Greene
County on Panther Creek, adjoining David Southerland. Richard Dots
Spraight at Newbern, 29 July 1793.


No. 1231         Page 407
For 50 shillings per 100 acres - to Benjamin Merret 300 acres in Greene
County on north side of Clinch River on Sycamore Creek, adjoining Thomas
King. Richard Dobspraight at Newbern, 29 July 1793.


No. 1012         Page 408
For 50 shillings per 100 acres - to Jasper Miller 200 acres in Greene
County, adjoining Lanty Armstrongs land. Alexander Martin at Newbern,
26 December 1791.


No. 362          Page 409
For 50 shillings per 100 acres - to James Milliken 150 acres in Greene
County on south fork of Cedar Branch of Lick Creek, adjoining Joseph
Henderson, John Odle, Perminees Taylor. Richard Caswell at Kinston,

20 September 1787.


No. 1244        Page 410
For 50 shillings per 100 acres - to James Galbreath 640 acres in Greene
County on Drafts of Richland Creek, adjoining John Gibson.  Richard
Dobspraight at Newbern, 29 July 1793.


No. 1264        Page 411
For 50 shillings per 100 acres - to Samuel Robertson 100 acres in Greene
County on north side of Nolachucky River on French Creek.  Alexander
Martin at Newbern, 27 November 1792.


No. 1065        Page 412
For 10 pounds per 100 acres - to Francis Alexander Ramsey 150 acres in
Greene County on north side of Nolachucky River and west side of Sinking
Creek, adjoining Joseph Whittenbarger.  Alexander Martin at Danbury, 11
May 1792.


No. 891         Page 413
For 10 pounds per 100 acres - to Robert Kirkpatrick 300 acres in Greene
County on Plumb Creek including the War Path, adjoining David Lindsey,
John Blair.  Alexander Martin at Fayetteville, 17 November 1799.


No. 984         Page 414
For 10 pounds per 100 acres - to John Wilson 100 acres in Greene County.
Alexander Martin at Newbern.


No. 865         Page 415
For 10 pounds per 100 acres - to Josiah Vansendtt 356 acres in Greene
County adjoining Hutchison, John Wilson.  Alexander Martin at Fayette-
ville, 17 November 1790.


No. 933         Page 416
For 10 pounds per 100 acres - to Isaac Vinsent 585 acres in Greene County
on south side of Nolichucky River on Cove Creek, adjoining John Lescollet,
Houston.  Alexander Martin at Newbern, 3 February 1794.


No. 932         Page 417
For 10 pounds per 100 acres - to Isaac Vinsant and James Pierce 210 acres
in Greene County on Cove Creek, south side of Nolachucky River, adjoining
Andrew Miller along end of Cove Mountain.  Alexander Martin at Newbern,
26 December 1791.


No. 1122        Page 418
For 10 pounds per 100 acres - to Sperling Bowman 100 acres in Greene
County adjoining McDonald line on watery fork of Camp Creek, Hopkins.
Richard Dobspraight at Newbern, 12 January 1793.


No. 1230        Page 419
For 50 shillings per 100 acres - to John Bull 550 acres in Greene County
at Bulls Gap of Bays Mountain.  Alexander Martin at Newbern, 27 November
1792.


No. 976         Page 420
For 50 shillings per 100 acres - to Thomas Gilespie 200 acres in Washington County on west side of Nolachucky River.  Alexander Martin at Newbern,
26 December 1791.

No. 925      Page 421
For 10 pounds per 100 acres - to Samuel Lewis 100 acres in Greene County
on McCartney's Branch, adjoining William Hannah. Alexander Martin at
Newbern, 16 December 1791.


No. 887      Page 421
For 10 pounds per 100 acres - to Thomas Johnston 640 acres in Greene
County on Bent Creek, including a Crab Orchard west side of Blue Spring
Fork of Bent Creek, adjoining James Roddy. Alexander Martin at Fayette-
ville, 17 November 1790.


No. 1255      Page 422
For 10 pounds per 100 acres - to Henry Willis 400 acres in Greene County
on south side of Nolachucky River, including his improvement, adjoining
Corren, Carr. Richard Dobspraight at Newbern, 29 July 1793.


BOOK 1-B


No. 1382      Page 1
For 10 pounds per 100 acres - to Job Sims 574 acres in Greene County on
both sides of Lick Creek. Samuel Ashe, 20 June 1796.


No. 433      Page 2
For 50 shillings per 100 acres - to Thomas Williams 200 acres in Washing-
ton County lying on first fork of Bluff Creek between creek and warpath.
Alexander Martin at Hillsboro, 13 October 1783.


No. 229      Page 3
For 50 shillings per 100 acres - to Robert Been 440 acres in Washington
County on a branch of Lick Creek, adjoining John Keeneys. Alexander
Martin at Fairfield, 24 October 1782.


No. 1318      Page 4
For 50 shillings per 100 acres - to Charles Hays 640 acres in Greene
County on Long Fork of Lick Creek, called Walnut Bottom, between Gideon
Morris and Matthew Harrises Plantation. Richard Dobbs Spaight at
Raleigh, 6 January 1795.


No. 709      Page 5
For 50 shillings per 100 acres - to Moses Kennedy 100 acres in Greene
County on Adcocks line, formerly Washington County, adjoining Lenoard
Adcock, John Ryan. Richard Caswell at Kinston, 6 October 1786.


No. 9      Page 6
For 50 shillings per 100 acres - to John Wallace 400 acres in Washington
County on Lick Creek near Great Knobb Licks, including a bottom and
valley where said branch sinks, adjoining Samuel Harris. Richard Caswell
at Kinston, 15 December 1778.


No. 217      Page 7
For 50 shillings per 100 acres - to Shadrach Morris 299 acres in Greene
County on branch of Lick Creek including Morris' old improvement, ad-
joining Bonds old claim, adjoining Charles Hays, Henry Cross. Alexander
Martin at Fairfield, 24 October 1782.


No. 23      Page 8
For 50 shillings per 100 acres - to Charles Hays 400 acres in Washington
County, now Greene County, including Aaron Burlesons old improvement.

No. 323　　　Page 9
For 50 shillings per 100 acres - to Robert Stephenson 45 acres in Washington County on Lick Fork of Lick Creek, adjoining Charles Hays line of his Manner (Manor) Place. Alexander Martin at Fairfield, 24 October 1782.


No. 447　　　Page 10
For 50 shillings per 100 acres - to Joseph Kerkendale 100 acres in Washington County on Roaring Fork of Lick Creek, adjoining William Dunn. Alexander Martin at Hillsboro, 13 October 1783.


No. 1226　　　Page 11
For 50 shillings per 100 acres - to Robert Walker 1200 acres in Greene County on south side of Elk River, adjoining William Wills No. 2181 containing 2500 acres. Richard Dobbs Spraight, 27 November 1793.


No. 1224　　　Page 11
For 50 shillings per 100 acres - to Robert and Samuel Walker 1000 acres in Greene County on south side of Elk River, adjoining William Hills 2000 acres No. 2649. Richard Dobbs Spaight, 15 September 1792.


No. 337　　　Page 12
For 50 shillings per 100 acres - to Benjamin Goodin 400 acres in Greene County on Roaring Fork of Lick Creek, adjoining Peter Harmon. Sealed by Richard Caswell, 20 September 1787.
SURVEY ALTERED: Survey of Matthew Cox to correct errors in Benjamin Goodin's 400 acres on Roaring Fork of Lick Creek, adjoining Rachel Anders, Harmon, John Carter, Daniel Carter. James Temple surveyor of Greene County, Isaac Armitage and Isaac Harmon chain bearers.


No. 1344　　　Page 13
For 50 shillings per 100 acres - to John Sevier 640 acres in Greene County on south side of French Broad River to waters of Spring Creek, east of Big Pigeon River. Richard Dobbs Spaight, 20 August 1795.


No. 1366　　　Page 14
For 50 shillings per 100 acres - to John Sevier Senr. 640 acres in Greene County on south side of Nolachucky River, adjoining Joseph McMurtrey. Samuel Ashe, 27 November 1795.


No. 102　　　Page 16
For 50 shillings per 100 acres - to Benjamin Gist 400 acres in Washington County on Lick Creek, including a cane break where Joseph Gist and Joseph Dunhams formerly meets. Alexander Martin at Fairfield, 23 October 1782.


No. 356　　　Page 17
For 50 shillings per 100 acres - to Andrew Reed 100 acres in Washington County on Cedar Fork of Lick Creek, including a large fall on said fork. Alexander Martin, 13 October 1783.


No. 1291　　　Page 18
For 50 shillings per 100 acres - to Samuel McKenney 150 acres in Greene County, adjoining James McMurtrey. Richard Dobbs Spaight, 15 September 1792.


No. 844　　　Page 20
For 50 shillings per 100 acres - to Isaac Davis 100 acres in Greene County on Double Lick Fork of Lick Creek. Alexander Martin at Fayetteville, 17 November 1790.

No. 270     Page 21
For 50 shillings per 100 acres - to Benjamin Gist 400 acres in Greene
County on north side of Nolachucky River on Gists Branch.  Richard
Caswell, 7 September 1787.


No. 189     Page 22
For 50 shillings per 100 acres - to Joseph Bogle 236 acres in Greene
County on Little Chuckey at mouth of Delaney's Creek, adjoining Gamble,
John Corbet.  Richard Caswell, 20 September 1787.


No. 1073     Page 25
For 50 shillings per 100 acres - to Joseph Whittenberger 300 acres in
Greene County, adjoining James Moore's land on Haley's Creek, James
Alexander, James Moore now Wilson's line.  Richard Dobbs Spaight, 26
December 1792.


No. 1261     Page 26
For 50 shillings per 100 acres - to Anthony Moore 200 acres in Greene
County on the head waters of Stonies Creek, adjoining Smith.  Richard
Dobbs Spaight, 29 July 1793.


No. 1391     Page 28
For 50 shillings per 100 acres - to John Collier and John Ryon 200 acres
in Greene County.  Samuel Ashe, 2 December 1796.


No. 1312     Page 29
For 50 shillings per 100 acres - to John Morris 100 acres in Greene
County on north side of Nolachucky River, adjoining Jacob Hise.  Richard
Dobbs Spraight in Raleigh, 6 January 1795.


No. 1444     Page 31
For 50 shillings per 100 acres - to John Morris 100 acres in Greene
County on north side Nolachucky River, adjoining Jacob Hise, Benjamin
Pickering, Howard.  Benjamin Williams at Raleigh, 10 May 1784.


No. 1129     Page 32
For 10 pounds per 100 acres - to Andrew Miller 100 acres in Greene County
on south side Nolachucky River at ford of Cove Creek, adjoining William
Wilson.  Richard Dobbs Spraight at Newbern, 12 January 1791.


No. 214     Page 34
For 10 pounds per 100 acres - to Joseph Bullard 140 acres in Greene
County on north side Lick Creek, adjoining himself, Daniel Carter.
Richard Caswell at Kinston, 20 September 1787.


No. 1065     Page 35
For 10 pounds per 100 acres - to James Galbreath 500 acres in Washington
County on Nolachucky River including mouth of Cove Creek, adjoining
William Wall.  Alexander Martin at Danbury, 11 May 1792.


No. 837     Page 37
For 10 pounds per 100 acres - to John Galbreath 10 acres in Washington
County on Sinking Creek adjoining Robert Parker, Alexander Galbreath.
Alexander Martin, 17 November 1790.


No. 1143     Page 38
For 50 shillings per 100 acres - to William Ford ___ acres in Greene
County on a branch of Lick Creek, adjoining Gillespie.  Richard Dobbs
Spraight at Newbern, 12 January 1793.

49

No. 158        Page 40
For 10 pounds per 100 acres - to Joseph Bullard 400 acres in Greene
County on a branch of Lick Creek, adjoining Daniel Carter, Abraham
Carter, Philemon Higgons, Jacob Carter. Kinston, 19 November 17__?


No. 167        Page 42
For 10 pounds per 100 acres - to Andrew Miller 300 acres in Greene County
on both sides of Cove Creek, adjoining Samuel Wilson. Richard Caswell at
Kinston, 20 September 1787.


No. 1062       Page 43
For 50 shillings per 100 acres - to James Galbreath 600 acres in Greene
County on Frankes Creek, adjoining James Martin. Alexander Martin at
Danbury, 11 May 1792.


No. 68         Page 45
For 10 pounds per 100 acres - to Major Temple 240 acres in Greene County
on a branch of Richland Creek. Richard Caswell at Kinston, 1 November
1786. The errors in this grant corrected and amended by the secretary.
Robert Houston, Secretary, 5 November 1786.


No. 315        Page 47
For 10 pounds per 100 acres - to Jacob Carter 200 acres in Greene County
on Roaring Fork of Lick Creek, including improvement, adjoining Joseph
Bullard. Richard Caswell at Kinston, 20 September 1787. Errors in
Grant amended and corrected, 20 September 1787, adjoining Benjamin
Anderson.


No. 1245       Page 50
For 10 pounds per 100 acres - to Isaac Bullard 340 acres in Greene County
on side of Lick Creek, with his own line. Richard Dobbs Spraight, 9
August 1792.


No. 652        Page 51
State of Tennessee, to John Gass 188 acres on Roaring Fork of Lick Creek,
entered in 6th District of No. 104 - 23 August 1808 - from No. 2439 to
John Gray Blount and Thomas Blount for 1000 acres, 10 February 1808, they
signed to Stokley Donelson and he to William Cathcart, he to William
Mitchell, and he to Spencer Griffin and he to John Gass, this enterer -
County of Green, District of Washington, adjoining John McPheran, Joshua
Kidwell. Willie Blount at Knoxville, 4 October 1809.


No. 653        Page 53
State of Tennessee, to John Gass on Lick Creek - 6th District No. 103 -
23 August 1808 - founded on a duplicate warrant No. 2439 issued by A.
Roane, Commissioner - County of Greene, District of Washington - adjoin-
ing Nathan Carter and Jacob Gray, known as Middle Hall Place. Willie
Blount at Knoxville, 4 October 1809.


No. 655        Page 54
State of North Carolina, to James Brown 60 acres in Washington County on
waters of Lick Creek - 18 April 1808 - Duplicate Warrant 2629 issued by
John Armstrong to Thomas Chiles for 1000 acres, 30 November 1784, sold
to James Patterson, Sheriff of Greene County, to James Galbreath highest
bidder. James Galbreath signed 60 acres to James Brown, enterer, adjoining James Campbell, Jacob Bowman, Abraham Williams, 10 May 1808.
Willie Blount at Knoxville, 4 October 1809.


No. 633        Page 56
State of Tennessee, to William Jolly 50 acres on Lick Creek, 1 August

1808 - Duplicate Warrant No. 910 - Issued A. Roane to James McBee 9
February 1808 - then to Israel McKee - Samuel Crawford, he 50 acres to
William Jolly the enterer - District of Washington - adjoining himself,
Thomas Brannon. Willie Blount, 29 September 1809.


No. 497      Page 57
For 10 pounds per 100 acres - to Andrew McPheran 250 acres in Greene
County on west side of Richland Creek, adjoining James Huston, Thomas
Tate, Robert Hood, Henry Farnsworth, William Willicks. Richard Caswell,
20 September 1787.


No. 377      Page 59
For 10 pounds per 100 acres - to James Henderson 200 acres in Greene
County on south side Nolachucky River on bank of river going downstream.
Richard Caswell at Kinston, 20 September 1787.


No. 447      Page 61
23 March 1808 - State of Tennessee, to Samuel Balch 61 acres on north
side of Nolachucky River - No. 22 issued to James Pearce 5 August 1786 -
assigned to Balch the enterer - County of Greene, District of Washington
- bank of Roppo, John Farnsworth's boat landing. John Sevier at Knoxville, 7 April 1809.


No. 445      Page 62
State of Tennessee, to Samuel Y. Balch 23 acres on Lick Creek - 2 March
1808 on Cert. No. 22 dated 5 August 1807 - Issued to James Pearce for
640 acres, he to Balch the enterer - County of Greene, Washington
District. John Sevier at Knoxville, 7 April 1809.


No. 627      Page 63
State of Tennessee, to Samuel Y. Balch 10 acres on south side of Nola-
chucky River, 19 December 1808, issued to Joseph Carter, to Balch the
enterer - County of Greene, District of Washington - including Watson
Dudley improvement, near main road leading from Baker's to Warm Springs.
Willie Blount at Knoxville, 23 May 1809.


No. 628      Page 64
State of Tennessee, to Samuel Y. Balch 10 acres at foot of Paint Creek
Mountain, issued to Joseph Carter for 200 acres land 9 April 1808 -
assigned by Carter to Balch enterer - County of Greene, District of
Washington, near Paint Creek at foot of Paint Creek Mountain on main
road Bakers to Warm Springs, fork of Curetons and Bakers Road in said
fork, including improvement where Molly Frisby lives. Willie Blount at
Knoxville, 25 September 1809.


No. 446      Page 66
State of Tennessee, to Samuel Y. Balch 50 acres on Roaring Fork of Lick
Creek, 2 March 1808 - on Cert. No. 22, to James Pierce for 640 acres -
County of Greene, District of Washington, originally granted to Matthew
Cox, deceased. John Sevier at Knoxville, 2 April 1809.


No. 642      Page 67
State of Tennessee, to Thomas William 84 acres on north side of Lick
Creek, from Entry No. 250, 9 March 1809 No. 1303 - by A. Roane, Com-
missioner for East Tennessee, 6 June 1808 - to Thomas Williams - County
of Greene, District of Washington - north side of Lick Creek, adjoining
John Pogue, Benjamin Williams, Caleb Carter, Christopher Kirbys. Willie
Blount at Knoxville, 29 September 1809.


No. 664      Page 70
State of Tennessee, to William Hannah 100 acres on Lick Creek, 21

November 1808, founded on Warrant No. 2356 to James Moore, Thomas Stewart to Hanna the enterer – District of Washington – adjoining Hannah, Johnson. Willie Blount at Knoxville, 6 October 1809.


No. 1848     Page 71
State of Tennessee, to Israel McBee 50 acres – District of Washington, County of Greene, 18 August 1808 – founded on Warrant No. 910, issued to Archibald Roane, to James McBee for 300 acres, 9 February 1808, James to Israel enterer, adjoining McBee, dividing Harrolds large spring. Willie Blount at Knoxville, 10 December 1810.


No. 743     Page 72
State of Tennessee – to Andrew Patterson 200 acres at mouth of Lick Creek – from Warrant #1478 dated 4 December 1779 – issued by John Carter to Zachariah Coward to James Stewart to Patterson the enterer – County of Greene, District of Washington – including Piburns Camps, adjoining Thomas Robinson, Alexander Newberry, Robertson. Willie Blount at Knoxville, 1 May 1810.


No. 1110     Page 73
For 10 pounds per 100 acres – to Hezekiah Balch 150 acres in Greene County on east side of Richland Creek, adjoining Major Temple, Matthew Leeper. Richard Dobs Spraight, 12 January 1793.


No. 1891     Page 74
State of Tennessee – to John Copeland 42 acres from Entry No. 182, 22 August 1808 – Warrant No. 2439, issued by Archibald Roane to John Gray and Thomas Blount for 1000 acres, dated 10 April 1808, to John Copeland enterer. County of Greene, District of Washington, north side Nolachucky River on Sinking Creek, adjoining himself, McAmish. Willie Blount at Knoxville, 4 April 1811.


No. 1557     Page 75
North Carolina, Washington County – 400 acres for Joshua English at mouth of Clear Creek running up creek – John Carter E.T. Certificate – Grant of Jacob Smelser No. 1229 Greene County, 12 June 1794, from writ 1520 – ripened into a grant to Thomas Rankin.


No. 1592     Page 76
State of Tennessee – to Samuel Crawford 70 acres on Lick Creek, founded on warrant No. 910, issued on Archibald Roane to James McBee for 300 acres, 9 February 1808 – to Israel McBee, to Samuel Crawford enterer – County of Greene, District of Washington – adjoining William Parker, William McDonald, waters of Lick Creek. Willie Blount at Knoxville, 2 July 1810.


No. 1889     Page 77
State of Tennessee – to heirs of John Carder 100 acres on the War Ford – Special Entry 731, 17 December 1778 – to William Holeman for 100 acres assigned to John Carder, County of Greene, District of Washington, on War Road, adjoining John English, James Whilars. Willie Blount at Knoxville, 4 April 1811.


No. 1890     Page 78
State of Tennessee – to heirs of John Carder 100 acres on Lick Creek on the Campaign Road – From #1905 for 100 acres, 22 October 1789 – County of Greene, District of Washington – adjoining William Walker, George Martin, Wheeler, Andrew Hannah, Martin. Willie Blount at Knoxville, 4 April 1811.

No. 2005      Page 80
State of Tennessee - to John Harmon 50 acres, adjoining himself and John
Gass - Entry No. 542 - Issued to Robert Wear for 50 acres land, 23
November 1809 - Robert Wear to John Harmon the enterer - County of Greene,
District of Washington.  Willie Blount at Knoxville, 2 October 1811.


No. 1968      Page 80
State of Tennessee - to James Haworth 100 acres on Horse Fork of Lick
Creek - From Entry No. 110, 30 August 1808, founded on Warrant No. 2439 -
Issued by A. Roan to John Gray and Thomas Blount for 1000 acres, 10
February 1808, they to James Haworth the enterer - County of Greene,
District of Washington - adjoining Thomas Babb, Thomas McCollum.  Willie
Blount at Knoxville, 30 January 1809.


No. 2009      Page 82
State of Tennessee - to Jesse Self 50 acres - Founded on Warrant No. 724
to James Guin to Henry Brown, Jesse Self the enterer - County of Greene,
District of Washington - at foot of Bays Mountain adjoining Thomas Self,
Joseph Self.  Willie Blount at Knoxville, 2 October 1811.


No. 2045      Page 83
State of Tennessee - to James Dinwiddie 50 acres on Big Limestone -
Founded on Warrant No. 2629, issued to John Armstrong to Thomas Childs
for 1000 acres, 30 November 1784, to James Dinwiddie the enterer - County
of Greene, District of Washington - adjoining Abel Loyd, Armstrong.
Willie Blount at Knoxville.


No. 2043      Page 84
State of Tennessee - to Solomon Stanberry 100 acres on Sinking Creek -
Entry No. 200, Warrant No. 528 - Issued by John Adair to Peter Morrison
for 150 acres, 16 February 1781 - District of Washington, County of
Greene - north side Chucky River on Little Sinking Creek, adjoining
Ellis Ellis, decd., Rees and Jones Frazier.  Willie Blount at Knoxville,
5 October 1811.


No. 1984      Page 85
State of Tennessee - to David Wilson 78 acres on Holleys Creek, waters of
Nolachucky River - No. 152, Warrant 1912 - Issued John Carter to Isaac
Taylor 250 acres, 29 April 1797, assigned by Adam Meek and John Sevier,
executors of Taylor, to William Henderson to David Wilson the enterer -
County of Greene, District of Washington - adjoining William Milburn,
David Robertson and Wilsons other land.  Willie Blount at Knoxville, 1
May 1811.


No. 1910      Page 87
State of Tennessee - to John Dodd 50 acres on Horse Fork of Lick Creek -
From Entry No. 369, 6 December 1809 - Cert. No. 30, Archibald Roane to
heirs of Andrew Greer for 1480 acres, 19 July 1808, 1926 acres assigned
to Nathaniel Taylor and 140 acres by Taylor to John Dodd enterer.  Greene
County, Washington District - adjoining Abraham Haynes, Andrew Patterson,
Drury Morris.  Willie Blount at Knoxville, 10 January 1810.


No. 1909      Page 88
State of Tennessee - to John Dodd 48 acres on Lick Creek - Entry No. 274,
Cert. No. 88 - Issued by A. Roane represenative of Daniel Dunham to
Aaron Newman and by him to John Dodd enterer - County of Greene, District
of Washington - adjoining Absalom Stonecypher, Thomas McCollum.  Willie
Blount at Knoxville, 12 April 1811.


No. 1923      Page 89
State of Tennessee - to John Dodd 40 acres on Lick Creek - Entry No. 275,
4 June 1809 - Cert. No. 88 by Archibald Roane to Daniel Dunham for 88

53

acres, 20 January 1809, assigned by Daniel Dunham to his agent John
Newman to Aaron Newman and by him to John Dodd enterer, adjoining Dutton
Lane, Drury Morris, including improvement at Young Spring. Willie Blount
at Knoxville, 18 January 1810.


No. 1923      Page 91
State of Tennessee, Washington District - to John Dodd 19 acres and 108
poles land on waters of Richland Creek, 5 March 1808 - Founded on Warrant
No. 2439, issued to Archibald Roane to John Gray Blount and Thomas Blount
for 1000 acres, 10 February 1808, to John Dodd enterer, adjoining David
Allison Junr. Willie Blount at Knoxville, 22 April 1811.


No. 1887      Page 92
State of Tennessee - to Philip Cole 60 acres on Limestone Fork of Lick
Creek - Entry 79, 12 August 1808 - Founded on Warrant No. 2464, issued
by John Carter to Thomas Mitchell for 100 acres, 10 March 1780 - 80
acres assigned to Philip Cole enterer. Surveyed 4 October 1808.


No. 2031      Page 93
State of Tennessee - to John Neese 50 acres on ____ - Entry No. 574,
Cert. No. 172 - Issued to Samuel Y. Blount for 188 acres, 21 May 1810,
entry dated 4 December 1810 - Balch to John Kennedy, 50 acres assigned
by Kennedy to said John Neese, where Neese now lives, adjoining John
Neese Senr. Surveyed 17 October 1811.


No. 1904      Page 94
State of Tennessee - to Samuel Y. Balch 30 acres on Big Gap Creek bounded
by a spur of Bays Mountain, south district - Entry No. 434, Warrant No.
967 - Issued by Archibald Roane to Francis Hughes for 100 acres, 6 July
1808, Hughes to Samuel Y. Balch, adjoining Balch 10 acre grant.


No. 1905      Page 95
State of Tennessee - to Samuel Y. Balch 10 acres on waters of Big Gap
Creek - Entry 183 dated 14 November 1808, founded on warrant No. 1307
- Issued to Joseph Carter for 200 acres, 6 April 1808, Carter to Sam
Y. Balch enterer, including mansion house and outhouses where Henry
Sullivan now lives. Willie Blount at Knoxville, 11 April 1811.


No. 1560      Page 96
State of Tennessee - to Isaac McAmish 40 acres on Slippery Branch of Lick
Creek - Entry No. 281, 16 June 1809, founded on warrant 1550, issued by
John Carter to John Smith for 200 acres, dated 11 November 1779 and
assigned by Smith to Samuel Y. Balch 88 acres and 8 poles - Andrew
Patterson 40 acres to Isaac McAmish enterer - Southside Lick Creek on
both sides of Slippery Branch, adjoining Caldwell and Carson.


No. 2004      Page 97
State of Tennessee - to Frederick Cutshall for 101 acres and 14 poles of
land on Matthews Flag Branch south side of Nolachucky River - Entry No.
485, certificate 106, issued to James Pierce for 267 acres, 27 March
1810 - Entry dated June 1810, assigned by Pierce to Frederick Cutshall
the enterer, being an occupant claim, adjoining Smithers, Emanuel
Parman.


No. 1860      Page 98
State of Tennessee - to John Temple on warrant No. 2439, issued by
Archibald Roane - John Gray Blount and Thomas Blount for 1000 acres,
dated 10 February 1808 - 100 acres assigned to John Temple the enterer,
north side Nolachucky River, north side ridge which divides waters of
Holleys and Richlands Creeks, adjoining John Temple, Milburn.

No. 641     Page 100
For 50 shillings per 100 acres - to Archibald Stoan 100 acres in Washing-
ton County on the Walnut Valley, east side of the former entry in Walnut
Valley. Alexander Martin at Newbern, 10 November 1784.


No. 2253     Page 101
State of Tennessee - to Henry Cross 150 acres and 20 poles on Cedar Fork
of Lick Creek - Entry No. 217, 26 July 1809 on Certificate No. 1 - Issued
by Archibald Roane to Christopher Houts for 173 acres and 100 poles, 6
May 1807 - a duplicate of that issued by Luke Lea, 29 February 1812 -
Certificate assigned by Houts to Henry Cross the enterer, adjoining John
Jones, Thompson, being an occupant claim.


No. 2136     Page 102
State of Tennessee - to Thomas Babb 116 acres on Horse Fork of Lick
Creek - based on Entry 201, Certificate 36 - Issued to Francis A. Ramsey
for 1000 acres, 25 October 1808 - to Thomas Babb the enterer by assign-
ment, adjoining Azariah Doty, Stonecypher, Babbs old line, Occupant
Claim, 6 June 1808.


No. 2390     Page 103
State of Tennessee - to Henry Cross 100 acres on Sinking Branch of Lick
Creek - from Entry No. 498, 6 August 1810 - founded on warrant 910 -
Issued to James McBee for 300 acres, dated 9 February 1808, assigned by
McBee to Henry Cross enterer, adjoining Ellis Pickering, near Michael
Brights line.


No. 2388     Page 104
State of Tennessee - to John Lescollet 150 acres land on both sides Cove
Creek, adjoining Hixons, to stake at foot of Paint Mountain. Surveyed
26 August 1808.


No. 880     Page 107
31 December 1778 - 300 acres on Sinking Creek to John Peble - surveyed
4 December 1792 - United States of America, South of River Ohio - to
John Peble, decd. - where widow now lives, bank of Nolachucky River,
adjoining Gillespie, Edmond Roberts, Emmet.


No. 1325     Page 107
For 50 shillings per 100 acres - State of North Carolina - to John Peeble
land on Sinking Creek, No. 880 above. Richard Dobs Spraight, 5 December
1794.


No. 2812     Page 108
State of Tennessee - to Valentine Sevier and Frederick C. Warnack 50
acres on south side of Nolachucky River on Cedar Creek - Entry 1280, 11
May 1812 - founded on Certificate ___, issued by D. McGavock to Nathaniel
Raylor, 1812 - 50 acres assigned by Taylor to Valentine Sevier and Frederick C. Warnack, including paper mill and mill dam and race, and dwelling house where Warnack now lives, adjoining John Freshour.


No. 2061     Page 109
State of Tennessee - to Henry Cross 200 acres on Lick Creek - Special
entry 402, dated 9 September 1778 - of warrant issued same to Shaderack
Morris on same No. for 200 acres, dated 7 March 1796 and assigned to
Henry Cross, on Lick Creek at mouth of a branch running from Double Licks,
adjoining John Woolsey, John Rhea, Crawford.


No. 2591     Page 110
State of Tennessee - to David Copeland 15 acres on Lick Creek - Entry No.
196, 21 December 1808, founded on warrant No. 2629 - Issued by John

Armstrong to Thomas Childs for 1000 acres, dated 30 November 1784, 50 acres of which is assigned to David Copeland enterer, adjoining Copelands old survey.


No. 1927     Page 111
State of Tennessee - to Henry Reynolds 99 acres on waters of Camp Creek - Entry No. 323, 8 September 1809 - on Warrant No. 81 - Issued by William Maclin to Henry Reynolds for 103 acres, 6 Decemter 1802. Occupant claim adjoining Eddleman, William McNew, Shaderach McNew.


No. 2126     Page 112
State of Tennessee - to James Wright for 10 acres on Richland Creek - Entry No. 280 - founded on Warrant 1550 - Issued by John Carter to John Smith, 24 August 1779 - Entry dated 16 June 1809 - 10 acres vested in James Wright enterer, adjoining himself, Hood.


No. 2221     Page 112
State of Tennessee - to Samuel Powel 80 acres on Gasses Creek - Entry No. 783 - founded on Certificate No. 294 to James P. Taylor for 80 acres - entered 1 August 1811, assigned by Taylor to Samuel Powel the enterer, adjoining Wyly, Pritchets, Gass.


No. 931     Page 113
State of North Carolina - for 10 pounds per 100 acres - to Robert Boid and William Logan for 600 acres in Washington County on north side of Nolachucky River on a Sinking Spring, adjoining John Keeny, Thomas Leatherdales. Alexander Martin, 26 December 1791.


No. 1919     Page 115
State of Tennessee - to Seth Babb 100 acres on Grassy Creek, waters of Lick Creek - Entry No. 521, 11 September 1810 - founded on Certificate No. 175 - Issued by Archibald Roane to Joseph Tipton for 259 1/2 acres, assigned by Tipton to John Kennedy and he to Seth Babb enterer.


No. 1916     Page 116
State of Tennessee - to Seth Babb 20 acres on Roaring Fork of Lick Creek - Entry No. 520, 11 September 1810 - founded on Certificate 175 - Issued by A. Roane to Joseph Tipton for 259 1/2 acres, 3 July 1810 - certificate assigned by Tipton to John Kennedy and he to Seth Babb enterer - north side of Bulls Gap Road, adjoining Jacob Bowman.


No. 1901     Page 117
State of Tennessee - to Bloomer White ___ acres on Horse Camp Fork of Lick Creek - Entry No. 54, 30 April 1808 - founded on to 2545 acres issued by Carter to John Bearden for 70 acres, 6 December 1782, assigned by Bearden to Bloomer White enterer, adjoining Thomas Johnston, David Rosy, David Bailes, Grubes.


No. 2189     Page 118
State of Tennessee - to Jonathan Humbard 149 1/2 acres on Horse Camp Fork of Lick Creek - No. 896, founded on warrant No. 2168 - Issued by John Armstrong - Anthony Moore for 400 acres, dated 30 November 1784 - Entry dated 23 November 1811, to Jonathan Humbard enterer - District of Washington, adjoining Hawkins, Eden Humbard, James Collens, Mauris. Occupant Claim.


No. 2218     Page 119
State of Tennessee - to William Milburn 6 acres on Jesse Mosley line - Entry No. 547 - founded on Certificate No. 30 - Issued to heirs of Andrew Greer for 2480 acres, 19 July 1808 - entry dated 29 October 1810 - 140 acres vested in William Milburn enterer, adjoining Jesse Mosley.

No. 2217    Page 120
State of Tennessee - to William Milburn 134 acres on Holleys Creek -
Entry No. 531 - to heirs of Andrew Greer enterer by assignment - adjoining
Edmondson, Wilson. Occupant Claim.


No. 2895    Page 121
State of Tennessee - to Frederick Trobaugh 50 acres on waters of Little
Chuckey - from Entry 1172, dated 20 March 1812 - founded on certificate
88 - issued by Luke Lea to William Shields for 5000 acres, 2 May 1812 -
50 acres vested in Frederick Trobaugh enterer - 50 acres including
house and improvements where James Gibson now lives.


No. 2920    Page 122
State of Tennessee - to Jesse Self 25 acres on Gasses Creek, No. 1163,
16 March 1812 - founded on Certificate issued to Luke Lea to William
Shields for 5000 acres - foot of Bays Mountain where Joseph Self now
lives.


No. 2916    Page 122
State of Tennessee - to Thomas Self 121 acres, 2 rods and 39 poles on
Gass Creek - from Entry No. 740, 5 August 1811 - founded on Certificate
No. 21 to Thomas Bailey, to Thomas Self the enterer, adjoining Bays
Mountain, Ellis Rutherford, including house spring and improvements.


No. 2918    Page 124
State of Tennessee - to Thomas Self 15 acres at Bays Mountain - from
Entry No. 743, 5 August 1811 - Warrant No. 1307, issued to Joseph Carter
for 200 acres - 25 acres assigned to Thomas Self enterer - 15 acres
granted - Bounded on every line by spurs on Bays Mountain, including
improvements made by Jacob Kile.


No. 2919    Page 124
State of Tennessee - to Thomas Self 10 acres on road leading from Snapp's
Ferry to Bulls Gap - Entry No. 742, dated 5 August 1811 - founded on No.
1307, dated 9 May 1811 - 25 acres to Thomas Self enterer, including
improvement made by John Brotherton.


No. 2853    Page 125
State of Tennessee - to Peter Baker 13 acres - Entry No. 1479, 1 October
1812 - founded on Certificate No. 88, issued to Luke Lea to William
Shields for 5000 acres, dated 2 March 1812 - 13 acres assigned to Peter
Baker, 9 October 1813.


No. 2922    Page 126
State of Tennessee - to Allen Gillespie 200 acres on both sides Big
Limestone Creek - Entry No. 702, 7 May 1811 - founded on Warrant No.
1874 - issued to Archibald Roane to Robert King, dated 25 July 1808
and assigned by enterer, adjoining Gillespie, Broils, Pevels?, Blakely,
George Gillespie, Thomas Gillespie.


No. 2185    Page 127
State of Tennessee - to John B. Hood 20 acres on Richland Creek near
town of Greeneville - Entry No. 484 - Certificate No. 116 - signed by
Lusk to John B. Hood enterer, adjoining Robert Hood, Robert Kerr, John
Russell and William Morrow, 1 October 1813.


No. 2785    Page 129
State of Tennessee - to John Russ_ll 5 acres on Richland Creek adjoining
town of Greeneville - Entry No. 43, 11 April 1808 - Warrant No. 2439 -
issued by Archibald Roane to John G. and Thomas Blount for 1000 acres,
10 February 1808. Two hundred acres vested in John Russell enterer by

assignment - 5 acres granted, adjoining Robert Kerr's old grant for 300 acres, No. 28, adjoining Morrow. 10 May 1813.


No. 2969     Page 130
State of Tennessee - to Joseph Mosley 25 acres adjoining Temples land - from Entry No. 1259, dated 6 May 1812 - founded on Certificate No. 33 - issued to heirs of Henry Earnest 555 acres, 18 December 1810 - 25 acres of which is assigned to Joseph Mosley enterer, adjoining Temple.


No. 2640     Page 131
State of Tennessee - to Samuel Lane 35 acres on Horse Camp Fork of Lick Creek - Entry No. 430, dated 9 March 1810 - on part of Warrant No. 30 - issued to heirs of Andrew Greer, decd., 19 July 1808 - granted to Samuel Lane assignee of heirs of Andrew Greer, decd - adjoining Azariah Doty, McCollum. 9 October 1812.


No. 747     Page 132
State of North Carolina - for 10 pounds per 100 acres - to David Copeland 300 acres in Greene County on head of Gass's Branch on waters of Lick Creek, adjoining Robert McCaul, Robert Kerr, Benjamin Gass. Certificate of survey No. 19, 2 December 1783.


No. 2923     Page 134
State of Tennessee - to Charles Myers 19 acres, 33 poles of land on waters of Cove Creek, south side of Nolachucky River - Entry No. 1209, 31 March 1812 - founded on Certificate No. 36 - issued by Luke Lea to James Greene for 83 acres, dated 25 September 1812 - 19 acres 5 poles granted by Tennessee to Charles Myers, adjoining Deaderick, the west side a branch of Cove Creek, Baker. 1 October 1813.


No. 1908     Page 134
State of Tennessee - to Andrew Patterson 148 1/2 acres on Horse Fork of Lick Creek - Entry No. 242, 17 March 1809 - founded on Warrant No. 2578 - issued by Archibald Roane to Edwin Ingram - assigned by Ingram to Thomas Stuart, by him to Charles Whitson, by him to Andrew Patterson enterer, adjoining George Vincent. Sealed 12 April 1811.


No. 3156     Page 135
State of Tennessee - to William Gladden 10 acres on Brush Creek - Entry No. 915, 9 December 1811 - founded on Warrant No. 4514 - issued to James Glasgow to Peter Shabese for 270 acres, 27 December 1796 - 10 acres assigned to William Gladden enterer - on both sides of Brush Creek between Paint Creek and Meadow Creek Mountains. Sealed 28 August 1814.


No. 3154     Page 136
State of Tennessee - to William Gladden 20 acres between Paint and Meadow Creek Mountains - from Entry No. 1179, dated 23 March 1812 - founded on Certificate No. 109 - issued to James Pearce for 190 acres, 27 March 1810 - 60 acres of which is assigned to William Gladden, the enterer. Sealed 28 August 1814.


No. 3155     Page 137
State of Tennessee - to William Gladden 24 acres on Brush Creek - Entry No. ____, 23 November 1810 - Certificate No. 109 - issued to James Pearce for 190 acres, dated 27 March 1810 - 60 acres of which is assigned to William Gladden containing 24 acres between Paint and Meadow Creek Mountains, including his house. Sealed 28 August 1814.


No. 3065     Page 138
State of Tennessee - to Bird Deatherage 25 acres on Lick Creek, adjoining his own land - Entry No. 1712, 6 March 1813 - founded on Certificate No.

483 - issued to Nathaniel Taylor for 100 acres, dated 25 November 1812 -
25 acres assigned to Bird Deatherage enterer. Sealed 3 May 1814.


No. 2392      Page 139
State of Tennessee - to William Whittenberg 15 acres on north side Nolachucky River - Entry No. 215, 20 January 1809 - Certificate No. 56 -
issued by Archibald Roane to James Wilson for 167 acres, dated 7 July
1808, assigned by Wilson to Andrew M. Lusk, to George Gordon - 15 acres
assigned by Gordon to William Whittenberg enterer - adjoining William
Tyrrell and a tract purchased of Robert Smith, adjoining Tyrrell, Gordon,
Smith. Sealed 23 June 1812.


No. 1911      Page 140
State of Tennessee - to Edwin Humberd 12 acres on Lick Creek - based on
Entry No. 42 - Warrant No. 2439 - issued by A. Roane to John G. and
Thomas Blount for 1000 acres, dated 10 February 1808 - 12 acres assigned
to Edwin Humbert enterer, adjoining Dinwoodie. Sealed 12 April 1811.


No. 1569      Page 141
State of Tennessee - to Jacob Beals 111 acres 80 poles land on head of
Sinking Creek - Entry No. 53, 30 April 1808 - Warrant No. 1550 - issued
by John Carter to John Smith for 200 acres, 11 November 1779 - assigned
to Samuel Y. Balch to Jacob Beals enterer - near head of Sinking Creek,
adjoining Shad Morris, Pickering, John Oren? An occupant claim. Sealed
2 July 1810.


No. 3070      Page 142
State of Tennessee - to James Patterson 100 acres on Churn Camp Creek -
based on Entry No. 952, 6 January 1812 - Certificate No. 20 - to John
McCampbell for 300 acres - 220 acres assigned to James Patterson - 100
acres on Churn Camp Creek, including house and improvement where Benjamin
Neil now lives, on Waggon Road. Sealed 4 May 1814.


No. 2861      Page 143
State of Tennessee - to David Rice 100 acres on Lick Creek - Entry No.
48, 18 April 1808 - founded on Warrant No. 2629 - issued by John Armstrong to Thomas Childs for 1000 acres, dated 30 November 1784 - 100
acres of which is assigned to David Rice enterer, adjoining Benjamin
Steward. Sealed 26 July 1813.


No. 2739      Page 144
State of Tennessee - to William Kilgore 30 acres north side of Nolachucky
River - Entry No. 1187, 23 March 1812 - founded on certificate No. 88 -
issued by Luke Lea to William Shields for 5000 acres, 2 May 1812 - 696
acres assigned by Shields to Thomas Thompson and by him to David Guin,
to William Kilgore enterer - 32 acres on north side Nolachucky River,
adjoining Walker, Widow Wilson, James Kilgore, to Charles Kilgore's
corner. Sealed 2 April 1813.


No. 2077      Page 145
State of Tennessee - to George Vincent 123 acres on Horse Fork of Lick
Creek - based on Entry No. 4 - certificate No. 9 - to John Morefield for
123 acres, he to George Vincent enterer, including grist and saw mill
built by Abraham Williams and all improvements, adjoining Drury Morris.
Sealed 30 October 1811.


No. 3330      Page 146
State of Tennessee - to Watson Dudley 40 acres on south side Nolachucky
River on Cove Creek - Entry No. 1343, dated 8 June 1812 - from certifi-
cate No. 109 - issued 27 March 1810 - 40 acres of which are assigned to
Watson Dudly enterer, including improvement where Dudley lives, adjoin-
ing Isaac Baker. Sealed 16 March 18__.

No. 3149     Page 147
State of Tennessee - to Jacob Dyke 50 acres on north side Nolachucky
River - Entry No. 633, 6 February 1811 - founded on certificate No. 66
- issued Alexander Outlaw 50 acres, 9 February 1810 - 50 acres assigned
to Jacob Dyke enterer, including house and improvement where Balem Sharp
formerly lived, adjoining Michael Woods. Sealed 28 August 1814.


No. 2917     Page 148
State of Tennessee - to Joseph Winters 20 acres on north side Nolachucky
River - Entry No. 679, 13 March 1811 - founded on certificate No. 22 -
issued to James Pearce for 640 acres, 5 August 1807 - 20 acres assigned
to Joseph Winters - adjoining William Hall, Samuel Y. Balch, Farnsworth.
Sealed 1 October 1813.


No. 2993     Page 149
State of Tennessee - to Robert Dobson 50 acres on a branch of Gasses
Creek, waters of Lick Creek - based on Entry No. 277, 10 June 1809 -
founded on Warrant No. 2439 - issued by A. Roane to John Gray and Thomas
Blount for 1000 acres, 10 February 1808 - 50 acres of which is assigned
to Robert Dobson enterer - on a branch of Gists Creek adjoining Wilson,
Robert Wyly. Sealed 10 August 1812.


No. 1954     Page 150
State of Tennessee - to Jacob Lung 35 acres on south side Nolachucky
River - based on Entry 438, dated 14 March 1810 - founded on certificate
No. 157 - issued by A. Roane to Thomas Davis for 85 acres - 35 acres to
Jacob Lung, adjoining Thomas Williamson, Jacob Bird. Sealed 1 May 1811.


No. 3566     Page 151
State of Tennessee - to James Jones 90 acres on Horse Camp Fork of Lick
Creek - based on Entry No. 1466 - certificate No. 90 for 72 1/4 acres,
20 January 1809 - issued by A. Roane to John Jones, to James Jones, also
on certificate No. 2050, 30 November 1784 - issued to David Stuart for
1000 acres - 90 acres assigned to James Jones enterer, adjoining Hoggit,
Isaac Doty, Reeds, Newman. Sealed 4 October 1815.


No. 2269     Page 153
State of Tennessee - to James Galbreath 66 acres on both sides of Gap
Creek - based on Entry No. 140, 9 September 1808 - founded on warrant
No. 2629 - issued by John Armstrong to Thomas Childs for 1000 acres,
dated 30 November 1784 - said warrant vested in James Galbreath enterer
by purchase at Sheriff's Sale, adjoining Robert Smith, Couch, being an
occupant claim. Sealed 10 June 1812.


No. 3373     Page 154
State of Tennessee - to Valentine Sevier 47 acres near Town of Greeneville
- Entry No. 310, 30 August 1809 - founded on warrant No. 2439 - issued by
A. Roane to John G. and Thomas Blount for 1000 acres, dated 4 February
1808 - 100 assigned to Joseph Brown enterer, adjoining Alexander Sevier,
Robertson, Rankin, Galbreath. Sealed 12 April 1815.


No. 3603     Page 155
State of Tennessee - to Thomas Self 30 acres on Lick Creek between spurs
of Bays Mountain - Entry No. 1254, dated 24 April 1812 - founded on
certificate No. 889 - issued to Nathaniel Taylor for 150 acres, 19
February 1812 - 30 acres assigned to Robert Reeder the enterer - assigned
by Rudder to Thomas Self. Sealed 6 October 1815.


No. 3681     Page 155
State of Tennessee - to Samuel McCurry 5 acres of land on both sides the
watery fork of the Caney Branch - Entry No. 1488, dated 13 October 1812
- founded on certificate No. 88 - issued by Luke Lea to William Shields

for 5000 acres land, dated 2 March 1812 - 5 acres of which are assigned to Samuel McCamey the enterer, adjoining Ellis. James McMinn at Nashville, 9 October 1815.

No. 3298        Page 156
State of Tennessee - to James Patterson and Daniel Guin 52 acres of land, an island in Nolachucky River known as Wyly's Island, 5 January 1810 - Entry No. 981, 3 February 1812 - certificate No. 21 - issued to John McCampbell for 300 acres - 64 acres assigned to Patterson and Guin, the enterers - 52 acres granted to Patterson and Guin, including an island by name of Loveladys, Roaches and afterwards Wyly's Island. Sealed 21 November 1814.

No. 3597        Page 157
State of Tennessee - to Christopher Lotspeich 50 acres on south side of Nolachucky River - based on Entry No. 1318, 4 June 1812 - founded on warrant No. 2666 - issued by Archibald Roane to Jacob Wilson for 100 acres, 23 March 1811 - 50 acres of which are assigned to Christopher Lotspeich the enterer - adjoining Haworth, Hughes, Allens corner, Broyles, Barnharts corner, Fox. Sealed 6 October 1815.

No. 3596        Page 159
State of Tennessee - to Christopher Lotspeich 28 acres north side of Horse Creek - Entry No. 1675, dated 6 March 1812 - founded on certificate No. 33 - issued by A. Roane to heirs of Henry Earnest for 550 acres, dated 18 December 1810 - 28 acres of which are assigned to Christopher Lotspeich the enterer - adjoining Broyles. Sealed 6 October 1815.

No. 3580        Page 160
State of Tennessee - to John Gass 15 acres on Roaring Fork of Lick Creek - based on Entry No. 2270 - certificate No. 268 - issued by Anthony Foster to David Faens heirs for 640 acres - 341 acres assigned to John Gass the enterer - 15 acres assigned to John Gass, adjoining his own lands, Babbs Mill Road to Greeneville. Joseph McMinn, 5 October 1815.

No. 2657        Page 161
State of Tennessee - to John Gass 15 acres on Roaring Fork of Lick Creek - warrant No. 20, dated 5 January 1810 - Survey No. 815, 4 October 1811 - to John Gass assignee of John McCampbell - 15 acres on Gass to Babbs Mill Road. Sealed 9 October 1812.

No. 3515        Page 162
State of Tennessee - to William Scruggs 50 acres north side Nolachucky River - based on Entry No. 1347, 20 June 1812 - founded on certificate No. 2 - issued to Frederick Scruggs for 600 acres - 50 acres assigned to William Scruggs enterer - adjoining Richard Scruggs corner. Sealed 1 September 1815.

No. 2865        Page 163
State of Tennessee - to John McCollum 20 acres on Raccoon Branch, waters of Lick Creek - Entry No. 916, 10 December 1811 - founded on certificate No. 333 - issued to George P. Gillespie for 20 acres, 1 October 1811 - assigned by Gillespie to Valentine Sevier and by him to John McCollum the enterer - including Carsners improvement where dwelling house stands. Sealed 27 July 1813.

No. 3677        Page 164
State of Tennessee - to Jacob Dykes 62 acres on north side Nolachucky River - Entry No. 1686, 14 April 1813 - founded on warrant No. 2052 - issued by John Armstrong to David Stuart and John Minos for 1000 acres, 30 November 1784 - 62 acres assigned to Jacob Dyke enterer - on river

bank opposite Tumbling Shoals then down stream. Sealed 9 October 1815.

No. 2248     Page 165
State of Tennessee - to Elijah Billingsley 8 acres south side Lick Creek
- based on Entry No. 208, 6 January 1809 - founded on certificate No. 72
- issued to Benjamin Mansfield for 18 acres, 21 October 1808 - assigned
to Thomas Brabson and by Brabson to Billingsley the enterer - as it
respects 8 acres adjoining Abraham Carter, Ballard. Sealed 8 June 1812.

No. 3674     Page 166
State of Tennessee - to John Cook 30 acres south side Nolachucky River,
west side of Cove Creek - Entry No. 2098, 20 August 1814 - founded on
certificate No. 88 - issued to Luke Lea to William Shields for 500 acres
- 30 acres of which are assigned to John Cook the enterer - adjoining
Pearce, Vinzant, Hawk, Morgan. Sealed 8 October 1815.

No. 3418     Page 168
State of Tennessee - to James McPheran 25 acres on the waters of Roaring
Fork of Lick Creek - Entry No. 1696, 22 April 1813 - founded on warrant
No. 268 - issued by Anthony Foster to David Fain heirs for 640 acres, 10
July 1809 - 49 acres of which are assigned to James McPheran the enterer
- adjoining Cavener. Sealed 22 May 1815.

No. 2915     Page 169
State of Tennessee - to Jacob Hise Senr. 29 acres north side Nolachucky
River - Entry No. 1156 - warrant No. 724 - issued by James Gaines to
David Russell for 100 acres, dated 1 January 1781 - assigned to Jacob
Hise Senr. enterer - adjoining Shannon, Ripley, Freeze. Sealed 20
September 1813.

No. 3590     Page 170
State of Tennessee - to John McCollum 9 acres south side Lick Creek -
based on Entry No. 2504, 10 March 1815 - founded on certificate No. 209
- issued to Richard Scruggs for 150 acres - 12 acres assigned to John
McCollum enterer. Sealed 6 October 1815.

No. 3591     Page 171
State of Tennessee - to John McCollum 3 acres on Raccoon Branch of Lick
Creek - based on Entry No. 2505, 10 March 1815 - certificate No. 209 -
issued by Nathan Shipley to Richard Scruggs for 150 acres which are
assigned to John McCollum the enterer - adjoining Frederick White.
Sealed 6 October 1815.

No. 3583     Page 172
State of Tennessee - to John Fincher 25 acres on Sinking Branch on east
side of Cornelius Newman's land - Entry No. 1002, 7 February 1812 -
founded on warrant No. 82 - issued by James Gaines to Nathaniel Taylor
for 250 acres - 25 acres of which are assigned to John Fincher enterer -
adjoining Cornelius Newman, Henry Cross, Ellis Pickering. Sealed 5
October 1815.

No. 3600     Page 173
State of Tennessee - to John Gragg 50 acres adjoining Graggs place he
now lives on - Entry No. 646, 8 February 1811 - founded on certificate
No. 30 - issued by A. Roane to heirs of Andrew Greer for 2400 acres, 19
July 1808 - 50 acres of which are assigned to John Gragg enterer - on
head of Charles Branch. Sealed 6 October 1815.

No. 3165     Page 174
State of Tennessee - to James Dinwiddie 20 1/2 acres on waters of Big

Limestone, adjoining his own land - based on Entry No. 1580, 23 January
1813 - founded on certificate No. 412 - issued to James Davidis for 83
1/3 acres - 22 1/2 acres of which are assigned to James Dinwiddie enterer
- adjoining his own land, Abner Frazier. Sealed 1 September 1814.


No. 3573     Page 175
State of Tennessee - to Jesse Self 30 acres on Stony Creek at foot of
Bays Mountain - Entry No. 825, 9 October 1811 - certificate No. 22 -
issued by Archibald Roane to Favis Reeve for 210 acres, dated 4 April
1810 - 30 acres of which are assigned to Richard Logan enterer, granted
by Tennessee - Jesse Self, assignee of said Logan and his heirs, a
tract containing 30 acres, adjoining Chivers, with spur of Bays Mountain,
Willoughbys. Sealed 5 October 1815.


No. 3586     Page 176
State of Tennessee - to Jesse Self 45 acres on waters of Big Creek on
the north side of Bays Mountain - Entry No. 1773, 16 August 1813 -
certificate No. 542 - issued to William Shields for 469 acres, 27 May
1813 - 45 acres assigned to Jesse Self enterer - adjoining Benjamin
Yates. Sealed 5 October 1815.


No. 3593     Page 178
State of Tennessee - to Philip Hinkle 200 acres south side Nolachucky
River - Entry No. 2440, 13 February 1813 - founded on certificate No.
168 - issued to George Gordon for 500 acres, 2 November 1814 - 200
acres of which are assigned to Philip Hinkle the enterer - adjoining
John Neece Junr., Thomas Gragg. Sealed 6 October 1815.


No. 3605     Page 179
State of Tennessee - to Maurice Morris 64 acres on both sides of Pigeon
Creek, waters of Chuckey River - Entry No. 1624, 4 March 1814 - founded
on certificate No. 88 - issued by Luke Lea to William Shields for 5000
acres, 2 March 1812 - 64 acres of which is granted to Maurice Morris -
adjoining Gibson Glasses corner. Sealed 6 October 1815.


No. 1877     Page 180
State of Tennessee - to Washington Henshaw 100 acres south side Nolachucky River, on Middle Creek - Entry No. 1319, 4 June 1812 - founded
on certificate No. 88 - issued by Luke Lea to William Shields for 500
acres, 2 March 1812 - 100 acres of which is assigned by said Shields
to Washington Hinshaw the enterer - including improvements where John
Hickson lives, adjoining Widdow Hickson, bank of Middle Creek. Sealed
29 July 1813.


No. 3748     Page 181
State of Tennessee - to George Brown 88 acres about 1 1/2 miles from
Town of Greeneville in Knoxville Road, adjoining Wylys Mill Dam and both
sides of the Great Road - Entry No. 2984, 2 October 1815 - certificate
No. 759 - to George Gordon for 500 acres, 2 November 1814 - 200 acres of
which is assigned to George Brown enterer. Granted by Tennessee, 88
acres to George Brown on both sides of road leading from Greeneville to
Bulls Gap, adjoining James Britten, Nicholas Trobaugh, heirs of Robert
Wyly, Joseph McRandles, Thomas Watson. Sealed 6 April 1816.


No. 3747     Page 182
State of Tennessee - to George Brown 70 acres, adjoining Thomas Mitchell,
James Britten and Thomas Watson - now the said George and Alexander
Browns, laying on the head waters of Little Chucky Creek, also joining
James Pattersons survey at the side of a Stony Ridge - based on Entry
No. 2985, 7 October 1815 - certificate No. 759 - issued to George Gordon
for 500 acres - 200 acres of which are assigned to George Brown enterer.
Sealed 6 April 1816.

No. 3803    Page 183
State of Tennessee - to George Brown 30 acres on Richland Creek about 1 mile from Greeneville on both sides main road from town to Greene Colledge, adjoining James Wrights place where he now lives - Entry No. 2837, 31 July 1815 - certificate No. 615 - issued to George Gordon for 100 acres - 40 acres assigned to George Brown. Thirty acres granted to George Brown, adjoining Robert Hood, David Russell, James Wright. Sealed 2 May 1816.


No. 3952    Page 184
State of Tennessee - to William McNew 100 acres on Camp Creek, adjoining said McNew - Entry No. 1068, 4 March 1812 - certificate No. 22 - issued to James Pearce for 640 acres - 100 acres of which is assigned to William McNew enterer - including improvement where Thomas Gibson, decd., formerly lived, adjoining McNew. Sealed 4 September 1816.


No. 3878    Page 185
State of Tennessee - to Joseph Brown 100 acres on north side Nolachucky River on the Draughts of Richland Creek - Entry No. 2221, 4 November 1814 - certificate No. 2439 - issued to John G. and Thomas Blount for 1000 acres, 10 February 1808 - 100 acres of which are assigned to Joseph Brown. The certificate is of No. 620, issued to George Gordon for 50 acres - the whole of which is vested in said Brown (by assignment) the enterer - adjoining Brown, Russell, Valentine Sevier, Alexander Sevier, heirs of David Robertson, Creamers corner. Sealed 3 July 1816.


No. 3585    Page 186
State of Tennessee - to Daniel Kirby 25 acres on Sinking Fork of Lick Creek - Entry No. 2141, dated 12 September 1814 - certificate No. 642 - issued to James P. Taylor for 150 acres - 25 acres of which are assigned to Daniel Kirby the enterer - adjoining Aaron Newman, John Fincher, Maltsbarger. Sealed 5 October 1815.


No. 3147    Page 187
State of Tennessee - to Joseph Shannon 50 acres on north side of Nolachucky River - Survey No. 838, 14 October 1811 - warrant No. 2666 - issued by A. Roane to Jacob Wilson - 100 acres of which is assigned to Joseph Shannon, adjoining Thomas Ripley, Doan. Sealed 28 August 1814.


No. 2225    Page 188
State of Tennessee - to Andrew English 100 acres on both sides Lick Creek - Entry No. 81 - warrant No. 772 - issued by John Carter to John English for 100 acres, dated 5 July 1794 - Entry 12 August 1808 - assigned by John English to James English and Michael Rawlings, executors of James English, to Andrew English the enterer - 100 acres granted to Andrew English - adjoining Phillip Cole, Joseph Robertson, James Johnston. Sealed 5 June 1812.


No. 1153    Page 189
State of North Carolina - for 50 shillings per 100 acres - to George House 150 acres in Greene County on waters of Lick Creek, beginning at a hickory above the Mill Seat, crossing Long Fork of Lick Creek. Richard Dobbs Spraight at Newbern, 4 July 1791.


No. 2862    Page 190
State of Tennessee - to William Reece 24 acres adjoining Reeces own land and Hugh Carters - Entry No. 47, 10 April 1808 - by John Armstrong to Thomas Childs - warrant No. 2629 for 1000 acres, 13 November 1784 - 24 acres assigned to William Reece the enterer - adjoining McClain. Sealed 26 July 1813.


No. 3577    Page 191
State of Tennessee - to James Johnson 6 acres on Limestone Form of Lick

64

Creek - Entry No. 871, 6 November 1811 - certificate No. 23 - issued by
Archibald Roane to George Himes for 259 acres, 17 April 1810 - 6 acres
of which are assigned to James Johnson enterer - adjoining Rhea, English.
Sealed 5 October 1815.


No. 3578     Page 192
State of Tennessee - to James Johnson 5 acres west side of Lick Creek -
Entry No. 2259, 19 November 1815 - based on certificate No. 754 - issued
by James Gains to Isaac Shelby for 265 acres, 14 February 1781 - 5 acres
of which are assigned to James Johnson - adjoining Francis Register.
Sealed 5 October 1815.


No. 3576     Page 193
State of Tennessee - to James Thompson 8 acres on Cedar Branch of Lick
Creek - Entry No. 2633, 13 April 1815 - founded on certificate No. 205
- issued by Nathan Shipley to John McGinnes for 180 acres, 29 August
1814 - 8 acres of which are assigned to James Thompson enterer - adjoining Newman, Alexander Thompson. Sealed 5 October 1815.


No. 3592     Page 194
State of Tennessee - to John Wilson 30 acres north side of Town of
Greeneville - Entry No. 2159, 20 September 1814 - founded on certificate No. 542 - issued to William Shields for 469 acres, 27 May 1813 -
a parcel of which is granted to John Wilson - adjoining Kerr. Sealed
6 October 1815.


No. 4036     Page 195
State of Tennessee - to John Russell 37 acres on east side of Richland
Creek - Entry No. 2022, dated 15 June 1814 - founded on certificate No.
550 - issued to John Russell for 50 acres, 26 June 1813 - 37 acres
granted to John Russell - adjoining land lately owned by William Morrow
- now the property of Valentine and Alexander Sevier, Joseph Brown, Hood
and Russell. Sealed 5 October 1816.


No. 2857     Page 196
State of Tennessee - to Daniel Guin 4 acres on Richland Creek - Entry No.
1271, 6 May 1812 - founded on certificate No. 33 - issued by A. Roane to
Henry Earnest heirs for 555 acres, dated 15 December 1810 - 182 acres of
which is assigned to Daniel Guin enterer - 4 acres of above tract, adjoining John B. Hood. Sealed 6 July 1813.


No. 2389     Page 197
State of Tennessee - to Andrew Hixon 100 acres on both sides Cove Creek -
Entry No. 719, 3 June 1811 - founded on certificate No. 4514 - issued by
I. Glasgow to Peter Shabiso for 274 acres, 22 December 1796, and assigned
by him to Stokely Donelson, by him to Joshua Hadley and by him to John
Huddleston, he to John Lescollet, he assigned 10 acres to Andrew Hixon
the enterer - adjoining Isaac Baker, John Lescollet. Sealed 23 June
1812.


No. 4073     Page 198
State of Tennessee - to John Harris 50 acres on waters of Kelleys Branch,
south side Nolachucky River - Entry No. 2703, 19 May 1814 - founded on
certificate No. 779 - issued to George Gordon for 500 acres, 2 November
1814 - 50 acres of which is assigned to John Harris enterer - adjoining
William Gragg. Sealed 28 November 1816.


No. 4074     Page 200
State of Tennessee - to William Gragg 40 acres south side of Nolachucky
River - Entry No. 2687, 8 May 1815 - founded on certificate No. 779 -
issued to George Gordon for 500 acres, 2 November 1814 - 40 acres of
which are assigned to William Gragg enterer - adjoining Graggs old tract,

adjoining John Harris. Sealed 28 November 1816.


No. 3059      Page 201
State of Tennessee - to John Bartley 35 acres on Mill Fork of Big Limestone - Entry No. 1534, 21 November 1812 - founded on certificate No. 189
- issued by Luke Lea to William Richey for 163 acres, 2 June 1812 - 35
acres of which is issued to John Bartley enterer - adjoining Daniel
Kennedy. Sealed 3 May 1814.


No. 5104      Page 202
State of Tennessee - to James Kilgore 20 acres on north side of Nolachucky River - Entry No. 1384, 3 August 1812 - founded on certificate
No. 88 - issued by Luke Lea to William Shields for 5000 acres, 2 March
1812 - 37 acres of which are assigned to John Shields enterer - 20
acres assigned to James Kilgore, adjoining Alexander Hall, Daniel Guin,
Widdow Wilson. Sealed 5 May 1817.


No. 2590      Page 203
State of Tennessee - to James Kilgore 4 acres on north side of Nolachucky
River - Entry No. 1079, 6 March 1812 - founded on warrant No. 85 - issued
by William Martin to Henry Reynolds for 100 acres, 6 December 1802 - 4
acres of which is vested in James Kilgore enterer - adjoining Charles
Kilgore, Daniel Guin. Sealed 10 August 1817.


No. 3930      Page 204
State of Tennessee - to Joseph Brown 33 acres on Draught of Richland
Creek, north side of Nolachucky River - Entry No. 3188, 5 March 1816
- founded on certificate No. 741 - issued to James Patterson for 1000
acres, 2 November 1814 - 33 acres of which are issued to Joseph Brown
enterer - adjoining Brown, John Russell and waggon road going from
Greeneville to Camp Creek Ironworks, Andrew Parks. Sealed 15 August
1815.


No. 3587      Page 205
State of Tennessee - to Aaron Newman 20 acres on Long Fork of Lick Creek
- Entry No. 969, 20 January 1812 - founded on certificate No. 178 - issued
to Thomas Hall for 50 acres, 26 December 1810 - 20 acres of which are
assigned to Aaron Newman enterer - adjoining Montieth. Sealed 5 October
1815.


No. 3759      Page 205
State of Tennessee - to David Logan 5 acres on Lick Creek - Entry No.
832, 28 December 1809 - founded on certificate No. 30 - issued to heirs
of Andrew Greer for 2480 acres, 19 July 1808 - 5 acres of which are
assigned to David Logan enterer - adjoining John Rodgers, David Logan.
Sealed 15 April 1816.


No. 814      Page 206
State of North Carolina - for 50 shillings per 100 acres - to Joseph
Harden 200 acres in Greene County on Roaring Fork of Lick Creek, where
Hardin formerly lived and sold to David Parkens and William McAmis line
and Samuel Blairs line - adjoining William McAmish line. Samuel John-
ston at Fairfield, 10 December 1789.


No. 5032      Page 208
State of Tennessee - to Joseph Shafer 50 acres on Puncheon Camp Creek,
south side of Bays Mountain - Entry No. 3219, 18 March 1816 - founded
on certificate No. 792 - issued to George Gordon for 500 acres, 2
November 1814 - 50 acres of which is assigned to Joseph Shafer enterer
- adjoining Moses Shank where Copeland now lives. Sealed 22 April 1817.

No. 3574     Page 209
State of Tennessee - to Benjamin Williams 18 acres on east side of Grassy
Creek - Entry No. 1013, 10 February 1812 - founded on warrant No. 15 - to
Archibald Roane to Michael Massingal for 300 acres, 18 January 1809 - 18
acres assigned to Benjamin Williams enterer - adjoining Richard Coffman,
Joseph Carter, Anthony Bewley. Sealed 5 October 1815.


No. 3066     Page 210
State of Tennessee - to James Daley 40 acres on Clear Fork of Lick Creek
- Entry No. 1556, dated 21 December 1812 - founded on warrant No. 189 -
issued by Luke Lea to William Richey for 160 acres, 2 June 1812 - 40
acres of which are assigned to James Daley enterer - including house and
spring where he now lives - adjoining Gray and Barnett Baxter. Sealed 3
May 1814.


No. 4080     Page 211
State of Tennessee - to Michael Bright 44 acres 54 poles on waters of
Lick Creek - Entry No. 1745, 7 June 1813 - founded in part on certificate No. 20 - issued to John McCampbell for 300 acres, dated 5 January
1810 - 54 acres of which are assigned to Michael Bright enterer - in
part founded on warrant No. 754, issued by James Gaines to Isaac Shelby
for 264 acres, 14 July 1781 - 25 acres of which are assigned to Michael
Bright - 40 acres 55 poles granted to Michael Bright. Sealed 5 March
1817.


No. 5291     Page 212
State of Tennessee - to Michael Bright 10 acres on waters of Sinking
Creek - Entry No. 2151, 15 September 1814 - founded on warrant No. 413
- issued by John Carter to George Taylor for 640 acres, 10 July 1792 -
10 acres of which are assigned to Michael Dittamore the enterer - issued
to Michael Bright (assignee of Dittamore), 10 acres adjoining his own
land, Samuel McNeese, Humbard and Michael Burger. Sealed 11 September
1817.


No. 5429     Page 213
State of Tennessee - to Thomas Ripley 20 acres on north side of Nolachucky River - Entry No. 3598, dated 30 November 1816 - founded on
certificate No. 372 - issued by Edward Scott to Jonathan Tipton for
150 acres, 18 December 1811 - 13 acres of which are assigned to Thomas
Ripley enterer - 20 acres granted to Thomas Ripley, adjoining John
Pebly, Jacob Hise and Adam Shovely. Sealed 23 October 1817.


No. 5177     Page 214
State of Tennessee - to Thomas Ripley 1 acre on north side of Nolachucky
River - Entry No. 435, 13 March 1810 - founded on certificate No. 36 -
issued by Archibald Roane to Francis A. Ramsey for 1000 acres, 25 October
1808 - 1 acre of which is assigned to Thomas Ripley enterer - adjoining
John Pebley, John Gillaspie. Sealed 16 June 1817.


No. 3793     Page 215
State of Tennessee - to Asa Gray 50 acres on Lick Creek - Entry No. 983,
3 February 1812 - founded on warrant No. 2625 - issued by John Carter to
Barney, Arthur and Emanuel Carter for 300 acres, dated 28 November 1784 -
50 acres of which are assigned to Asa Gray enterer - 50 acres granted to
Asa Gray, adjoining his own land, Marshall. Sealed 9 May 1816.


No. _____     Page 216
State of North Carolina - for 10 pounds per 100 acres - to John Pebley
300 acres in Greene County, adjoining Gillaspie, including plantation
where Widdow Pebley now lives, adjoining Edmond Robeson and Armants.
Richard Dobbs Spraight, 5 December 1794.

No. 2746     Page 217
State of Tennessee - to John Williams for 100 acres on Lick Creek, on
west fork of Camp Creek - Entry No. 846, 23 October 1811 - founded on
certificate No. 351 - issued to John Williams for 100 acres, 16 October
1811 - 100 acres granted to John Williams, adjoining Alexander Williams,
Joseph Brown, Henry Rowan, being an Occupant Claim. Sealed at Nashville,
3 April 1813.


No. 5214     Page 218
State of Tennessee - to Thomas Conway 3 1/2 acres on an island in Nolachucky River - Entry No. 1139, 11 March 1812 - founded on certificate No.
234 - issued to Adam Huntsmar for 1000 acres, 6 April 1811 - 3 1/3 acres
of which are assigned to Thomas Conway enterer - adjoining Allen Ragan.
Sealed 30 June 1817.


No. 5028     Page 219
State of Tennessee - to John Munsher 100 acres on south side of Nolachucky River on Camp Creek - Entry No. 3259, 29 April 1816 - founded on
certificate No. 793 - issued to George Gordon for 500 acres, 2 November
1814 - 100 acres assigned to John Munsher enterer - adjoining Samuel
Snapp, Marton Waddle and Aaron Hopton, Bowman. Sealed 8 April 1817.


No. 1924     Page 220
State of Tennessee - to William Kelly 50 acres on Browns Fork of Mill
Creek, adjoining Kelly and others - Entry No. 260, 21 March 1809 -
founded on warrant No. 2326 - issued to Archibald Roane to Thomas
Gillaspie for 150 acres, 19 October 1808 - 50 acres assigned by
Gillaspie to William Kelley enterer - adjoining said Kelley, Frazier
and Cowan. Sealed 24 April 1811.


No. 5432     Page 221
State of Tennessee - to Aaron Newman for 25 acres on Sinking Branch of
Lick Creek, including John Finchers improvement - Entry No. 970, 20
January 1812 - founded on certificate No. 178 - issued to Thomas Hall
for 50 acres, dated 26 December 1810, the whole of which is assigned
to Aaron Newman enterer - adjoining Black and Bickers, Henry Cross.
Sealed 5 October 1817.


No. 5675     Page 222
State of Tennessee - to Philip Cole 58 acres on Limestone Fork of Lick
Creek - Entry No. 922, 24 December 1811 - founded on warrant No. 754 -
issued to Isaac Shelby for 265 acres, 14 February 1781 - the whole of
which is assigned to Philip Cole enterer - including what were formerly
Hutchisons and Susan Dicksons improvements - adjoining James Johnson,
Andrew English, Cole. Sealed 23 February 1818.


No. 277     Page 224
State of North Carolina - for 10 pounds per 100 acres - to George Doherty
400 acres in Greene County on south side of Nolachucky River on Wolfe
Branch - beginning below mouth of Wolfe Branch, adjoining James Jack.
Richard Caswell at Kinston, 20 September 1787.


No. 3164     Page 225
State of Tennessee - to James Patterson 100 acres, including house and
improvement of said Blair on both sides Camp Creek - Entry No. 705, 10
May 1811 - founded on warrant No. 820 - issued by John Carter to Jordan
Daves for 200 acres, 9 July 1792 - 100 acres of which is assigned to
John Blair Senr. enterer and the survey is assigned to James Patterson.
Sealed 1 September 1814.


No. 133     Page 226
State of North Carolina - for 50 shillings per 100 acres - to John McAdow

200 acres in Greene County on Bullards Creek, formerly Washington County, including where he lives. Sealed 22 January 1779.

No. 5082    Page 227
State of Tennessee - to Joseph Gaston 42 acres on Roaring Fork of Lick Creek - Entry No. 589, 5 January 1811 - founded on certificate No. 30 - issued to A. Roane to Francis A. Ramsey for 1000 acres, 25 December 1808 - 42 acres of which is assigned to Joseph Gaston - adjoining Gass. Sealed 26 April 1817.

No. 5306    Page 228
State of Tennessee - to James McMurtrey 30 acres on south side of Nola-chucky River - Entry No. 2706, 19 May 1815 - founded on certificate No. 766 - issued to George Gordon for 500 acres, 2 November 1814 - 30 acres of which is assigned to James McMurtrey enterer - adjoining McMurtrey, Thomas Gragg. Sealed 13 September 1817.

No. 5096    Page 229
State of Tennessee - to Adam Lonis 26 acres on Churn Camp Creek - Entry No. 1230, 6 April 1812 - founded on warrant No. 15 - issued by A. Roane to Michael Mysinger for 300 acres, 18 January 1809 - 26 acres of which are assigned to Adam Lonis, including improvement of Henry Long. Sealed 2 May 1817.

No. 5586    Page 230
State of Tennessee - to Josiah Harrison for 34 acres on south side of Nolachucky River - Survey No. 1998, 2 June 1814 - issued by John Carter to Thomas Bailey for 300 acres, 25 June 1799 - 53 acres assigned to Josiah Harrison enterer - adjoining where Harrison now lives. Sealed 14 January 1818.

No. 3662    Page 231
State of Tennessee - to Major Farnsworth 14 acres on south side of Nola-chucky River on Little Lick Creek - Entry No. 3084, 29 November 1815 - founded on certificate No. 759 - issued to George Gordon for 500 acres, 2 November 1814 - 14 acres of which are assigned to Major Farnsworth the enterer, including an improvement where George H__rvey? now lives. Sealed 21 February 1818.

No. 5574    Page 232
State of Tennessee - to Hugh Cavner 22 1/2 acres on Lick Creek, adjoining his own land - Entry No. 3023, 18 October 1815 - founded on certificate No. 225 - issued by Nathan Shipley to John Rhea for 45 acres, 25 July 1815, the whole issued to Hugh Cavner the enterer - 24 1/2 acres granted to Hugh Cavner, adjoining his own land, James McPheran. Sealed 8 January 1818.

No. 5111    Page 233
State of Tennessee - to Benjamin Johnston 9 acres on branches of McCart-ney's Creek, waters of Nolachucky River - Entry No. 142, 9 September 1808 - founded on warrant No. 2629 - issued by John Armstrong to Thomas Childs for 1000 acres, 30 November 1784 - 9 acres of which are assigned to Benjamin Johnston enterer - 9 acres granted to Benjamin Johnston, adjoin-ing Fryes, waggon road, Stanfield. Sealed 26 May 1817.

No. 5988    Page 234
State of Tennessee - to John Kennedy 60 acres on headwaters of Sinking Creek - Entry No. 2827, 22 July 1815 - warrant No. 220 - issued by James Gains to Nathaniel Taylor for 640 acres, 21 February 1780 - 76 acres of which are assigned to John Kennedy enterer - granted to him 60 acres adjoining Michael Burgner, Peter Sellers, Hendersons corner, Michael Dittamore. Sealed 6 May 1818.

No. 5786     Page 235
State of Tennessee - to John Kennedy 2 acres on draught of Sinking Creek
- Entry No. 2375, 21 January 1815 - founded on warrant No. 220 - issued
by James Gains to Nathaniel Taylor for 640 acres, 21 February 1780 - 76
acres of which was assigned to John Kennedy enterer - 2 acres granted to
John Kennedy, adjoining Burger. Sealed 6 May 1818.


No. 5665     Page 236
State of Tennessee - to David Gerdner 50 acres on south side of Nolachucky River - Entry No. 3078, 27 November 1815 - founded on certificate No. 791 - issued to George Gordon for 500 acres, 2 November 1814
- 50 acres of which are assigned to David Girdner enterer - 50 acres
granted to David Girdner, adjoining Solomon Wilhite, including cleared
land and spring where Paulser Hawk now lives. Sealed 21 February 1818.


No. 5689     Page 237
State of Tennessee - to John Olinger 10 acres on north side Lick Creek -
Entry No. 3407, 31 August 1816 - founded on certificate No. 741 - issued
to James Patterson for 1000 acres, 2 November 1814 - 70 acres of which
are assigned to John Olinger enterer - adjoining Archibald Campbell,
Frederick Sauda, Christopher Houts, including Pattersons Meeting House
and improvement and spring around it. Sealed 5 March 1818.


No. 5668     Page 237
State of Tennessee - to Michael Bright 20 acres on Lick Creek - Entry No.
2099, 22 August 1814 - founded on certificate No. 642 - issued to James
P. Taylor for 250 acres, 5 April 1814 - 20 acres assigned to John Dickson enterer. To Michael Bright, assignee of John Dickson, 20 acres
lying between Michael Bright and Martin Bailey, including an improvement
where Isaac Hope now lives. Sealed 1 February 1818.


No. 1994     Page 238
State of Tennessee - to Ephraim Broyles 10 acres on south side of Nolachucky River on Higgins Branch, adjoining Thomas Prather and Philip Bird
- based on Entry No. 377, 21 December 1809 - founded on warrant No. 2411
- issued by John Carter to Henry McKenney for 100 acres, 10 January 1795
- assigned by McKenney to Jacob Bird and by Bird, 10 acres to Ephraim
Broyles enterer. Sealed 18 December 1811.


No. 6026     Page 239
State of Tennessee - to William Luster 100 acres on Lick Creek - Entry
No. 3987, 10 July 1817 - based on certificate No. 867 - issued by A.
Foster to Edward Mead for 640 acres, 16 December 1815 - 100 acres of
which are assigned to William Luster enterer - granted by Tennessee -
adjoining Hugh Carter and William Crumley. Sealed 16 December 1818.


No. 5518     Page 240
State of Tennessee - to Zachariah Kennamon 18 acres on north side of
Sinking Creek - Entry No. 1726, 20 May 1813 - founded on certificate
No. 88 - issued by Luke Lea to William Shields for 5000 acres, 2 March
1812 - 10 acres of which are assigned to Zachariah Kinnamon enterer -
adjoining William Whittenberger, Kinnamons old survey. Granted 11
December 1817.


No. 3569     Page 241
State of Tennessee - to Simon Pope 50 acres on Lick Creek - Entry No.
2423, dated 8 February 1815 - founded on certificate No. 215 - issued
by Nathan Shipley to John Billingsley for 50 acres, 24 December 1814
- whole amount assigned to Simon Pope enterer - adjoining James Mathes
and William McAmish. Granted 4 October 1815.

No. 3568    Page 242
State of Tennessee - to Simon Pope 25 acres on Lick Creek, adjoining his own land - Entry No. 2424, 8 February 1815 - founded on certificate No. 105 - issued by Nathan Shipley to David Perry for 35 acres, 2 January 1815 - whole amount assigned to Simon Pope enterer. Granted 4 October 1815.

No. 5516    Page 243
State of Tennessee - to Simon Pope 50 acres on Sinking Creek - Entry No. 2748, 9 June 1815 - founded on certificate No. 754 - issued by James Gains to Isaac Shelby for 264 acres, 14 February 1781 - 50 acres of which are assigned to Simon Pope enterer - adjoining John English, James Mathes. Granted 10 December 1817.

No. 3567    Page 244
State of Tennessee - to Simon Pope 10 acres on Lick Creek, adjoining himself - Entry No. 2425, 8 February 1815 - certificate No. 105 - issued by Nathan Shipley to David Perry for 35 acres, 2 January 1815 - amount of acres assigned to Simon Pope enterer. Granted 4 October 1815.

No. 5503    Page 245
State of Tennessee - to Simon Pope 51 acres on Piburns Creek, adjoining John Woolsey and his own land - Entry No. 870, dated 6 November 1811 - founded on certificate No. 23 - issued by Archibald Roane to George Hines for 259 acres, 17 April 1810 - 51 acres assigned to Simon Pope enterer - adjoining Graham. Granted 6 December 1817.

No. 1597    Page 246
State of Tennessee - to Simon Pope 5 acres on Piburns Creek, waters of Lick Creek - Entry No. 273, 24 May 1809 - founded on warrant No. 910 - issued by Archibald Roane to James McBee for 300 acres, 9 February 1808 - assigned by McBee to Samuel Crawford and 150 acres by Crawford to Simon Pope - 30 acres of the said 100 to Simon Pope enterer. Granted 2 July 1810.

No. 2866    Page 247
State of Tennessee - to Hugh Carter 74 acres on Lick Creek - Entry No. 49, 18 April 1808 - founded on warrant No. 2629 - issued by John Armstrong to Thomas Childes for 1000 acres, 30 November 1784 - 75 acres of which are assigned to Hugh Carter enterer - adjoining Thomas McAmish. Granted 7 July 1813.

No. 5634    Page 248
State of Tennessee - to David Rice 100 acres on Roaring Fork of Lick Creek - Entry No. 569, 30 November 1810 - founded on certificate No. 38 - issued by Archibald Roane to Joseph Brown for 100 acres, 7 January 1809, the whole of which are assigned to David Rice, enterer - adjoining Robert Maloney and Rice. Granted 5 February 1818.

No. 5035    Page 249
State of Tennessee - to Nicholas Ealy for 50 acres adjoining Samuel Denwoody survey - Entry No. 2257, 18 November 1814 - founded on certificate No. 542 - issued by Edward Scott to William Shields for 469 acres, 27 May 1813 - 50 acres of which are assigned to Nicholas Ealy. Granted 22 April 1817.

No. 2210    Page 250
State of Tennessee - to Zachariah Tate 59 3/4 acres on Mill Fork of Big Limestone - Entry No. 800 - founded on certificate No. 124 - issued to A. P. Fore for 400 acres, 11 June 1810 - which certificate is assigned by Fore to George T. Gillespie enterer, 18 September 1811 - a plot

assigned to Zachariah Tate. Granted 3 June 1812.


No. 2135     Page 251
State of Tennessee - to Joseph Shannon 48 acres on Draughts of Sinking
Creek - Entry No. 302 - founded on certificate No. 3 - issued to Francis
A. Ramsey for 1000 acres, 21 August 1809 - 60 acres vested in Joseph
Shannon enterer by assignment - adjoining Delany, Hicks. Granted 30
March 1812.


No. 287     Page 252
State of North Carolina - for 10 pounds per 100 acres - to John Waggoner
200 acres in Greene County on a fork of Camp Creek and Middle Creek.
Granted 20 September 1787.


No. 5999     Page 253
State of Tennessee - to David Rice 15 acres adjoining himself, Hugh
Cavner and Jacob Hoyle - Entry No. 4252, 31 January 1818 - founded on
certificate No. 1294 - issued to James P. Taylor for 300 acres, 1 May
1817 - 15 acres of which are assigned to David Rice, enterer. Granted
2 November 1818.


No. 5198     Page 254
State of Tennessee - to John Wilson 10 acres on south side of Nolachucky
River near town of Greeneville, adjoining his own land - Entry No. 2532,
16 March 1815 - founded on certificate No. 766 - issued to George Gordon
for 500 acres, 2 November 1814 - 10 acres of which are assigned to John
Wilson enterer - adjoining Valentine Sevier, John Balch. Granted 21
June 1817.


No. 5447     Page 255
State of Tennessee - to William Gladden 74 acres on south side Nolachucky
River on Cove Creek, adjoining Paint Mountain - Entry No. 2158, 17 September 1814 - founded on certificate No. 172 - issued by Archibalc Roane
to Samuel Y. Balch for 188 acres, 21 May 1810 - 22 acres assigned to
James Patterson, one of the enteries and partly on certificate No. 88,
issued by Luke Lea to William Shields for 500 acres, 2 March 1812 - the
whole of which is assigned to Daniel Guin, the other enterer, assigned
to Gladden and Guin - 74 acres including house, spring and improvement
whereon Thomas Wilson and Isaac Wilson now live, across Cove Creek and
Warm Spring Road. Granted to William Gladdin, assignee of said
Patterson and Guin, 29 October 1817.


No. 5160     Page 256
State of Tennessee - to Elliot Rutherford 10 acres on waters of Gap
Creek, north side of Bays Mountain - Entry No. 2084, 10 August 1814 -
founded on certificate No. 542 - issued to William Shields for 469
acres, 27 May 1813 - 10 acres of which are assigned to Elliot Rutherford enterer. Granted 14 June 1817.


No. 820     Page 257
State of North Carolina - for 10 pounds per 100 acres - to James Love
100 acres in Greene County on north side Nolachucky River on Sinking
Creek, adjoining John Johnston. Granted by Samuel Johnson at Fayetteville 17 November 1789.


No. 6319     Page 258
State of Tennessee - to Nehemiah Woolsey 200 acres on south side Nolachucky River on waters of Little Lick Creek - Entry No. 4110, 8 August
1817 - founded on certificate No. 1194 - issued to William Nelson for
200 acres, 2 March 1816 - all of which is assigned to Nehemiah Woolsey
enterer - adjoining David Reynolds, John Kelley, Moses Hughes and his
own land, including his improvement. Granted 26 October 1819.

No. 6318    Page 259
State of Tennessee - to Gilbert Woolsey 29 acres on south side Nolachucky
River - Entry No. 4453, 30 June 1818 - founded on warrant No. 1083 -
issued to heirs of Robert Campbell for 200 acres, 30 May 1809 - 49 acres
assigned to Gilbert Woolsey enterer - adjoining Moses Hughes and said
Woolsey.  Granted 26 October 1819.


No. 6313    Page 260
State of Tennessee - to Gilbert Woolsey 20 acres on south side Nolachucky
River - based on Entry No. 4452, 30 June 1818 - founded on certificate No.
1083 - issued to heirs of Robert Campbell for 200 acres, 30 May 1809 -
49 acres of which are assigned to Gilbert Woolsey enterer - 20 acres
granted to Gilbert Woolsey, adjoining William Woolsey, including improvement made by John Brasure.  Granted 26 October 1819.


No. 6322    Page 261
State of Tennessee - to Michael Bright 16 acres on Lick Creek on north
side Lick Creek Road from Snapps Ferry to Bulls Gap - Entry No. 2895,
2 September 1815 - founded on warrant No. 754 - issued by James P. Gains
to Isaac Shelby for 265 acres, 14 February 1781 - all of which is assigned
to Philip Cole enterer.  Granted by Tennessee to Michael Bright, assignee
of said Cole - 16 acres adjoining Andrew English Senr.  Granted 27
October 1819.


No. 6362    Page 262
State of Tennessee - to David Logan 18 acres on north side Lick Creek -
Entry No. 4008, 4 August 1817 - founded on certificate No. 1294 - issued
by Jacob Lipton to James P. Taylor for 300 acres, 1 May 1817 - 18 acres
of which are assigned to David Logan enterer - adjoining Logan and John
Olinger, along spurs of Lust Mountain.  Granted 11 November 1819.


No. 6341    Page 263
State of Tennessee - to David Logan 10 acres on Lick Creek adjoining
John Rogers and Logans other lands - Entry No. 4046, 4 November 1817
- founded on certificate No. 928 - issued to the heirs of Samuel
McCorkle for 150 acres, 2 June 1815 - 10 acres of which are assigned
to David Logan enterer.  Granted 15 November 1819.


No. 6352    Page 265
State of Tennessee - to Alexander English 26 acres on south side of Lick
Creek joining his own land and Elizabeth Campbell and Andrew English -
Entry No. 3893, 15 May 1817 - founded on certificate No. 1176 - issued
by Jacob Tipton to James P. Taylor for 50 acres, 5 March 1816 - all of
which is assigned to Andrew English enterer.  Granted 10 November 1819.


No. 6353    Page 266
State of Tennessee - to Alexander English 13 acres on Limestone Fork of
Lick Creek - Entry No. 3897, 14 May 1817 - founded on certificate No.
1176 - issued by Jacob Tipton to James P. Taylor for 50 acres, 5 March
1816 - all of which is assigned to Andrew English enterer - Andrew
English 13 acres a late entry of Philip Cole on both sides of a path
leading from English's house to Sarah Cole's cabbin, adjoining English,
Thomas Coulson.  Granted 10 November 1819.


No. 6351    Page 267
State of Tennessee - to Alexander English for 7 acres on Clear Fork of
Lick Creek - Entry No. 4065, 13 September 1817 - founded on certificate
No. 1176 - issued to James P. Taylor for 50 acres, 5 May 1816 - all of
which is assigned to Andrew English enterer - 7 acres granted to Andrew
English, between lands of James English, decd. and lands formerly owned
by Robert Crockett, now William Mc~onald, including house where Crockett
lived, adjoining English Mill Survey.  Granted 10 November 1819.

No. 6378    Page 268
State of Tennessee – to John McRogers 25 acres on Dales Branch of Lick
Creek – Entry No. 4462, 21 July 1818 – founded on certificate No. 2553
– Issued by David McGavock to James P. Taylor for 500 acres – granted
to John McRogers and his heirs, 21 acres, adjoining his own land and
the mountain, including the Freestone Spring. Granted 14 November 1819.

No. 6055    Page 269
State of Tennessee – to Thomas Williamson 27 acres on Horse Creek, south
side of Nolachucky River – based on Entry No. 3352, 5 August 1816 –
founded on certificate No. 794 – Issued to George Gordon for 500 acres,
2 November 1814 – 30 acres of which are assigned to Thomas Williamson
enterer – 27 acres granted to Williamson, adjoining William Kinder Senr.,
Joseph Newberry and his own land. Granted 15 February 1819.

No. 6296    Page 270
State of Tennessee – to Samuel Snapp 37 acres on south side of Nolachucky
River – Entry No. 3959, 11 June 1817 – founded on certificate No. 1192 –
Issued to Elkannah R. Dulaney for 100 acres, 10 October 1815 – 50 acres
of which are assigned to Samuel Snapp enterer – 37 acres adjoining John
Farnsworth and Samuel Snapp, including old improvement made by Stapleton.
Granted 24 October 1819.

No. 6323    Page 271
State of Tennessee – to Elias Houff 3 acres joining his own land – based
on Entry No. 4564, 31 October 1818 – founded on certificate No. 727 –
Issued to James P. Taylor for 300 acres, 30 August 1814 – 3 acres of
which are assigned to Elias Houff enterer. Granted 27 October 1819.

No. 6381    Page 271
State of Tennessee – to Adam Lonis 20 acres adjoining Edward Jones' old
survey – based on Entry No. 2554, 21 March 1815 – founded on certificate
No. 794 – Issued to George Gordon for 500 acres, 2 November 1814 – 20
acres of which are assigned to Adam Lonis, assignee of said Edward Jones
enterer. Granted 12 November 1819.

No. 5044    Page 273
State of Tennessee – to James Parsons 20 acres on north side Nolachucky
River, adjoining his old survey – Entry No. 2987, 2 October 1815 –
founded on certificate No. 791 – Issued to George Gordon for 500 acres,
2 November 1814 – 55 acres of which are assigned to James Parsons
enterer – 20 acres adjoining Farmer, Williamson survey. Granted 22
April 1817.

No. 6317    Page 274
State of Tennessee – to John Lints 50 acres adjoining his own land and
others – Entry No. 3850, 31 March 1817 – founded on certificate No. 1186
– Issued by Jacob Tipton to George Gordon for 100 acres, 11 March 1816 –
50 acres of which are assigned to John Lints enterer – adjoining Elias
Clifton and Widow Smith and his own land. Granted 26 October 1819.

No. 6314    Page 275
State of Tennessee – to Peter Whittenberg 50 acres on Richland Creek,
north side of Nolachucky River – Entry No. 2555, 21 March 1815 – founded
on certificate No. 794 – Issued to George Gordon for 500 acres, 2
November 1814 – 50 acres of which are assigned to Peter Whittenberg
enterer – adjoining his own land, Major Temple and James Whittenberg.
Granted 26 October 1819.

No. 6325    Page 276
State of Tennessee – to John Fincher 25 acres on Limestone Fork of Lick
Creek – Entry No. 923, 24 December 1811 – founded on warrant No. 754 –

by James Gains to Isaac Shelby for 264 acres, 14 February 1781 - all of
which is assigned to Philip Cole enterer - 20 acres on both sides Limestone Fork of Lick Creek, including an improvement claimed by James
Moore. Granted 27 October 1819.


No. 6387      Page 277
State of Tennessee - to Watson Dudley 10 acres on south side Nolachucky
River on Cove Creek - Entry No. 3118, 16 December 1815 - founded on
certificate No. 1083 - issued by Archibald Roane to heirs of Robert
Campbell for 200 acres - 10 acres of which are assigned to Watson Dudley
enterer - between Dudley and Andrew Stephens. Granted 13 November 1819.


No. 6053      Page 278
State of Tennessee - to Daniel Guin 110 acres on south side Nolachucky
River near waters of Horse Creek - Entry No. 3914, 2 May 1817 - founded
on warrant No. 2974 - issued by John Carter to James Clinkham for 640
acres, 17 December 1797 - 110 acres assigned to Daniel Guin enterer -
adjoining Thomas Williamson and Jacob Broyles, including Chestnut Ridge,
heirs of Lewis Broyles. Granted 15 February 1819.


No. 5021      Page 279
State of Tennessee - to Saymore Catching 100 acres including where James
Matthews lives - Entry No. 1176, 21 March 1812 - founded on certificate
No. 88 - issued by Luke Lea to William Shields for 5000 acres, 2 March
1812 - 100 acres of which are assigned to Saymore Catching enterer -
including house spring and improvement where James Mathes now lives.
Granted 24 March 1817.


No. 6054      Page 280
State of Tennessee - to Thomas Williamson 2 1/4 acres on Horse Creek,
on south side Nolachucky River - Entry No. 4292, 9 March 1818 - founded
on certificate No. 794 - issued to George Gordon for 500 acres, 2
November 1814 - 30 acres assigned to Thomas Williamson enterer - 2 1/4
acres on Horse Creek, adjoining John Rynals, Williamson's own land.
Granted 15 February 1819.


No. 6321      Page 281
State of Tennessee - to Solomon Bails 7 1/2 acres adjoining his own and
John Frakers lands - Entry No. 4241, 29 January 1818 - founded on warrant
No. 552 - issued by John Carter to John Vech? for 640 acres, 1 August
1793 - 25 acres of which are assigned to Solomon Beals enterer - 7 1/2
acres granted 26 October 1819.


No. 6373      Page 282
State of Tennessee - to William Reynolds 10 acres land on Paint Creek -
Entry No. 2819, 20 July 1815 - founded on warrant No. 1083 - issued by
Archibald Roane to heirs of Robert Campbell for 200 acres, 30 May 1809
- 20 acres of which are assigned to William Reynolds enterer. Granted
12 November 1819.


No. 6382      Page 283
State of Tennessee - to William Reynolds 10 acres on south side of Nola-
chucky River on Paint Creek - Entry No. 2818, 20 July 1815 - founded on
certificate No. 1083 - issued by Archibald Roane to heirs of Robert
Campbell for 200 acres, 30 May 1809 - 20 acres of which are assigned to
William Reynolds enterer. Granted 13 November 1819.


No. 6380      Page 284
State of Tennessee - to William Reynolds 8 acres on south side of Nolachucky River on Brush Creek - Entry No. 2830, 26 July 1815 - founded on
certificate No. 791 - issued to George Gordon for 500 acres, 2 November
1814 - 20 acres of which are assigned to William Gladden enterer - 8

75

acres assigned to William Reynolds, assignee of Benjamin Martney?, assignee of said Gladden and his heirs. Granted 12 November 1819.


No. 6150      Page 285
State of Tennessee - to Joseph Self 10 acres on Gap Creek - Entry No. 1814, 20 October 1813 - based on certificate No. 542 - issued to William Shields for 469 acres, 27 May 1813 - 10 acres of which are assigned to William Brown enterer - Joseph Self, assignee of William Brown, granted 10 acres where Snapps Road crosses branch of Gap Creek, adjoining James McCullough. Granted 29 July 1819.


No. 6114      Page 286
State of Tennessee - to John Simpson 20 acres on Little Sinking Creek - Entry No. 3468, 3 October 1816 - based on certificate No. 116 - issued by Nathan Shipley to James P. Taylor for 640 acres, 20 July 1815 - 20 acres of which are assigned to John Simpson enterer. Granted 18 May 1819.


No. 6366      Page 287
State of Tennessee - to Allen Gillespie 30 acres on Big Limestone - Entry No. 3644, 24 December 1816 - based on certificate No. 2974 - issued by John Carter to James Clinkham for 640 acres, 17 December 1797 - 30 acres of which are assigned to Allen Gillespie enterer - adjoining John Pebly and George H. Gillespie. Granted 11 November 1819.


No. 6350      Page 288
State of Tennessee - to John Robinson 25 acres on Limestone Fork of Lick Creek - Entry No. 3640, 23 December 1816 - founded on certificate No. 1254 - issued to James P. Taylor for 300 acres, 1 November 1816 - 25 acres of which are assigned to John Robinson enterer - adjoining Alexander English, said Robinson, Stothard Neal. Granted 10 November 1819.


No. 6376      Page 289
State of Tennessee - to James Jones 15 acres on Lick Creek - Entry No. 4064, 12 September 1817 - founded on certificate No. 2553 - issued to James P. Taylor for 500 acres, 17 December 1816 - 25 acres of which are assigned to James Jones enterer. Granted 15 acres, 12 November 1819.


No. 6042      Page 290
State of Tennessee - to Phillip Rinker 17 acres on south side of Lick Creek - Entry No. 3030, 2 November 1815 - founded on certificate No. 741 - issued to James Patterson for 1000 acres, 2 November 1814 - 45 acres of which are assigned to Philip Rinker enterer - 17 acres adjoining a tract whereon Rachel Gray now lives, David Perkens. Granted 1 January 1819.


No. 6041      Page 291
State of Tennessee - to Philip Rinker 20 acres on or near Lick Creek - Entry No. 3183, 4 March 1816 - founded on certificate No. 745 - issued to James Patterson for 1000 acres, 2 November 1814 - 45 acres of which are assigned to Philip Rinker enterer - 20 acres adjoining Jones. Granted 1 January 1819.


No. 5112      Page 292
State of Tennessee - to George Morelock 1 acre on Sinking Creek - Entry No. 93, 16 August 1808 - based on warrant No. 2629 - issued by John Armstrong to Thomas Childs for 1000 acres, 30 November 1784 - 1 acre assigned to Michael Burger the enterer. Granted by Tennessee, George Morelock, assignee, 26 May 1817.


No. 5288      Page 293
State of Tennessee - to John Moyers 45 acres on Draughts of Jockeys Creek

- Entry No. 3202, 8 March 1816 - founded on certificate No. 117 - issued by Nathan Shipley to James P. Taylor for 640 acres, 20 July 1815 - 113 acres of which are assigned to John Moyers enterer - 45 acres adjoining Jonathan Nare and William Kelly. Granted 11 September 1817.


No. 5287     Page 294
State of Tennessee - to John Moyers 68 acres adjoining Edward Doltson and John Roberts - Entry No. 3207, 12 March 1816 - founded on certificate No. 117 - issued by Nathan Shipley to James P. Taylor for 640 acres, 20 June 1815 - 113 acres assigned to John Moyers enterer - 68 acres granted to John Moyers, 11 September 1817.


No. 6389     Page 295
State of Tennessee - to Benjamin Parker 25 acres near Lick Creek - Entry No. 1593, 1 February 1813 - founded on certificate No. 88 - issued by Luke Lea to William Shields for 5000 acres, 2 March 1812 - 24 acres of the above was assigned to Benjamin Parker, on the certificate 51 acres assigned to Benjamin Parker enterer. Tennessee granted 15 acres to Benjamin Parker, adjoining Absalom Temple, James Trim. Granted 13 November 1819.


No. 6342     Page 296
State of Tennessee - to Farmer Pogue 40 acres on Lick Creek - based on Entry No. 3738, 10 February 1817 - founded on certificate No. 1243 - issued to Jacob K. Snapp for 100 acres, 12 August 1816 - 40 acres of which are assigned to Farmer Pogue enterer - adjoining John Hartley and Pogue. Granted 9 November 1819.


No. 6374     Page 297
State of Tennessee - to Farmer Pogue 25 acres on Lick Creek - Entry No. 3236, 30 March 1816 - founded on certificate No. 782 - issued to George Gordon for 500 acres, 2 September 1814 - 25 acres of which are assigned to Farmer Pogue - adjoining Hartley and said Pogue. Granted 12 November 1819.


No. 6344     Page 298
State of Tennessee - to Thomas Dodd 10 acres on Horse Camp Fork of Lick Creek - Entry No. 3702, 20 January 1817 - based on certificate No. 279 - issued to James P. Taylor for 10 acres, 13 May 1811, all of which is assigned to Thomas Dodd enterer - adjoining lands of said Dodd, Abraham Haynes. Granted 9 November 1819.


No. 6312     Page 299
State of Tennessee - to John Crawford 4 acres on Lick Creek adjoining his own land - Entry No. 4097, 6 October 1817 - founded on warrant No. 476 - issued to John McAdow for 640 acres, 2 April 1780 - 4 acres of which are assigned to John Crawford enterer - adjoining Thomas Coulson, Alexander English and Barnetts. Granted 26 October 1819.


No. 6216     Page 300
State of Tennessee - to Thomas Caldwell 15 acres near Lick Creek - Entry No. 3139, 8 January 1816 - founded on certificate No. 792 - issued to George Gordon for 500 acres, 2 November 1814 - 27 acres of which are assigned to Thomas Caldwell enterer - 15 acres on both sides of path leading from Caldwells to John Robenson. Granted 15 October 1819.


No. 6218     Page 301
State of Tennessee - to Thomas Caldwell for 12 acres near Lick Creek - Entry No. 3140, 8 January 1816 - founded on certificate No. 792 - issued to George Gordon for 500 acres, 2 November 1814 - 27 acres of which are assigned to Thomas Caldwell enterer - 12 acres, adjoining himself and Samuel Caldwell. Granted 15 October 1819.

No. 6376     Page 302
State of Tennessee - to Thomas Collier 15 acres on head of Clear Fork of
Lick Creek - Entry No. 3652, 28 December 1816 - founded on certificate
No. 476 - issued to John McAdow for 640 acres, 24 April 1780 - 15 acres
of which are assigned to Thomas Collier enterer - adjoining John Collier
and John Ryan.  Granted 11 November 1819.


No. 6384     Page 303
State of Tennessee - to John Olinger 60 acres on Lick Creek - Entry No.
4203, 8 January 1818 - founded on certificate No. 1183 - issued to
George Gordon for 500 acres, 7 March 1816 - 60 acres of which are
assigned to John Olinger enterer - adjoining Thomas McCollum and Archibald Campbell.  Granted 13 November 1819.


No. 6377     Page 304
State of Tennessee - to James Johnson 40 acres on Limestone Fork of Lick
Creek - Entry No. 3894, 15 May 1817 - founded on certificate No. 1254 -
issued to James P. Taylor for 300 acres, 1 November 1816 - 40 acres of
which are granted to James Johnson enterer - adjoining John Rhea and
Johnson.  Granted 12 November 1819.


No. 6371     Page 305
State of Tennessee - to Robert Hays 40 acres on Lick Creek - Entry No.
3331, 30 July 1816 - based on certificate No. 1181 - issued by Jacob
Tipton to George Gordon for 200 acres, 7 March 1816 - 40 acres of which
are assigned to Robert Hays enterer - adjoining Joseph Hays and Robert
Hays.  Granted 11 November 1819.


No. 6375     Page 306
State of Tennessee - to Robert Hays 42 acres on Lick Creek - Entry No.
2142, 14 September 1815 - based on certificate No. 789 - issued to George
Gordon for 500 acres, 2 November 1814 - 42 acres of which are assigned to
Robert Hays, adjoining Alexander English.  Granted 12 November 1819.


No. 6354     Page 307
State of Tennessee - to Stoddard Neil 19 acres on Clear Fork of Lick
Creek - Entry No. 3142, 15 January 1816 - founded on certificate No.
189 - issued by Luke Lea to William Richey for 163 acres, 2 June 1812
- 19 acres assigned to Stoddard Neil, adjoining John Robinson, James
Daley and said Neal.  Granted 10 November 1819.


No. 5763     Page 308
State of Tennessee - to John Stine for 20 acres on Nolachucky River -
Entry No. 449, 7 April 1810 - founded on certificate No. 56 - issued by
Archibald Roane to James Wilson for 100 acres, 7 July 1808 - 70 acres of
which are assigned to John Stine enterer - adjoining John Ottinger.
Granted 10 April 1818.


No. 5764     Page 309
State of Tennessee - to John Stine 50 acres adjoining John Ottinger on
Nolachucky River - based on Entry No. 450, 7 April 1810 - founded on
certificate No. 56 - issued by Archibald Roane to James Wilson for 160
acres, 7 July 1808 - 70 acres of which are assigned to John Stine
enterer - 50 acres adjoining John Ottinger.  Granted 10 April 1818.


No. 5791     Page 310
State of Tennessee - to John Willoughby 50 acres on Fergusons Lick Branch
- Entry No. 826, 9 October 1810 - founded on certificate No. 22 - issued
by Archibald Roane to David Reese for 210 acres, 4 April 1810 - 80 acres
of which are assigned to John Willoughby enterer - 50 acres granted, 6
May 1818.


78

No. 5790    Page 311
State of Tennessee - to Benjamin Willoughby 10 acres on Lick Creek - Entry No. 1765, 2 August 1813 - founded on certificate No. 542 - issued to William Shields for 469 acres, 27 May 1813 - 10 acres of which are assigned to Mary Etter, enterer, her assignee, Benjamin Willoughby. Granted 6 May 1818.


No. 6319    Page 312
State of Tennessee - to Jonathan Justice 5 acres on Horse Camp Fork of Lick Creek - Entry No. 2805, 8 July 1815 - founded on certificate No. 759 - issued to George Gordon for 500 acres, 2 November 1814 - 5 acres of which are assigned to Jonathan Justice, enterer - adjoining Anthony Hoggatt, Azariah Doty. Granted 12 November 1819.


No. 6363    Page 313
State of Tennessee - to Jonathan Justice 20 acres on Horse Camp Fork of Lick Creek - Entry No. 3949, 10 June 1817 - founded on certificate No. 2553 - issued to James P. Taylor for 500 acres, 11 December 1816 - 20 acres of which are assigned to Jonathan Justice, enterer - adjoining Azariah Doty, Samuel Milligan and Wright. Granted 11 November 1819.


No. 6332    Page 314
State of Tennessee - to John Glass 20 acres on Richland Creek - Entry No. 3044, 7 November 1815 - founded on certificate No. 980 - issued to Peter Parsons for 320 acres, 22 July 1815 - 20 acres of which are assigned to Benjamin H. Champlaens, enterer, Glass his assignee - adjoining John Brown. Granted 28 October 1819.


No. 5963    Page 315
State of Tennessee - to Turner Sharp 10 acres on Little Chuckey Creek - Entry No. 1166, 18 March 1812 - founded on certificate No. 88 - issued by Luke Lea to William Shields for 5000 acres, 2 March 1812 - 10 acres of which are assigned to Turner Sharp, including house and spring where John Cobble now lives. Granted 25 September 1818.


No. 6045    Page 316
State of Tennessee - to Peter Pitsenberger 41 acres on both sides of Lick Creek - Entry No. 1082, 7 March 1812 - founded on certificate No. 88 - issued by Luke Lee to William Shields for 5000 acres, 2 March 1812 - 41 acres assigned to Peter Pitsenberger, adjoining Widow Gray, John Fry. Granted 2 January 1819.


No. 6315    Page 316
State of Tennessee - to heirs of John Williams 50 acres on north side of Nolichuckey River - Entry No. 3103, 14 December 1815 - founded on warrant No. 1675 - issued by John Carter to Samuel Bowman for 200 acres, 2 February 1784 - 50 acres of which are assigned to John Williams, decd., adjoining his own land. Granted 26 October 1819.


No. 5711    Page 318
State of Tennessee - to William Mitchell 60 acres on Lick Creek - based on Entry No. 3097, 8 December 1815 - founded on warrant No. 980 - to Peter Parsons for 300 acres, 22 July 1815 - 60 acres of which are assigned to William Mitchell, enterer, adjoining William Western and John Harmon. Granted 20 March 1818.


No. 3159    Page 319
State of Tennessee - to Robert Maloney 40 acres adjoining David Rice and Hugh Cavener - Entry No. 1298, 23 May 1812 - certificate No. 88 - issued by Luke Lea to William Shields for 5000 acres, 2 August 1812 - 40 acres assigned to Robert Maloney, enterer. Granted 29 August 1814.

No. 6052     Page 320
State of Tennessee - to John Kindel 180 acres on south side of Nolachucky
River - Entry No. 4262, 2 February 1818 - certificate No. 2974 - issued
by John ____ to James Cleckham for 640 acres, 17 December 1797 - 180
acres of which are assigned to John Kindel, enterer - adjoining John
Cotter, Martin Click and Washington Hinshaw, William Chanley. Granted
15 February 1819.


No. 6385     Page 321
State of Tennessee - to Zephaniah St. John 9 acres on south side of Nolachucky River on Brush Creek - Entry No. 2864, 11 August 1815 - certificate No. 782 - issued to George Gordon for 500 acres, 2 November 1814 -
9 acres assigned to Joseph Gladden, enterer - Tennessee to Zephaniah
St. John, assignee of Benjamin Marberry, assignee of Joseph Gladen and
his heirs. Granted 13 November 1819.


No. 5636     Page 322
State of Tennessee - to Thomas Mansfield 30 acres on Draughts of Sinking
Creek - Entry No. 141, dated 9 September 1808 - certificate No. 2629 -
issued by John Armstrong to Thomas Childs for 1000 acres, 13 November
1784 - 30 acres of which are assigned to Joseph Johnson, enterer -
Tennessee granted to Thomas Stanfield, assignee, adjoining John Delaney.
Granted 5 February 1818.


No. 3588     Page 323
State of Tennessee - to David Paulsel 20 acres on Cedar Branch, north
side of Nolachuckey River - Entry No. 286, 28 June 1809 - certificate
No. 2856 - issued by Archibald Roane to John Carter's heirs for 300
acres, 24 October 1808 - 20 acres of which are assigned to David Paulsel,
enterer, adjoining Brumley, including mouth of Cedar Branch. Granted 6
October 1815.


No. 5657     Page 324
State of Tennessee - to Turner Smith 50 acres on waters of Lick Creek -
Entry No. 3356, 7 October 1816 - certificate No. 1222 - issued to John
R. McKinney for 150 acres, 19 June 1816 - 50 acres of which are assigned
to Turner Smith, enterer, adjoining John Rhea, Thomas Coulson and Thomas
Nelson. Granted 20 February 1818.


No. 5658     Page 325
State of Tennessee - to Turner Smith for 40 acres on waters of Lick Creek
- Entry No. 3402, 31 August 1816 - certificate No. 1211 - issued to James
P. Taylor for 40 acres, 12 April 1816 - the whole of which is assigned to
Turner Smith, enterer, adjoining Thomas Nelson and part of Martin Prewits
old field. Granted 20 February 1818.


No. 6369     Page 326
State of Tennessee - to William McBride 135 acres on Little Chuckey,
adjoining Widow Crowleys land and Robert Russell - Entry No. 2782, 26
June 1815 - certificate No. 762 - issued to George Gordon for 500 acres,
2 November 1814 - 350 acres of which are assigned to William McBride,
enterer. Granted 11 November 1819.


No. 6368     Page 327
State of Tennessee - to William McBride 50 acres adjoining Samuel Dunwoody and John Ramsey - Entry No. 3788, 15 March 1817 - founded on
certificate No. 762 - issued to George Gordon for 500 acres, 2 November
1814 - 350 acres assigned to William McBride, enterer. Granted 11
November 1819.


No. 6426     Page 328
State of Tennessee - to William Dickson 13 acres on Pigeon Creek adjoin-

ing Dickson and Widow Isabella Temple - Entry No. 4545, 21 October 1818 -
certificate No. 758, 2 November 1814 - to George Gordon for 500 acres -
13 acres assigned to William Dickson, including house and improvement
made by Benjamin A. Champlain. Granted 22 December 1819.


No. 5656    Page 329
State of Tennessee - to Joseph Hays 75 acres on waters of Long Fork of
Lick Creek, adjoining himself and George Cunningham - Entry No. 3325,
22 July 1816 - certificate No. 1222, 19 June 1816 - to John A. McKinney
for 150 acres, the whold of which is assigned to Joseph Hays. Granted
20 February 1818.


No. 5659    Page 330
State of Tennessee - to Joseph Hays 70 acres on Long Fork of Lick Creek,
adjoining where Hays now lives - Entry No. 2611, 4 April 1814 - warrant
No. 2733, 15 October 1796 - issued by John Carter to John Thomas for 632
acres - 70 acres of which are assigned to Joseph Hays, enterer. Granted
20 February 1818.


No. 3802    Page 331
State of Tennessee - to William Jones for 20 acres and 25 poles of land
on Lick Creek, adjoining his own land and Joseph Carter's - Entry No.
2433, 9 February 1815 - certificate No. 794 - issued to George Gordon
for 500 acres, 2 November 1814 - 20 acres assigned to William Jones,
adjoining Jones, Joseph Carter. Granted 20 May 1816.


No. 3801    Page 332
State of Tennessee - to William Jones 78 acres on waters of Grassy Creek,
adjoining Joseph Carter and Christopher Kirby - Entry No. 2432, 9 February 1815 - certificate No. 794, issued to George Gordon, 2 November
1814 for 500 acres - 78 acres of which are assigned to William Jones,
enterer. Granted 20 May 1816.


No. 5524    Page 333
State of Tennessee - to Thomas Gragg 45 acres on south side of Nolachucky
River, adjoining John Neas land - Entry No. 2096, 15 August 1814 - founded
on certificate No. 708 - issued to Robert Gordon for 100 acres, 24 June
1814 - 50 acres of which are assigned to Thomas Gragg, enterer - 45 acres
granted to Thomas Gragg, adjoining John Welty. Granted 11 December 1817.


No. 3581    Page 334
State of Tennessee - to Nancy McChaughen 20 acres adjoining William
Stanley, on Small Spring Branch that runs to Gasses Creek - Entry No.
2127, 5 September 1814 - founded on certificate No. 268 - issued by
Anthony Foster to David Fains heirs for 640 acres, 10 July 1809 - 20
acres of which are assigned to William Brown, assignee of Nancy
McClaughen and her heirs. Granted 5 October 1815.


No. 6397    Page 335
State of Tennessee - to Henderson Trim 15 acres adjoining James Trim's
land - Entry No. 4295, 11 March 1818 - founded on certificate No. 785 -
issued to George Gordon for 500 acres, 2 November 1814 - 15 acres of
which arc assigned to Henderson Trim, enterer. Granted 9 December 1819.


No. 1888    Page 336
State of Tennessee - to John Robertson 20 acres on north side of Lick
Creek - Entry No. 127, dated 8 September 1808 - certificate No. 2464 -
issued by John Carter to Thomas Mitchell for 100 acres, 10 March 1780
- 20 acres of which are assigned to John Robertson, enterer - adjoining
Francis Register, Joseph Robertson. Granted 4 April 1811.

No. 6108    Page 337
State of Tennessee - to John Harmon 25 acres land on Lick Creek, joining
Harmons own land and an Entry of William Westens - Entry No. 3902, 16 May
1817 - founded on certificate No. 3749 - issued by A. Foster to David
Clagg for 274 acres, 13 September 1808 - 25 acres of which are assigned
to John Harmon, enterer. Granted 26 April 1819.


No. 6464    Page 338
State of Tennessee - to Jacob Dyches 190 acres on north side of Nola-
chuckey River, adjoining himself and Isaac Baker - Entry No. 3616, 9
December 1816 - founded on certificate No. 3175 - issued to Jonathan
Tipton for 190 acres, 18 December 1811 - the whole amount assigned to
Jacob Dyche, enterer, heirs of Kennamus Dyche at the Skillet Shoals
above Tumbling Shoals, down river to include an island. Granted 9
February 1820.


No. 6337    Page 339
State of Tennessee - to William Hendry 57 1/2 acres near headwaters of
Lick Creek, adjoining lands where Hendry lives on - Entry No. 4473, 7
August 1818 - certificate No. 88 - issued to William Shields for 5000
acres, 2 March 1812 - 57 1/2 acres of which are assigned to William
Hendry, enterer. Granted 28 October 1819.


No. 2592    Page 340
State of Tennessee - to William Reynolds 15 acres on both sides Paint
Creek at Paint Mountain - Entry No. 784, 2 September 1811 - founded on
certificate No. 2603 - issued by John Carter to James Goodrich for 340
acres, 6 December 1794 - 15 acres of which is assigned to William
Reynolds, enterer. Granted 10 August 1812.


No. 6390    No. 341
State of Tennessee - to Solomon Beals 30 acres on waters of Sinking Creek,
adjoining his own and Robert Gray - Entry No. 4147, dated 13 November
1817 - founded on certificate No. 4147, dated 29 August 1814 - issued by
Nathan Shipley to John McGinnis for 180 acres - 30 acres of which are
assigned to Solomon Beals, enterer - adjoining Pickering. Granted 21
November 1819.


No. 5859    Page 342
State of Tennessee - to John Carter 10 acres on Lick Creek adjoining John
Carter Senr. - Entry No. 2619, 8 April 1815 - founded on certificate No.
761 - issued to George Gordon for 500 acres, 2 November 1814 - 40 acres
of which are assigned to John Carter, enterer. Granted 30 May 1818.


No. 6403    Page 343
State of Tennessee - to Meshack Hale for 50 acres on Clear Fork of Lick
Creek, adjoining himself and Stoddard Neil - Entry No. 3693, 14 January
1817 - founded on certificate No. 1848 - issued by John Carter to Moses
and Samuel Looney for 300 acres, 2 November 1797 - 50 acres granted to
Meshack Hale, 20 December 1819.


No. 316    Page 344
State of North Carolina - for 50 shillings per 100 acres - to Edmond
Roberts 200 acres in Greene County on Cedar Branch, waters of Big
Limestone, adjoining Gillaspie, John Peaveley. Granted by Alexander
Martin at Fairfield, 4 October 1782.


No. 6463    Page 345
State of Tennessee - to Thomas Caldwell 30 acres on Clear Fork of Lick
Creek - Entry No. 2073, 2 August 1814 - founded on certificate No. 689
- issued to Samuel Caruthers for 30 acres, 1 June 1814 - all of which
is assigned to Thomas Caldwell, enterer. Granted 9 February 1820.

No. 5887    Page 346
State of Tennessee - to William Hall 40 acres on Richland Creek on north
side of Nolachuckey River - Entry No. 3409, 31 August 1816 - founded on
certificate No. 762 - issued to George Gordon for 500 acres, 2 November
1814 - 40 acres of which are assigned to William Hall, enterer - adjoining Hall and James Pearce, near waggon road leading from Bakers Ferry to
Greeneville. Granted 25 June 1818.


No. 174    Page 347
State of North Carolina - for 50 shillings per 100 acres - to William
Donelson 250 acres in Greene County on Little Sinking Creek, adjoining
James Moore, Samuel Moore, Thomas Mitchell, Joseph Eaton. Granted 12
September 1787.


No. 5067    Page 349
State of Tennessee - to Reuben Peters 200 acres on Pigeon Creek, including
improvement where Emanuel Peters lives on - Entry No. 3214, 16 March 1816
- founded on certificate No. 792 - issued by Edward Scott to George Gordon
for 500 acres, 2 November 1814 - 200 acres of which are assigned to
Emanuel Peters, enterer. Granted by Reuben Peters, assignee of Emanuel
Peters, 24 April 1817.


No. 5874    Page 350
State of Tennessee - to William Westen 30 acres on Lick Creek - Entry No.
236, 19 January 1815 - founded on certificate No. 617 - issued to George
Gordon for 100 acres, 28 March 1814 - 30 acres of which are assigned to
William Weston, enterer - adjoining Christian Dyche. Granted 5 June
1818.


No. 3133    Page 351
State of Tennessee - to James McPheran 16 acres, adjoining himself -
Entry No. 2927, 13 September 1815 - founded on certificate No. 758 -
issued to George Gordon for 500 acres, 2 November 1814 - 16 acres of
which are assigned to James McPheran, enterer. Granted 13 June 1817.


No. 6401    Page 352
State of Tennessee - to John Crawford 10 acres on Lick Creek, adjoining
himself - Entry No. 3478, 7 October 1816 - founded on certificate No.
116 - issued by Nathan Shipley to James P. Taylor for 640 acres, 20 July
1815 - 10 acres assigned to John Crawford, enterer. Granted 9 December
1819.


No. 6763    Page 353
State of Tennessee - to Thomas Ripley 1 acre on north side of Nolachucky
River, adjoining a former entry of Ripley and John Pebley - Entry No.
3419, 6 September 1816 - founded on warrant No. 295 - issued by John
Carter, E. T., to Simon Todd for 320 acres, 11 March 1795 - 1 acres of
which is assigned to Thomas Ripley, enterer. Granted 25 July 1821.


No. 6913    Page 354
State of Tennessee - to George Brown 70 acres on Holley's Creek in
draughts thereof, adjoining John McGaughey, Merriman Payne and others -
based on Entry No. 3743, 3 February 1817 - founded on certificate No. 88
- issued by Luke Lea to William Shields for 5000 acres, 2 March 1812 -
70 acres of which are assigned to George Brown - bound by William
Milburn, Thomas Murphey, John Temple, Andrew Park, Joseph Brown, Widow
Robertson and Mosley. Granted 7 October 1821.


No. 6922    Page 355
State of Tennessee - to Robert Henry for 25 acres on Mill Creek, a branch
of Big Limestone - Entry No. 1355, 27 June 1812 - founded on warrant No.
201 - issued by Luke Lee, Commissioner, to heirs of John Winegard? for

640 acres, 8 July 1812 - 25 acres of which are assigned to Robert Henry, enterer - adjoining himself, Adam Dinwiddie decd., John Doan and Edward Ross. Granted 9 October 1821.


No. 6729    Page 358
State of Tennessee - to Michael Bright 30 acres on Sinking Fork of Lick Creek - Entry No. 2931, 13 September 1815 - founded on certificate No. 784 - issued to George Gordon for 500 acres, 2 November 1814 - 100 acres assigned to Michael Bright, enterer. Granted to Michael Bright and his heirs, 30 acres, adjoining himself. Granted 10 March 1821.


No. 6727    Page 359
State of Tennessee - to Michael Bright 27 acres on Sinking Fork of Lick Creek - Entry No. 2932, 13 September 1815 - founded on certificate No. 784 - issued to George Gordon for 500 acres, 2 November 1814 - 100 acres of which are assigned to Michael Bright, enterer. Twenty-seven acres granted to Michael Bright, 10 March 1821, adjoining himself, Ellis, Robertson, John Dickson.


No. 5101    Page 360
State of Tennessee - to James Shields 100 acres on waters of Little Chuckey - Entry No. 3026, 1 October 1815 - founded on certificate No. 541 - issued by Edward Scott to William Shields for 475 acres land, of which are assigned to James Shields, enterer, 100 acres - where George Brown formerly lived adjoining Sharp. Granted 5 May 1817.


No. 2008    Page 361
State of Tennessee - to James Shields 30 acres on both sides Lick Creek - Entry No. 489 - founded on certificate No. 116 - issued to Andrew M. Lusk for 50 acres, 12 May 1810 - Entry dated 24 July 1810 - 30 acres of which are assigned to James Shields, enterer - adjoining Widow Missemer, David Copeland. Granted 2 October 1811.


No. 6876    Page 362
State of Tennessee - to James Shields 25 acres on Lick Creek - Entry No. 2468, 25 February 1815 - certificate No. 727 - issued by Edward Scott to James P. Taylor for 300 acres, 30 August 1814 - 25 acres of which are assigned to James Shields, enterer. Granted 2 October 1821.


No. 6904    Page 363
State of Tennessee - to James Shields 20 acres on Lick Creek - Entry No. 3536, 20 October 1816 - certificate No. 541 - issued by Edward Scott to William Shields for 475 acres, 27 May 1813 - 440 acres of which are assigned to James Shields, enterer. Granted 5 October 1821.


No. 6906    Page 365
State of Tennessee - to James Shields 20 acres on south bank of Lick Creek - Entry No. 1260, 30 April 1815 - certificate No. 88 - issued by Luke Lea to William Shields for 5000 acres, 2 March 1812 - 20 acres of which are assigned to James Shields, enterer. Granted 5 October 1821.


No. 6905    Page 366
State of Tennessee - to James Shields 15 acres on Blue Spring Branch - Entry No. 4110, dated 10 January 1818 - founded on certificate No. 541 - issued by Edward Scott to William Shields for 475 acres, 27 March 1813 - 474 acres assigned to James Shields, enterer. Granted 5 October 1821.


No. 6142    Page 367
State of Tennessee - to Thomas Mitchell 8 acres adjoining himself, Henry Dyches and Henry Myers, not far from George and Abner Brown's land - Entry No. 2936, 14 September 1815 - founded on certificate No. 761 -

issued to George Gordon for 500 acres, 2 November 1814 — 8 acres of which are assigned to Thomas Mitchell, enterer. Granted 15 July 1819.

No. 8005     Page 368
State of Tennessee — to John Rhea for 50 acres on waters of Lick Creek, west side thereof — Entry No. 4952, dated 1 November 1819 — founded on certificate No. 1306 — issued to John Rhea for 224 acres, 2 June 1817 — 50 acres of which are granted to John Rhea, adjoining himself, Thomas Nelson, Simon Pope and John Woolsey. Granted 3 July 1822.

No. 8006     Page 369
State of Tennessee — to John Rhea 30 acres on west side of Lick Creek — Entry No. 4933, 1 November 1819 — founded on certificate No. 1306 — issued to John Rhea for 224 acres, 2 June 1817 — adjoining himself. Granted 3 July 1822.

No. 6451     Page 370
State of Tennessee — to John Lauderdale 8 acres on north side of Nola-chucky River — Entry No. 2311, 24 December 1814 — founded on certificate No. 2168 — issued to Anthony Moore for 400 acres, 30 November 1784 — 8 acres of which are assigned to John Lauderdale, enterer. Granted 8 February 1820.

No. 8065     Page 371
State of Tennessee — to John Lauderdale 30 acres on north side of Nola-chucky River — Entry No. 1590, 1 February 1813 — founded on warrant No. 2052 — issued to Savid Stuart and John Mines for 1080 acres, 30 November 1784 — 329 acres assigned to James Galbreath, enterer — assigned by Galbreath to John Lauderdale. Granted 19 July 1822.

No. 1109     Page 372
State of North Carolina — for 50 shillings per 100 acres — to George Gillaspie for 400 acres in Greene County on McCartneys Branch, adjoining Milburn, himself. Granted 12 January 1793.

No. 5445     Page 373
State of Tennessee — to Absalom Haworth Junr. for 35 acres on north side of Nolachucky River on both sides Big Sinking Creek, adjoining John Oliphant and David Paulsel — founded on two warrants — Entry No. 2109, 29 August 1814 — founded partly on warrant No. 2168, issued to Anthony Moore for 400 acres, 30 November 1784 — 25 acres of which are assigned to Absalom Haworth Junr., enterer — and partly on warrant No. 413, issued to George Taylor for 600 acres, 10 July 1792 — 20 acres of which are assigned to Absalom Haworth. Granted 8 October 1817.

No. ___     Page 374
State of North Carolina — for 50 shillings per 100 acres — to James Mitchell 200 acres in Greene County on Lick Creek, head of Little Gap Creek, foot of Bays Mountain. Surveyed for James Mitchell, 3 October 1783.

No. 1247     Page 375
State of North Carolina — for 50 shillings per 100 acres — to James Mitchell 200 acres in Greene County on Lick Creek, waters of Gap Creek, adjoining Thomas Bayley. Richard Dobbs Spraight, 27 January 1793.

No. 6348     Page 375
State of Tennessee — to Caleb Carter 20 acres on Lick Creek — Entry No. 2578, 27 March 1815 — founded on certificate No. 794 — to George Gordon for 500 acres, 2 November 1814 — 20 acres granted to Caleb Carter, ad-joining John Pogue survey. Granted 16 November 1819.

No. 1593       Page 376
State of Tennessee - to Simon Pope 25 acres on Piburn Creek, waters of
Lick Creek - based on Entry No. 272, dated 24 May 1809 - founded on
warrant No. 910 - issued by Archibald Roane to James McBee to Israel
McBee, 150 acres assigned by Israel McBee to Samuel Crawford - 30 acres
of that assigned to Simon Pope, enterer - in District of Washington,
adjoining John Olinger, Woolsey and his own lands.   Granted 2 July 1810.


No. 2398       Page 378
State of Tennessee - to Henry Rader 100 acres on Lick Creek - Entry No.
501, 11 August 1810 - founded on certificate No. 21 - issued to John
McCampbell for 300 acres, 5 January 1810 and assigned by him to Martin
McBride - 100 acres assigned by McBride to Andrew McPheron, enterer -
he to Henry Rader - adjoining Smiley, Love, Walkers condition, William
McPheron, being an Occupant Claim.   Granted 4 June 1812.


No. 8659       Page 379
State of Tennessee - to Thomas Frazier 5 acres on Lick Creek - Entry No.
4095, 6 October 1817 - founded on warrant No. 476 - issued by James Goens
E. S. to John McAdow for 600 acres, 12 April 1780 - 5 acres of which are
assigned to Thomas Frazier, enterer.   Granted 27 September 1820.


No. 2596       Page 380
State of Tennessee - to David Frazier 19 acres on north side Lick Creek -
Entry No. 602, 17 January 1811 - founded on certificate No. 172 - issued
by Archibald Roane to Samuel Y. Balch for 188 acres, 21 May 1810 - 19
acres of which is assigned to David Frazier, enterer - adjoining David
Parkens, Thomas Frazier Senr.   Granted 10 August 1812.


No. 8651       Page 381
State of Tennessee - to David Frazier 20 acres on Lick Creek - Entry No.
4094, 6 October 1817 - founded on certificate No. 1245 - issued to Jacob
K. Snapp for 100 acres, 12 August 1816 - 20 acres of which are assigned
to David Frazier, enterer.   Granted 25 September 1823.


No. 8660       Page 382
State of Tennessee - to David Frazier 20 acres on Lick Creek - Entry No.
4093, 6 October 1817 - founded on warrant No. 2974 - by John Carter, E.L.
to James Clinkham for 640 acres, 17 December 1797 - 20 acres of which
are assigned to David Frazier, enterer - adjoining Thomas Frazier.
Granted 27 September 1823.


No. 8647       Page 383
State of Tennessee - to Joseph White 20 acres on Sinking Fork of Lick
Creek - based on Entry No. 972, 20 January 1812 - founded on warrant No.
2416 - issued by John Carter to John Smith for 150 acres, 22 August 179_
- 40 acres of which are assigned to Joseph White, enterer - 50 acres
granted to Joseph White, 25 September 1823.


No. 8648       Page 384
State of Tennessee - to Joseph White 20 acres on Sinking Fork of Lick
Creek - Entry No. 791, 20 January 1812 - based on warrant No. 2416 -
issued by John Carter to John Smith for 150 acres - 40 acres of which
are assigned to Joseph White, enterer.   Twenty acres granted to Joseph
White, 25 September 1823.


No. 6349       Page 385
State of Tennessee - to Dutton Lane 30 acres, adjoining William Ford
Senr. and James Wright - Entry No. 3181, 2 March 1816 - founded on
certificate No. 762 - issued to George Gordon for 500 acres, 2 November
1814 - 30 acres of which are assigned to Dutton Lane, enterer - adjoining
William Ford and James Wright.   Granted 10 November 1819.

No. 6320     Page 386
State of Tennessee - to Jesse Davis for 15 acres on Lick Creek, adjoining
Joseph Reynolds and others - based on Entry No. 2963, 26 September 1815 -
founded on certificate No. 791 - issued to George Gordon for 500 acres, 2
November 1814 - 15 acres of which are assigned to Dutton Lane, enterer -
Jesse Davis is assignee of Dutton Lane. Granted 26 October 1819.


No. 8640     Page 387
State of Tennessee - to Jesse Davis 20 acres on Lick Creek - Entry No.
4180, 12 December 1817 - founded on certificate No. 1367 - issued to
James P. Taylor for 300 acres, 31 October 1817 - 20 acres assigned to
Jesse Davis, adjoining Seth Babbs. Granted 24 September 1823.


No. 8641     Page 388
State of Tennessee - to Jesse Davis 10 acres on Lick Creek, adjoining
Seth Babb - Entry No. 4179, 12 December 1817 - founded on certificate
No. 1376 - issued to James P. Taylor for 300 acres, 31 October 1817 -
60 acres assigned to Jesse Davis, enterer - 10 acres granted to Jesse
Davis, adjoining Seth Babb, Jacob Bowman, 24 September 1823.


No. 1064     Page 389
State of North Carolina - for 50 shillings per 100 acres - to Nathaniel
Davis 200 acres in Greene County on Lick Creek, 27 June 1793. No. 1120
entered 21 January 1779. Drawing of Plat.


No. 174     Page 391
State of North Carolina - for 50 shillings per 100 acres - to William
Donelson 250 acres in Greene County on Little Sinking Creek on Nolachucky
River, adjoining James Moore, Samuel Moore, Thomas Mitchell, Joseph
Eaton. Sealed by Richard Caswell at Raleigh, 20 September 1787.


No. 7040     Page 393
State of Tennessee - to John Maloney Senr. 250 acres on Lick Creek -
Entry on warrant No. 1022 - issued to John Waggoner for 250 acres, 7
June 1784 and assigned by Waggoner to John Maloney - adjoining said
Waggoner, Francis Hamilton, Jacob Bowman. Granted 25 February 1822.


No. 5081
State of Tennessee - to David Windle 50 acres on Nolachucky River - Entry
No. 1819, dated 8 January 1814 - founded on certificate No. 1485 - to
Harmon King for 100 acres, 23 April 1814, the whole of which is assigned
to David Windle, enterer - adjoining Hugh Neilson decd. and Philip Hale.
Granted 5 April 1817.


No. 6598     Page 396
State of Tennessee - to John Doan 52 acres near Mill Creek, adjoining an
entry made by George F. Gillespie, John Miller, Daniel Creamer, Samuel
Duncan - based on Entry No. 4353, 11 April 1818 - founded on certificate
No. 794 - issued to George Gordon for 500 acres, 2 November 1814 - 52
acres of which are assigned to John Doan, enterer. Granted 21 June 1820.


No. ____     Page 397
State of North Carolina - to William McPheran 250 acres on Roaring Fork
of Lick Creek, north side of Nolachucky River on Rich Hill and Rich
Hollow, adjoining John Price. Granted 3 September 1825.


No. 462     Page 398
State of North Carolina - to William McPheran 250 acres on Roaring Fork
of Lick Creek. Granted 12 September 1787.

No. 10750    Page 399
State of Tennessee - to Jacob Bible for 6 acres on north side Nolachucky
River, adjoining said Bible - based on Entry No. 5774, 11 April 1823 -
founded on warrant No. 2961 - issued by John Carter to George Leonard
for 580 acres, 4 September 1794 - 6 acres of which are assigned to Jacob
Bible, enterer - adjoining John Bible. Granted 21 March 1825.


No. 12136    Page 400
State of Tennessee - to Stephen Alexander 100 acres on Clear Fork of Lick
Creek - based on Entry No. 475, 2 August 1824 @ 12½ cents per acre, where
R. K. Pickering lives and saw mill, adjoining E. T. Coulson. Granted 6
December 1825.


No. 11901    Page 401
State of Tennessee - to Frederick Weaver 25 acres on Pigeon Creek, north
side of Nolachucky River - Entry No. 5682, 30 December 1822 - founded on
certificate No. 2136 - issued to heirs of Landon Carter for 1280 acres,
7 April 1822 - 25 acres of which are assigned to Frederick Weaver,
enterer, adjoining Swatsel. Granted 15 September 1825.


No. 10970    Page 403
State of Tennessee - to James McMurtrey 100 acres on Dry Fork of Cany
Branch, adjoining McMurtrey, J. Henderson and George Cook - based on
Entry No. 168, dated 27 May 1824 @ 12½ cents per acre. Granted 14
May 1825.


No. 10980    Page 405
State of Tennessee - to James McMurtrey 15 acres on Caney Branch, south
side of Nolachucky River, adjoining Richard Ellis and his own land -
Entry No. 169, 29 May 1824 @ 12½ cents per acre. Granted 16 May 1825.


No. 11321    Page 405
State of Tennessee - to George Brown 10 acres on Draughts of Delaney's
Creek on branch adjoining Philip Woolover, John Woolover, David Russell
and William McBride. Granted 9 June 1825.


No. 10998    Page 406
State of Tennessee - to George Brown 25 acres on Draughts of Delaney's
Branch, on waters of Little Chuckey Creek, adjoining William McBrides
old place, John and Philip Woolover, George Brown on Warrensburgh Road
5 miles from the town of Greeneville - based on Entry No. 354, 5 June
1824 @ 12½ cents per acre. Granted 17 May 1825.


No. 6874    Page 408
State of Tennessee - to Michael Dearstone 100 acres, adjoining John Reece,
William Hale, William Gibson, on Newport Road from Greeneville - Entry No.
2374, 21 January 1815 - founded on warrant No. 220 - issued by Nathan
Shipley to Nathaniel Taylor for 640 acres, 4 November 1814 - 100 acres of
which are assigned to Michael Dearstone, enterer. Granted 1 October 1821.


No. 6875    Page 409
State of Tennessee - to Michael Dearstone 50 acres adjoining Gibson and
said Dearstone on Newport Road leading from Greeneville - Entry No. 3098,
8 December 1815 - founded on Certificate No. 783 - to George Gordon for
500 acres, 2 November 1814 - 50 acres of which are assigned to William
Hale, enterer, assigned to Michael Dearstone. Granted 1 October 1820.


No. 9212    Page 410
State of Tennessee - to Michael Dearstone 50 acres on Pigeon Creek,
adjoining his own land - based on Entry No. 5, 5 April 1825 @ 12½ cents
per acre. Granted 30 August 1824.

No. 8812     Page 411
State of Tennessee - to Jacob Basinger 60 acres on Pigeon Creek adjoining
George Ealy - Entry No. 848, 24 October 1811 - founded on certificate No.
1511 - issued for 60 acres, 23 November 1809, the whole amount assigned
to Jacob Bassinger, enterer.  Granted 26 May 1824.


No. 13362     Page 413
State of Tennessee - to John Rhea 456 acres on both sides of Lick Creek
and both sides of Clear Fork of Lick Creek, including mouth of said
creek and 5 tracts of said Rhea's - Entry No. 886, 8 March 1826 - by
John Rhea 3 tracts granted to Edmund Stephens, 2 tracts to himself.
Granted 4 September 1826.


No. ___     Page 414
State of North Carolina - Peter Flemen Testimonial - October 9, 1779 in
Washington County, South Branch of Lick Creek - 200 acres granted 6
August 1827.  Grant No. 118.


No. 6691     Page 417
State of Tennessee - to William Dickson 20 acres on head of Short Creek,
adjoining Bays Mountain - Entry No. 2860, 10 August 1815 - founded on
certificate No. 762 - issued to George Gordon for 500 acres, 2 November
1814 - 50 acres of which are assigned to John Hartley, enterer - William
Dickson, purchaser at Sherriffs Sale of Hartley's Int., adjoining Farmer
Pogue.  Granted 8 January 1821.


No. 10616     Page 418
State of Tennessee - to Nathaniel D. Moore 25 acres on north bank of
Nolachucky River, adjoining William Moore Senr. and Farensworth's survey
- Entry No. 2941, 14 September 1815 - founded on certificate No. 784 -
issued to George Gordon for 500 acres, 2 November 1814 - 25 acres of
which are assigned to William Moore, enterer, assigned by him to
Nathaniel D. Moore.  Granted 28 February 1825.


No. 9181     Page 419
State of Tennessee - to William Dickson 140 acres on north side of Lick
Creek, adjoining Moses Harmon and others.  Entry No. 29, 5 April 1824 @
12½ cents per acre.  Granted 27 August 1824.


No. 13125     Page 420
State of Tennessee - to William Dickson 60 acres on Big Ridge between
Lick Creek and Grassy Creek, adjoining George Rinker, Samuel P. Bayles
and George McCrary - Entry No. 605, 12 March 1825 - by Samuel P. Bayles,
assigned by Alfred Hunter, Sheriff, to William Dickson.  Granted 10
August 1826.


No. 14550     Page 421
State of Tennessee - to George Brown 42 acres on Draughts of ____, on
waters of Little Chucky, adjoining George Brown and others - Entry No.
5766, 8 March 1823 - founded on certificate No. 759 - issued to George
Gordon for 500 acres, 2 November 1814 - 200 acres of which are assigned
to George Brown, enterer - 42 acres granted to George Brown, adjoining
grant of 5000 acres to Stokley Donelson, John and Philip Woolover.
Granted 13 July 1827.


No. 15028     Page 422
State of Tennessee - to Joseph Cutler, Charles A. Russell, Daniel M.
Russell, Thomas F. A. M. Russell for 440 acres on both sides Richland
Creek, adjoining A. Sevier, J. Hood, J. Wright, A. Patterson, Alexander
and others - Entry No. 991, 25 November 1826 - also adjoining Rocky
Ridge.  Granted 31 January 1828.

No. 15029    Page 423
State of Tennessee - to Joseph Cutler, Charles A. Daniel M. and Thomas
F. A. M. Russell for 160 acres on Richland Creek, adjoining Merryman
Payne, Andrew Patterson and others - Entry No. 990, 22 December 1826 to
the said Russells, 160 acres including dwelling house, E. Birdwell.
Granted 31 January 1828.


No. 13517    Page 424
State of Tennessee - to Michael Myers 55 acres on Big Gap Creek, adjoining
John Couch, Christopher Myers and his own land - Entry No. 659, 24 January
1826 - 50 acres granted 10 October 1826.


No. 373    Page 425
State of North Carolina - for 10 pounds per 100 acres - to Robert Oar
100 acres in Greene County on south side of Nolachucky River and north
side the dividing line between Lick Creek and the head of Cove Creek.
Richard Caswell at Kinston, 20 September 1787.


No. 15030    Page 426
State of Tennessee - to David McCormick for 78 acres, adjoining David
Deaderick, Hoods old tract, Widow Clawson, heirs of Russell Trobaugh's
old place, George Brown, William K. Vance and George T. Gillespie and
town of Greeneville - Entry No. 936, 17 July 1826 - by George Brown,
agent for David McCormick. Granted 31 January 1828.


No. 15621    Page 426
State of Tennessee - to William Dickson 30 acres on north side of Lick
Creek, adjoining Ezekiel Carter, Elisha Carter and said Dickson - from
Entry No. 1130, 28 January 1828. Granted 24 December 1828.


No. 15622    Page 428
State of Tennessee - to Henry Keller 50 acres on north side of Lick
Creek, adjoining his own lands - Entry No. 587, 11 February 1825.
Granted 24 December 1828.


No. 15624    Page 429
State of Tennessee - to Alexander Williams 77 acres adjoining land of
the heirs of Robert Wyly, decd., Daniel Trobaugh and Charles Dyches -
Entry No. 835, 7 February 1826. Granted 24 December 1828.


No. 15623    Page 430
State of Tennessee - to Alexander Williams 100 acres on north side of
Lick Creek, adjoining George Weems, William Dickson - Entry No. 667,
24 January 1826. Granted 24 December 1828.


No. _____    Page 431
State of Tennessee - to William Dickson 25 acres on north side of Nola-
chucky River, adjoining his own land, Hugh Wilson, John McAmish, David
Farnsworth and John Roberts - Entry No. 1225, 25 September 1828.
Granted 14 October 1829.


No. _____    Page 432
State of Tennessee - to George Brown 5 acres adjoining lands of David
McCormick, Robert Hoods survey, Nicholas Trobaugh, Robert Kerr's old
300 acre survey, and town of Greeneville - Entry No. 758, 2 November
1814 - founded on certificate No. 758 - issued to George Gordon for
500 acres, 2 November 1814 - 5 acres assigned to George Brown. Granted
17 October 1829.

No. 8803    Page 433
State of Tennessee - to Joseph Shannon 12 acres adjoining Thomas Ripley's land - Entry No. 895, 23 November 1811 - founded on certificate No. 36 - issued to Francis A. Ramsey for 1000 acres, 25 October 1808 - 60 acres of which are assigned to Joseph Shannon, enterer. Granted 26 May 1824.

No. 8462    Page 434
State of Tennessee - to Henry Yokley 5 acres on Lick Creek, adjoining Anthony Hoggatt and James Jones - Entry No. 5696, 14 January 1823 - founded on certificate No. 1367 - issued to James P. Taylor for 300 acres, 31 October 1817 - 5 acres of which are assigned to Henry Yokley, enterer. Granted 4 September 1823.

No. ___    Page 435
State of North Carolina - to James Richardson 300 acres, adjoining Hood - warrant No. 916, 7 June 1784. North Carolina Governors Testimonial, 20 June 1831.

No. 6902    Page 436
State of Tennessee - to John Lauderdale 12 acres on north side of Nola-chucky River at mouth of Pigeon Creek, adjoining Lauderdale's own land and land of Henry Thompson - Entry No. 4157, 27 November 1817 - founded on certificate No. 88 - issued by Luke Lea, Commissioner, to William Shields for 5000 acres, 2 March 1812 - 12 acres of which are assigned to John Lauderdale, enterer. Granted 5 October 1821.

No. 16877    Page 437
State of Tennessee - to Samuel Lauderdale 16 acres on north side of Nola-chucky River, adjoining A. Susong and Thompsons land - Entry No. 1077, 30 May 1826 - by James and Samuel Lauderdale. Sixteen acres granted 14 September 1831.

No. 16878    Page 438
State of Tennessee - to James Lauderdale and Samuel Lauderdale 3 acres on south side of an island in Chucky River - Entry No. 1068, 4 April 1827. Granted 14 September 1831.

No. 6895    Page 439
State of Tennessee - to John S. Reed 21 acres on Roaring Fork of Lick Creek, adjoining said Reed, David Key and William Jones - Entry No. 4810, 10 May 1819 - founded on certificate No. 1184 - issued to George Gordon for 500 acres, 7 March 1816 - 21 acres of which are assigned to John S. Reed, enterer - on Greeneville to Rogersville Road. Granted 4 October 1821.

No. 11021    Page 440
State of Tennessee - to John S. Reed - 8 acres on Roaring Fork of Lick Creek, adjoining Reed, J. Ross and William Jones - Entry No. 284, 1 July 1824 @ 12½ cents per acre. Granted at Murfreesboro, 18 May 1825.

No. 16847    Page 441
State of Tennessee - to Andrew Stephens for 12¼ acres on north side of Nolachucky River, adjoining James Lauderdale, including 2 islands - Entry No. 1155, 13 September 1828, by Andrew Stephens Jr. Granted 14 September 1831 at Nashville.

No. 9502    Page 442
State of Tennessee - to Nimrod C. Willett - 140 acres on Little Chuckey, adjoining his own land, Guins and Weese - Entry No. 12, 5 April 1848 @ 12½ cents per acre. Granted at Murfreesborough, 9 October 1824.

No. 16174     Page 443
State of Tennessee - to Nimrod Willet - 20 acres on south side of Little
Chucky, adjoining John Weese - Entry No. 5982, 30 April 1823 - founded on
warrant No. 2228 - issued to David Perry for 50 acres, 26 January 1809 -
20 acres of which are assigned to Nimrod Willett, enterer. Granted 15
October 1829.

No. 16794     Page 444
State of Tennessee - to Mary Debusk - 35 acres on Little Chuckey, adjoin-
ing George Lonas, Frederick Wampler and Mary Debusk - Entry No. 1237, 9
November - by Mary Debusk and her heirs. Granted at Nashville, 13
September 1831.

No. 15868     Page 445
State of Tennessee - to James Smith - 100 acres on Little Chuckey, adjoining Laughner, George Andes, said Smith and Murphy - Entry No. 484,
21 August 1824 by James Smith. Granted at Nashville, 24 August 1829.

No. 15759     Page 446
State of Tennessee - to Thomas W. Williamson - 72 acres on Middle Creek,
south side of Nolachucky River, adjoining William Jennings, John Wilhoit,
John Jennings et al. - Entry No. 488, 30 August 1824 by Thomas W.
Williamson - 22 acres granted to Williamson. Granted at Nashville, 10
June 1829.

No. 8639     Page 447
State of Tennessee - to David Key - 20 acres on Roaring Fork of Lick
Creek, adjoining Key and Armitage's land - Entry No. 2410, 6 February
1815 - founded on certificate No. 758 - issued to George Gordon for 500
acres, 2 November 1814 - 20 acres of which are assigned to John McKee,
enterer - assigned by said John to David Key. Granted at Murfreesborough, 24 September 1823.

No. 9462     Page 448
State of Tennessee - to David Key - 10 acres on Lick Creek, adjoining
Isaac Armitage, Samuel Keller and said Key's lands - Entry No. 101, 10
April 1824 @ 12½ cents per acre. Granted at Murfreesborough, 6 October
1824.

No. 18140     Page 449
State of Tennessee - to William Malone - 2½ acres on Lick Creek, adjoining himself and Bruner land - Entry No. 868, 20 February 1826. Granted
at Nashville, 14 September 1833.

No. 15773     Page 449
State of Tennessee - to William Evans - 50 acres on Lick Creek, adjoining
George Smelser and himself - Entry No. 816, 1 February 1826. Granted at
Nashville, 12 June 1829.

No. 6356     Page 450
State of Tennessee - to Thomas and Stephen Alexander - 15 acres on Nola-
chucky River - Entry No. 1533, 13 March 1813 - founded on certificate
No. 88 - issued by Luke Lea to William Shields for 5000 acres, 2 March
1812 - 20 acres assigned to Thomas and Stephen Alexander, enterers.
Granted at Murfreesborough, 10 November 1819.

No. 18566     Page 451
State of Tennessee - to Elizabeth Paulsell - 50 acres on Cedar Branch,
north side of Nolachucky River - Entry No. 1443, 21 December 1831 - by
Elizabeth Paulsell and her heirs, adjoining David Paulsell, purchased

from Stephen Brooks, Thomas Oliphant, Joseph Night and Wyly heirs. Granted at Nashville, 14 April 1834.


No. 41198    Page 452
State of Tennessee - to Samuel Dodson and Thomas Crozier - 218 acres on Big Gap Creek - Entry No. 1643, 27 January 1834. Granted at Nashville, 26 October 1835.


No. 6275    Page 453
State of Tennessee - to John Maloney - 10 acres on Roaring Fork of Lick Creek - Entry No. 3992, 21 July 1817 - founded on warrant No. 2974, 17 December 1797 - 10 acres of which are assigned to John Maloney, enterer. Granted at Murfreesborough, 22 October 1819.


No. 21214    Page 454
State of Tennessee - to Elim Carter - 50 acres on Lick Creek - Entry No. 716, 24 January 1826. Granted at Nashville, 23 September 1837.


No. 15081    Page 455
State of Tennessee - to John Gass, Senr. - 250 acres on south side of Lick Creek - Entry No. 893, 17 March 1826 - adjoining Curtis Williams, Joseph Brown, F. T. Winkle, Harmon, Crumly. Granted at Nashville, 7 February 1828.


No. 22861    Page 456
State of Tennessee - to Alexander Jones - 1200 acres - Entry No. 1897, 8 April 1837 - adjoining Phineas Jones on a ridge dividing waters of Paint and Camp Creek, State Line and Murphey. Granted at Nashville, 30 September 1839.


No. 22439    Page 457
State of Tennessee - to John Bowman - 17 acres adjoining Bowman, Henderson and Bright - Entry No. 1798, 24 March 1836. Granted at Nashville, 27 February 1839.


BOOK II

Land Transfers - State of Franklin
1784 - 1797


Page 1
Isaac Barton to Absalom Hayworth - 11 acres on Nolachucky River, 2 February 1785 - Greene County, North Carolina - for 100 pounds - 94 acres.


Page 2
Isaac Barton to Absalom Hayworth - Greene County, North Carolina, 2 February 1785 - 100 acres - 100 pounds.


Page 3
14 February 1785 - Joseph Wilson Esq., County of Washington, State of Franklin, to Samuel and George Wilson, County of Greene, State of Franklin - for 50 pounds current State of Franklin money - 100 acres, part in Washington County and part in Greene County, adjoining William McBride, William Moore. Land granted to Joseph Wilson, 13 October 1783.


Page 4
4 February 1786 - Deed of Gift - James English to Michael Rawlings - 100 acres, County of Greene, State of Franklin, for natural love and affec-

tion for Michael Rawlings, his son-in-law. Witnesses: John Newman, John Tadlock. Signed: James English, Elizabeth English.


Page 5
8 September 1785 - Asahel Rawlings to James Patterson - 500 acres - 40 pounds - 3 tracts in Greene County, State of Franklin, on each side of Cann Creek and each side of War Path - 200 acre tract. Witnesses: Charles Hays, Henry Stiers.


Page 7
7 February 1785 - Charles Hays to Waightstill Avery, Attorney at Law of Burke County, North Carolina - both sides of Lick Creek, including mouth of Raccoon Branch - 30 pounds. Hays got land grant, October 1783. Witnesses: Robert and David Hays, Henry Stiers.


Page 8
8 May 1786 - Alexander Millican to Christopher Houts - 40 pounds - 300 acres on Lick Fork of Lick Creek, including Double Lick. Test: James Patterson, James Bowen.


Page 9
11 March 1785 - William Stockton, of Greene County, North Carolina, to Dutton Lane - 20 pounds - 300 acres granted to Stockton by North Carolina. Test: John Gass, Edward Hughes.


Page 10
16 January 1787 - William McGaughey, Sevier County, to David Robinson, planter of Greene County - 150 pounds - 200 acres by estimation on west side of Holley's Creek. Witnesses: Joseph Posey, William Willock.


Page 12
8 February 1787 - Gideon Morris to Thomas Pierce - 99 acres on a Branch of Lick Creek - 50 pounds - Greene County, North Carolina. Witnesses: John Newman, Nineon Steel.


Page 14
3 October 1784 - Francis Holley, Wilkes County, State of Georgia, to Laurence Glaize, Greene County, North Carolina - 100 acres on south side Nolachucky River, adjoining Henry Earnest - 60 pounds specia paid by Laurence Glaize. Witnesses: Charles Deviny, Mathias Selcer, Phillip Sherrill, Samuel Leather. Signed: Francis Holly, Mathene (her mark) Holly.


Page 15
17 May 1787 - William Reed to Robert Kerr - 100 acres on Little Chuckey, adjoining Samuel Vance, Charles Lowery - 40 pounds. Witnesses: Joseph Lusk, Elizabeth Kerr, Adam Sherrill. Signed: William Reed.


Page 16
4 May 1787 - Joseph Harden to John Liggett - 400 acres on Big Gap Creek, Lick Creek, for 100 pounds - having been granted to Harden, 9 November 1786. Witnesses: William Hannah, Joseph Hardin Junr., John Hardin. Signed: Joseph Hardin.


Page 18
10 March 1786 - John Richey to James Pickens - 198 acres at Fork of Lick Creek, known as Hans Improvement - 100 pounds specia - granted to Richey, No. 3441, 20 October 1782.

Page 19
16 January 1787 - William McGaughey, of Sevier County, to David Robertson, of Greene County - 100 acres on Holleys Creek, branch of Nolachucky River, for 50 pounds.


Page 21
1 September 1786 - Aaron Lewis, of Virginia, to Joseph Walker, of Greene County, State of Franklin - 20 pounds paid for land on both sides of Lick Creek, adjoining James English.


Page 22
8 April 1782 - Charles Harrington, of Sullivan County, North Carolina, to Peter King, of Washington County, North Carolina - 260 pounds specia - 300 acres on Dunhams Fork, both sides Indian Path.


Page 24
9 September 1783 - William Murphy, of Washington County, to Isaac Barton, of Greene County - 100 acres on Nolachucky River.


Page 25
29 September 1783 - William Murphy, of Washington County, to Isaac Barton, of Greene County - 94 acres on Nolachucky River.


Page 26
20 March 1784 - William Randals to James Keel - 200 acres on south side of Nolachucky River.


Page 27
4 May 1784 - James Englis to James Hays - 40 pounds - 200 acres on Limestone Fork of Lick Creek.


Page 28
4 May 1784 - James English to Reuben Riggs - 200 acres on Lick Creek, adjoining Leonard Adcock.


Page 29
4 May 1783 - Robert Blackburn, of Washington County, to John Hughes - for 70 pounds, 150 acres on Horse Camp Creek, waters of Lick Creek. Granted to Blackburn by Grant No. 3371, 24 October 1782.


Page 31
20 December 1782 - Dutton Lane to John Hornback - for 50 pounds, 100 acres on Lick Creek, adjoining Mulkey.


Page 32
20 December 1783 - Dutton Lane to John Legate (Ligit) - 100 acres on Lick Creek, on Aruntons Mill Shole Creek. Granted to Lane, 23 October 1782.


Page 33
14 August 1784 - Adam Wilson Senr., of Washington County, to James Pickens, of Greene County - for 100 pounds, 200 acres on Lick Creek at head of Daniel Kenedys Creek. Granted to Wilson, No. 114, 4 October 1782.


Page 35
19 March 1787 - Alexander Outlaw to Richard Pierce, of Russell County, Virginia - 3000 acres on north side of Holston River near mouth of

Holston - 400 pounds Virginia Currency.


Page 36
5 July 1787 - Alexander Galbreath of Greene County, State of Franklin;
Thomas Galbreath, Millright; John Galbreath, yeoman; William Galbreath,
yeoman, of Virginia; James Galbreath, of Virginia and Samuel Galbreath
of Virginia to Samuel Miller - 5 shillings each - 260 acres on a branch
of Gumton's Creek, Pennsylvania - James Dunwoody of Campbell County,
Virginia and his wife, Isabel; Andrew Field of Campbell County, Virginia
and his wife, Margaret; James McAmish of Greene County, Tennessee and
his wife, Agnes. The said Alexander, Thomas, John, William, James,
Samuel, Isabel, Margaret and Agnes are grandchildren of Thomas Miller,
late of Mountbethel Township in Northampton County, Pennsylvania,
deceased, by his daughter Agnes, also deceased, intermarried with
Alexander Galbreath late of the same place, yeoman - 8 April 1747 and
25 June 1811 Thomas Miller became seized of tracts - now bounded by
William Miller, Thomas Miller and now or late of Samuel Neilson.


Page 39
15 August 1787 - Francis Hughes to Robert Wilson - 50 pounds Virginia
money - 99 acres on waters of Sinking Creek, adjoining Joseph Martin.
Granted to Hughes at Fairfield, Grant No. 262, 4 October 1782.


Page 40
19 May 1787 - Joseph Hardin to John Ligel - for 100 pounds, 400 acres on
waters of Lick Creek, on Big Gap Creek.


BOOK III

North Carolina Grants

Page 1        No. __
For 50 shillings per 100 acres - Jonathan Evans - 500 acres on Little
Sinking Creek, adjoining William McGill, Kailihan, John Elley, James
McGill. Sealed by Richard Caswell at Kinston, 20 September 1787.


Page 2        No. 607
For 10 pounds per 100 acres - John Evans - 150 acres on south side of
Holston River. Samuel Johnston at Kinston, 33 August 1788.


Page 3        No. 638
For 10 pounds per 100 acres - John Evans - 112 acres on south side of
Holston River, opposite Millikens Island, Isaac Cloud. Samuel Johnston
at Edinton, 23 August 1788.


Page 4        No. 408
Ebenezer Byrum - 300 acres on waters of Little Chucky, adjoining William
Reed. Richard Caswell at Kinston, 20 September 1797.


Page 4        No. 423
David Copeland - 200 acres on south side Holston River, North east Fork
of Turkey Creek. Richard Caswell at Kinston, 20 September 1787.


Page 5        No. 473
David Copeland - 200 acres on south side Holston River on Cedar Creek,
adjoining McAmish. Richard Caswell at Kinston, 20 September 1787.


Page 6        No. 519
Nicholas Hays - 100 acres on a branch of Sinking Creek. Richard Caswell

at Kinston, 20 September 1787.

Page 7        No. 325
William Reed - 400 acres on Beaver Dam Creek.  Richard Caswell at Kinston,
12 September 1787.

Page 7        No. 609
James Woods Lackey - 300 acres on south side Clinch River, second bottom
above Chatta Ford, adjoining Linn.  Johnston at Edinton, 23 August 1788.

Page 8        No. 533
Joseph Bird - 300 acres on Oven Creek, south side Nolachucky River,
including his improvements, adjoining Veitch, George McKee.  Richard
Caswell at Kinston, 20 September 1737.

Page 9        No. 292
John Lyons - 250 acres on south side Holston River on Long Creek.  Richard
Caswell at Kinston, 20 September 1787.

Page 10       No. 144
Adam Meek - 100 acres on south side Holston River at mouth of Lost Creek.
Richard Caswell at Kinston, 23 April 1787.

Page 10       No. 149
Adam Meek - 100 acres on south side Holston River at mouth of a creek
that empties opposite to the end of Clinch Mountain.  Richard Caswell
at Kinston, 23 April 1787.

Page 11       No. 328
David Hailey - 315 acres on north side Holston River on Richland Creek.
Richard Caswell at Kinston, 20 September 1787.

Page 12       No. 484
David Hailey - 250 acres on north side Holston River including mouth of
Richland Creek where Hailey now lives.  Richard Caswell at Kinston, 20
September 1787.

Page 13       No. 316
John Patterson - 100 acres on headwaters of Holleys Creek, entered by
Anthony Moore, adjoining Andrew Martin.  Richard Caswell at Kinston, 20
September 1787.

Page 13       No. 394
John Patterson - 300 acres on south side Holston River on West Fork of
Flat Creek.  Richard Caswell at Kinston, 20 September 1787.

Page 14       No. 459
John Walker - 100 acres on Meadow Creek, adjoining Robert Craford,
Charles Kilgores corner and line.  Richard Caswell at Kinston, 20
September 1787.

Page 15       No. 113
Isaac Taylor - 4000 acres on north side Tennessee River, including
Pleasant Garden, to Turkey Creek, Swift Creek.  Richard Caswell at
Kinston, 1 November 1787.

Page 16     No. 613
Isaac Taylor - 640 acres on south side Clinch River on Tennants Creek,
adjoining Annanias McCoy's 400 acre tract. Richard Caswell at Kinston,
3 August 1788.


Page 16     No. 510
William McGill - 200 acres on north side Nolachucky River on Sinking
Creek, adjoining Jonathan Evans, Thomas Brumley. Richard Caswell at
Kinston. Registered 11 September 1789.


Page 17     No. 376
Robert Parress - 100 acres on Sinking Creek, adjoining himself. Richard
Caswell at Kinston, 20 September 1787. Registered 11 September 1789.


Page 18     No. 527
Robert Parris - 100 acres on Sinking Creek, adjoining John Galbreath.
Richard Caswell at Kinston, 20 September 1787.


Page 19     No. 460
Archibald McCaleb - 150 acres on north side French Broad River on Leaths
Creek, running downbranch. Richard Caswell at Kinston, 20 September
1787.


Page 19     No. 350
George Waggoner - 400 acres on both sides Lick Creek, adjoining John
Hurshey, John Carter, Daniel Carter. Richard Caswell at Kinston, 20
September 1787.


Page 20     No. 400
Alexander Gilbreath - 50 acres on Sinking Creek, adjoining Gilbreath,
formerly Alexander McFarland's line, Evan Jones. Richard Caswell at
Kinston, 20 September 1787.


Page 21     No. 722
David Stewart - 155 acres on Big Pigeon and French Broad River, to David
Stewart, John McNabb, William Crowson, Abraham Denton, James Baldridge
and John Elliott. Johnston at Edenton, 11 July 1788.


Page 22     No. 729
David Stewart and Permands Taylor - 640 acres on south side Holston River
on Hornsbacks Creek, near John Hornsback. Johnston at Edenton, 11 July
1788.


Page 22     No. 769
David Stewart and Thomas Huff - 200 acres on south side Holston River on
Middle Fork of Buffalo Creek. Richard Caswell at Kinston, 7 August 1787.


Page 23     No. 317
George Hayworth - 300 acres on Nolachucky River on Buffalo Branch of
Pigeon Creek, adjoining William Wyatt, Samuel McGill, William McGill.
Richard Caswell at Kinston, 20 September 1787.


Page 24     No. 310
William Whitefield, Joseph Greene and Nathan Whitefield - 2500 acres on
Tennessee River. Richard Caswell at Kinston, 20 September 1787.


Page 25     No. 427
Charles Hays - 500 acres on north side Tennessee River on Swift Creek,

adjoining Isaac Taylor.  Richard Caswell at Kinston, 20 September 1787.


Page 25      No. 670
Constantine Perkins - 640 acres on north side Holston River including
mouth of First Creek, below Rock House Spring.  Johnston at Edenton, 11
July 1788.


Page 26      No. 759
John Gilliland - 640 acres at mouth of Big Pigeon River, down French
Broad River, Synoteries Turmins line, James Turmins line.  Johnston at
Fairfield, 11 July 1788.


Page 27      No. 678
John Gillaland - 66 acres on French Broad River in an island at the War
Ford, joining Gillaland.  Johnston at Fairfield, 11 July 1788.


Page 28      No. 742
John Gilliland - 240 acres between French Broad and Big Pigeon Rivers.
Johnston at Fairfield, 11 July 1789.


Page 29      No. 752
John Gilliland - 100 acres adjoining himself, including spring at War
Ford.  Johnston at Fairfield, 11 July 1788.


Page 29      No. ___
Moses Carson - 100 acres on Lick Creek, adjoining Benjamin Killiam.
Richard Caswell at Kinston, 20 September 1787.


Page 30      No. 297
Moses Carson - 200 acres on Lick Creek, adjoining Nathaniel Davis.
Richard Caswell at Kinston, 20 September 1787.


Page 31      No. 666
John Stevenson and Henry Jones - 500 acres on east side Big Pigeon River.
Johnston at Fairfield, 11 July 1788.


Page 32      No. 502
Edward Riggs - 445 acres between French Broad and Holston Rivers.
Richard Caswell at Kinston, 20 September 1787.


Page 32      No. 428
Edward Riggs - 1000 acres on south side Holston River below Indian Path
from head of Dumplin Creek where it comes through knobs, adjoining Gideon
Morris, Joseph Gilbreath, Swelten's Creek.  Richard Caswell at Kinston,
20 September 1787.


Page 33      No. 294
Jesse Riggs - 70 acres on south side Holston River on Fall Creek, including Falls.  Richard Caswell at Kinston, 20 September 1787.


Page 34      No. 660
Edward Riggs - 200 acres on south side Holston River on Dry Fork.
Johnston at Fairfield, 11 July 1788.


Page 35      No. 556
Charles Gilgore (Kilgore?) - 300 acres on north side Nolachucky River,
including his improvement, adjoining Higgins McFarlin.  Richard Caswell

at Kinston, 20 September 1787.


Page 35      No. 646
John Huff - 400 acres on north side French Broad River.  Johnston at
Fairfield, 11 July 1788.


Page 36      No. 436
Richard Webb - 150 acres on north side Chuckey River opposite mouth of
Caney Creek.  Richard Caswell at Kinston, 20 September 1787.


Page 37      No. 535
Jacob Jackson - 200 acres on Long Creek including his improvement, running
down creek, adjoining Nathaniel Evans, Christopher Myers, Joseph Lines.
Richard Caswell at Kinston, 20 September 1787.


Page 37      No. 568
John McNabb - 432 acres on Big Pigeon River, including Old Indian Town,
a large spring and James Henry's improvement, adjoining Spencer Coleman,
at foot of Iron Mountain, adjoining William Crowson.  Richard Caswell at
Kinston, 20 September 1787.


Page 38      No. 740
William Crowson - 400 acres on north ease side Big Pigeon.  Johnston at
Fairfield, 11 July 1788.


Page 39      No. 658
Thomas White - 350 acres on east side Big Pigeon River, adjoining William
Crowson.  Johnston, 11 July 1788.


Page 40      No. 23
Amos Balch - 1000 acres on north side Duck River (in our Middle District)
above mouth of Shugar Creek, adjoining William Gilbreath, Jeremiah
Chamberlain, Samuel Patten Senr., Robert Hays.  Johnston at Fairfield,
10 July 1788.


Page 41      No. 394
John Patterson - 100 acres on Holleys Creek (Francis Holleys Creek),
adjoining Robert Harold, Jacob Smelser.  Richard Caswell at Kinston,
20 September 1787.


Page 42      No. 733
William Whitson - 282 acres on Big Pigeon River, adjoining William
Coleman.  Johnson at Fairfield, 11 July 1788.


Page 42      No. 661
William Colman - 150 acres on Big Pigeon River.  Johnston at Fairfield,
11 July 1788.


Page 43      No. 641
Robert McFarland - 400 acres on south side Sinking Creek, including John
Crouch Cabbin.  Johnston at Edenton, 23 August 1788.


Page 44      No. 818
Robert McFarland - 200 acres on south side Nolachucky River.  Johnston
at Edenton, 11 August 1789.

Page 45    No. 379
John McAdoo - 50 acres on Chestnut Ridge, adjoining Anthony Berry.
Richard Caswell at Kinston, 20 September 1787.


Page 45    No. 811
James Bryan - 200 acres on Branch of Coplands Creek.  Johnston at Edenton,
11 August 1788.


Page 46    No. 555
William Bigham - 500 acres on north side French Broad River on Clear
Creek, adjoining John Basking, Nicholas Neal, William Boulston.  Richard
Caswell at Kinston, 20 September 1787.


Page 47    No. 352
Joseph McFarland - 228 acres on south side Chuckey River.  Richard
Caswell at Kinston, 20 September 1787.


Page 47    No. 813
James McEmis - 200 acres on Sinking Creek, corner to John Hays, adjoining
Samuel Gibson.  Johnston at Edenton, 11 August 1789.


Page 48    No. 551
Benjamin Cox - 140 acres between Holston and French Broad Rivers.
Richard Caswell at Kinston, 20 September 1787.


Page 49    No. 315
Jacob Carter - 200 acres on Roaring Fork of Lick Creek, including his
improvement, adjoining Joseph Bullard.  Richard Caswell at Kinston, 20
September 1787.


Page 50    No. 668
Gasser Daggy - 200 acres on south side French Broad River, including the
Warm Springs.  Johnston at Fairfield, 11 July 1788.


Page 50    No. 819
Mary Edmondson - 150 acres on Little Chuckey, adjoining Thomas Watson,
James Thompson.  Johnston at Fayetteville, 27 November 1789.


Page 51    No. 565
Nicholas Davice - 300 acres on Little Chuckey.  Richard Caswell at
Kinston, 20 September 1787.


Page 52    No. 811
Jesse Greene - 300 acres on north side French Broad River.  Johnston at
Fayetteville, 27 November 1789.


Page 53    No. 389
Archibald Blackburn - 400 acres on Little Lick Creek, south side Nolachucky River.  Richard Caswell at Kinston, 20 September 1787.


Page 53    No. 549
Robert Caldwell - 300 acres on Camp Creek, adjoining Hughes.  Richard
Caswell at Kinston, 20 September 1787.


Page 54    No. 813
James Dunlap - 300 acres on Little River, adjoining Mary Odd, Tommy Hawk
marks standing ___ 5 miles above Christian War Ford.  S. Johnston.

Page 55      No. 816
James Dunlap - 640 acres near Sever Court House.  Johnston.


Page 56      No. 824
Ephraim Dunlap - 640 acres on Little River and Christians War Ford, adjoining Lewis.  Johnston at Fayetteville, 27 November 1789.


Page 56      No. 822
William King - 640 acres on Little River, corner to Robert Lewis at
Snoddy's Ford.  Johnston at Fayetteville, 27 November 1789.


Page 57      No. 826
William King - 300 acres on Little River to John Chesolm's land, south
east corner.  S. Johnston at Fayetteville, 27 September 1789.


Page 58      No. 570
Hugh Kelsey - 225 acres on north side of French Broad River, adjoining
his own land, Michael Coons.  Johnston at Edenton, 23 August 1788.


Page 59      No. 747
David Copeland - 300 acres on north side Nolachucky River on Gasses
Branch on Lick Creek, adjoining Robert McCall, Robert Kerr, Benjamin
Gass (Gesse).  S. Johnston at Fairfield, 11 July 1788.


Page 60      No. 868
George Martin - 100 acres on Lick Creek on head of Martins Spring Branch.
Johnston at Fayetteville, 26 November 1789.


Page 61      No. 814
John Hackett - 250 acres in Fork of Clinch and Tennessee Rivers.  Johnston at Edenton, 11 August 1789.


Page 62      No. 203
James Lackey - 276 acres on French Broad River above mouth of Big Pigeon
River, nearly opposite mouth of Sinking Cain Valley.  Richard Caswell at
Kinston, 20 September 1787.


Page 62      No. 539
Owen Owens - 150 acres on Sinking Creek, on Nolachucky River in Washing-
ton County, adjoining Thomas West, Samuel Moore.  Alexander Martin at
Newbern, 10 November 1784.


Page 63      No. 817
James Bryans - 400 acres on French Broad River, including his improvement.  Alexander Martin at Fayetteville, 24 November 1790.


Page 64      No. 173
Abednego Inman - 100 acres on south side Holston River, adjoining himself.  Richard Caswell at Kinston, 20 September 1787.


Page 64      No. 69
Abednego Inman - 150 acres on south side Holston River.  Richard Caswell
at Kinston, 1 November 1786.


Page 65      No. 404
Thomas Brown - 200 acres on Brown Creek.  Richard Caswell at Kinston,
20 September 1787.

Page 66        No. 813
William Henderson - 300 acres north of Little Pigeon River where he now
lives. Alexander Martin at Danberry, 25 September 1790.


Page 67        No. 816
William Henderson - 300 acres on Little Pigeon River, adjoining his
former 300 acre entry of 24 February 1788. Alexander Martin at Danberry,
25 September 1790.


Page 67        No. 679
James Baldridge - 5000 acres in fork of Big Pigeon River and French
Broad River, adjoining Henry, John Stevenson, William Bell, James Lackey,
Benjamin White. S. Johnston at Fairfield, 11 July 1788.


Page 69        No. 504
Elisha Baker - 640 acres on north side Holston River below mouth of
French Broad River. Richard Caswell at Kinston, 20 September 1787.


Page 69        No. 569
James Martin Lewis - 640 acres on north side French Broad River, adjoin-
ing James Randolph, James Hubbard. Alexander Martin at Fayetteville, 18
December 1789.


Page 70        No. 829
Adam Meek - 600 acres on Dividing Ridge that divides Holston and French
Broad Rivers. Alexander Martin at Danberry, 5 October 1790.


Page 71        No. 817
Alexander Melone - 1000 acres on First Sinking Branch below John Cowans.
Alexander Martin at Fayetteville, 6 December 1790.


Page 71        No. 211
Joseph McCullah - 500 acres on south side Holston River, including his
improvement. Richard Caswell at Kinston, 20 September 1787.


Page 72        No. 359
James Mahan - 300 acres on Lick Creek, including Charles Arton improvement, adjoining Drury Hodge. Richard Caswell at Kinston, 20 September
1787.


Page 73        No. 851
William Morrow - 400 acres on Nine Mile Creek, including Crossroads.
Martin at Kinston, 6 October 1790.


Page 73        No. 729
Robert Steel - 150 acres in Washington County, adjoining John Gillilan
as entry he sold to Steel at head of Sinking Creek, adjoining James
Wilson, Gid Morris, John Bearden, Robert Wear. Richard Caswell at
Kinston, 26 October 1786.


Page 74        No. 698
Robert Steel - 200 acres below Joseph Martins entry in Washington County,
adjoining John Bearden, Archibald Sloan. Richard Caswell at Kinston, 26
October 1786.


Page 75        No, 822
James Stinson - 150 acres on Lick Creek on Joseph Gists Fork of Lick
Creek, adjoining Alexander Lowry, Thomas Davis. Alexander Martin at

Fayetteville, 19 November 1790.


Page 76     No. 679
William Steel - 150 acres on Sinking Creek - Washington County - corner
to Robert Wear, James Alexander.  Richard Caswell at Kinston, 26 October
1786.


Page 77     No. 553
Hosea Stout - 200 acres on south side Nolachucky River on both sides
Little Lick Creek, corner to John Morris land.  Richard Caswell at
Kinston, 20 September 1787.


Page 77     No. 81
George Bean - 400 acres on Little Chucky, adjoining Marmaduke Viceroy.
Alexander Martin at Danberry, 7 March 1790.


Page 78     No. 820
William Bell - 150 acres at mouth of Nolachucky River, north side French
Broad River including an island.  Alexander Martin at Danberry, 5 October
1790.


Page 79     No. 401
William Berry - 150 acres on head of Sinking Creek - Washington County -
adjoining John Morris, Asahel Rawlings.  Alexander Martin at Hillsboro,
13 October 1783.


Page 80     No. 368
William Berry - 25 acres on Mill Fork of Limestone, adjoining Daniel
Kennedy's survey.  Alexander Martin at Hillsbro, 13 October 1783.


Page 80     No. 464
William Berry - 150 acres on head of Sinking Creek - Washington County -
adjoining John Morris and Asahel Rawlings, Chedd Morris.  Alexander
Martin at Hillsbro, 13 October 1783.


Page 81     No. 199
John Beard - 100 acres on Flat Creek, north side Holston River.  Richard
Caswell at Kinston, 20 September 1787.


Page 82     No. 843
George Edger - 400 acres on Bens Branch on Holston River.  Alexander
Martin at Fayetteville, 24 November 1790.


Page 82     No. 544
Thomas Ishmael - 200 acres adjoining John Francisco.  Richard Caswell at
Kinston, 20 September 1787.


Page 83     No. 508
Andrew English - 200 acres on Lick Creek, adjoining Chimney Top Mountain.
Richard Caswell at Kinston, 20 September 1787.


Page 84     No. 174
William Donelson - 250 acres on Sinking Creek, adjoining Samuel Moore,
corner to James Moore, Thomas Mitchell.  Richard Caswell at Kinston, 20
September 1787.

Page 85       No. 165
Samuel Thompson - 200 acres on north side French Broad River above mouth
of Little Pidgeon River.  Richard Caswell at Kinston, 20 September 1787.


Page 85       No. 821
Isaac Taylor - 300 acres on Dumpling Creek, adjoining McCleary, Bank of
French Broad River, including island.  Alexander Martin at Danberry, 5
October 1790.


Page 86       No. 824
Isaac Taylor, assignee of Hugh Beard - 300 acres on north side French
Broad River.  Alexander Martin at Danberry, 5 October 1790.


Page 87       No. 228
Isaac Taylor - 200 acres on Bradshaws Gap.  Alexander Martin at Danberry,
5 October 1790.


Page 87       No. 822
Isaac Taylor - 300 acres on Kelseys Creek, adjoining Hackett, McGivits,
McCammon.  Alexander Marton at Danberry, 5 October 1790.


Page 88       No. 817
Isaac Taylor - 300 acres on Dumplins Creek above Beaver Dam, on a Sinking
Creek.  Alexander Martin at Danberry, 5 October 1790.


Page 89       No. 251
Isaac Taylor - 400 acres on Tennessee River, adjoining Alexander Outlaw.
Richard Caswell at Caswell, 20 September 1787.


Page 90       No. 205
James Hubbard - 250 acres on French Broad River below Christans War Path.
Richard Caswell at Kinston, 20 September 1787.


Page 90       No. 266
James Hubbard - 100 acres on Dumplin Creek at Upper War Ford, known as
Mill Seat Place.  Richard Caswell at Kinston, 20 September 1787.


Page 91       No. 652
James Hubbert - 200 acres on Dumplin Creek below mouth of Sinking Spring.
Johnston at Fairfield, 11 July 1788.


Page 92       No. 822
William Horner - 100 acres on Bent Creek.  Alexander Martin at Danberry,
13 February 1791.


Page 92       No. 129
Jonathan Holley - 100 acres in Washington County on Holleys Creek.
Alexander Martin at Fairfield, 24 October 1782.


Page 93       No. 106
James Hays - 30 acres on Limestone Fork of Lick Creek, adjoining James
English.  Richard Caswell at Kinston, 1 November 1786.


Page 94       No. 835
Hugh Henry - 100 acres on Dumplin Creek, adjoining his old survey.
Alexander Martin at Danberry, 13 February 1790.

Page 94      No. 546
Samuel Hubbard - 246 acres on Alexander Branch of Lick Creek, including
his improvement, adjoining William T. Lewis, James Mahan.  Richard Caswell at Kinston, 20 September 1787.

Page 95      No. 826
William Cowan - 250 acres on south side Little River at mouth of Crooked
Creek, adjoining George Evans - Rockingham County Court House.  Alexander
Martin, 6 October 1790.

Page 96      No. 837
Thomas Cannon - 100 acres on Sinking Fork of Long Creek, including John
Craig improvement, adjoining Robert Biggs.  Alexander Martin at Danberry,
13 February 1791.

Page 97      No. 183
Abner Chapman - 640 acres on Russells Creek and Powels River, adjoining
John Horner.  Richard Caswell at Kinston, 20 September 1787.

Page 97      No. 182
Abner Chapman - 400 acres on Russells Creek, adjoining David Stewart.
Richard Caswell at Kinston, 20 September 1787.

Page 98      No. 300
John Carter - 100 acres on Roaring Fork of Lick Creek.  Richard Caswell
at Kinston, 20 September 1787.

Page 99      No. ___
Lewis Roberson - 200 acres on Holston River including his own improvement,
adjoining James Short.  Richard Caswell at Kinston, 20 September 1787.

Page 100     No. 651
Charles Robertson - 300 acres on Cove Creek, adjoining Joseph Kyler,
John Cunningham, Frethias Wall.  S. Johnston at Fairfield, 11 July 1788.

Page 100     No. 867
Asahel Rawlings - 400 acres in Sinking Creek - Washington County - includ-
ing two springs near Joseph Martins claim, adjoining his other entry.
Alexander Martin at Fayetteville, 16 November 1790.

Page 101     No. 868
Asahel Rawlings - 200 acres on Lick Creek, adjoining or near other survey,
including Pruits Camp.  Alexander Martin at Fayetteville, 16 November
1790.

Page 102     No. 870
Asahel Rawlings - 200 acres on Lick Creek in Washington County, including
Benjamin Pruits Camp.  Sealed by Alexander Martin at Fayetteville, 16
November 1790.

Page 103     No. 820
Jacob Vanhoozer - 70 acres on Bent Creek, adjoining Valentine Vanhoozer
and his other land.  Alexander Martin at Danberry, 13 February 1791.

Page 103     No. 801
William Asher - 640 acres on Bent Creek, adjoining Tidence Lane, James
Roddy, William Horner and John Smith.  Samuel Johnston at Fayetteville,
17 November 1788.

Page 104     No. 258
John Patterson - 200 acres on a Branch of Long Creek.  Richard Caswell
at Kinston, 20 September 1787.

Page 105      No. 547
Jacob Fishback - 400 acres on Nolachucky River on Cedar Branch, south
side Nolachucky River, beginning at Cedar Spring, adjoining Bennet,
Goforth, Brison.  Richard Caswell at Kinston, 20 September 1787.


Page 106      No. 449
John Wright - 100 acres in Washington County on Browns Creek, adjoining
Thomas Brown.  Alexander Martin at Hillsbro, 13 October 1783.


Page 106      No. 836
Jesse Kimbrough - 250 acres on Kelsay's Creek, waters of French Broad
River, including where he lives, adjoining James Randle, Amos Balch.
Alexander Martin at Danberry, 13 February 1791.


Page 107      No. 507
Andrew Kinkade - 200 acres on north side Holston River opposite Robert
Kings Plantation on south side of river, adjoining William Cocke.
Richard Caswell at Kinston, 20 September 1787.


Page 108      No. ___
John Johnston - 100 acres on Clay Lick Creek - French Broad River above
Thomas Christians.  Richard Caswell at Kinston, 20 September 1787.


Page 109      No. 818
Robert Oneal - 400 acres on Horse Creek where he now lives, adjoining
Nolachucky River, English.  Alexander Martin at Danberry, 15 October
1790.


Page 109      No. 710
Robert Oneal - 200 acres in Washington County on south side Nolachucky
River, adjoining Michael Borders.  Richard Caswell at Kinston, 26
October 1786.


Page 110      No. 31
Nicholas Neal - 200 acres on Clear Creek, adjoining Isaac Taylor,
Swaggerty.  Richard Caswell at Kinston, 1 November 1786.


Page 111      No. 806
Samuel Gragg - 100 acres on Meadow Creek, adjoining Thomas Gragg.  Samuel
Johnston at Edenton, 18 May 1789.


Page 112      No. ___
Thomas Gillespy - 100 acres on Middle Creek.  Richard Caswell at Kinston,
1 November 1786.


Page 113      No. 345
John Gass - 400 acres on both sides of Lick Creek, adjoining Andrew
Mitchell, John Baldwin.  Richard Caswell at Kinston, 20 September 1787.


Page 113      No. 193
Joseph Long - 300 acres on Fall Creek, on south side Clinch River in
Hinds Valley, south side Falls Creek.  Richard Caswell at Kinston, 20
September 1787.


Page 114      No. 841
Michael Coons - 640 acres on French Broad River where Coons now lives,
adjoining Charles Gentry, Hugh Kelso, Robert Carson.  Alexander Martin
at Fayetteville, 24 November 1790.


Page 115      No. 531
Abraham Fulkerson - 500 acres on north side French Broad River, including
head springs of First Creek.  Richard Caswell at Kinston, 20 September
1787.

Page 116     No. 56
Samuel Patten Junr. - 1500 acres on Duck River, adjoining George Martin,
Amos Balch, Richard Martin.  Samuel Johnston at Fairfield, 10 July 1788.

Page 116     No. 824
Thomas Brown - 250 acres on Long Creek, on head of Sinking Fork.
Alexander Martin at Danberry, 13 February 1791.

Page 117     No. 827
Henry Payne - 350 acres on north side French Broad River, known as Logans
improvement, on head of McCleary's Branch.  Alexander Martin at Hillsborough, 16 November 1790.

Page 118     No. 473
Aaron Lewis - 200 acres in Washington County.  Alexander Martin at Newbern,
10 November 1782.

Page 119     No. 479
Aaron Lewis - 150 acres in Washington County on Limestone Fork of Lick
Creek, adjoining James English.  Alexander Martin at Newbern, 10 November
1780.

Page 119     No. 477
Aaron Lewis - 146 acres in Washington County on Cedar Spring.  Alexander
Martin at Newbern, 10 November 1784.

Page 120     No. 476
Aaron Lewis - 100 acres in Washington County on both sides Limestone Fork
of Lick Creek, above James English.  Alexander Martin at Newbern, 10
November 1794.

Page 121     No. 820
John Douglass - 250 acres on French Broad River near Jonathan Langdons
land.  Samuel Johnston at Edenton, 11 August 1789.

Page 122     No. 893
Charles Robertson - 600 acres on Clear Creek, adjoining Peter Fine.
Alexander Martin at Danberry, 6 September 1791.

Page 123     No. 821
Jonathan Langdon - 200 acres on French Broad River, adjoining Neelus.
Samuel Johnston at Edenton, 11 August 1789.

Page 123     No. 458
Isaac Hammer - 200 acres on Limestone Fork of Tuckahoe Creek.  Richard
Caswell at Kinston, 20 September 1787.

Page 124     No. 428
Bartholomew Woods Junr. - 400 acres in Washington County on Little Nolachucky River.  Alexander Martin at Hillsborough, 13 October 1783.

Page 125     No. 320
James Armstrong - 200 acres on Dry Fork of Lick Creek, near Wild Cat
Branch.  Richard Caswell at Kinston, 20 September 1787.

Page 126     No. 60
Samuel Flanaken - 200 acres in Washington County on north side Nolachucky
River on a creek below Boxes, opposite Vances land, adjoining William
Randle, Cox, Dealy, The Barrens?  Alexander Martin at Fairfield, 23
October 1782.

Page 126     No. 635
John Darmond - 200 acres on North Fork of Emry's River, at foot of

Cumberland Mountain, adjoining William Blount. Samuel Johnston at Edenton, 23 August 1788.


Page 127    No. 581
James Robinson - 300 acres on Arntons Fork of Lick Creek - Washington County - adjoining Jesse Bond. Alexander Martin at Newbern, 10 November 1784.


Page 128    No. 825
Joseph Colvill - 400 acres on Crooked Creek where he lives now, adjoining William Lowry, Wierr, McMurry. Alexander Martin at Hillsborough, 15 April 1790.


Page 129    No. 818
David Craig - 640 acres on north bank French Broad River, including Second Island above mouth of river. Alexander Martin at Fayetteville, 2 December 1790.


Page 130    No. 840
Ephraim Dunlap - 200 acres on south side Nolachucky River on the War Path, including a small marshy meadow and spring, known as Indian Camps. Alexander Martin at Danberry, 13 February 1791.


Page 130    No. 839
Ephraim Dunlap - 640 acres on north side Nolachucky River. Alexander Martin at Danberry, 13 February 1791.


Page 131    No. 411
Alexander Williams - 411 acres on Lick Creek and Camp Creek, adjoining Peter News, Hugh Brown, Andrew Mitchell, Claudius Bailey. Richard Caswell at Kinston, 20 September 1789.


Page 132    No. 823
Samuel Wier - North Fork of Crooked Creek. Alexander Martin at Hillsborough, 15 April 1790.


Page 133    No. 525
Samuel Wier - 200 acres in Washington County on Mill Fork of Big Limestone, adjoining John Gillihan, Lancelot Armstrong and Taylor. Alexander Martin at Newbern, 10 November 1784.


Page 134    No. 817
Josiah Leath - 225 acres adjoining Leath's 640 acre survey. Samuel Johnston at Edenton, 11 August 1789.


Page 135    No. 18
David Campbell - 600 acres on French Broad River, adjoining John Beard, including three islands downriver. Richard Caswell at Kinston, 1 November 1786.


Page 135    No. 818
Anthony Patten - 8 acres on Island in French Broad River, known as Bungans Island, opposite Beach Bottoms formerly claimed by Robert Lamb. Samuel Johnston at Fayetteville, 27 November 1789.


Page 135    No. 822
George Doughterty - 20 acres on Island in French Broad River. Samuel Johnston at Edenton, 11 August 1789.


Page 136    No. 812
Francis Dean - 50 acres on north side French Broad River, adjoining Lewis. Samuel Johnston at Edenton, 11 August, 1789.

Page 137     No. 816
Andrew Lewis - 640 acres on French Broad River, including a large island
in river and 2 small ones, also his improvements on the outlands.  Andrew
Lewis, orphan of John Lewis.  Samuel Johnston at Edenton, 11 August 1789.


Page 138     No. 590
James Creswell - 50 acres on south side Holston River.  Samuel Johnston
at Edenton, 13 August 1788.


Page 139     No. 428
Bartholomew Woods Junr. - 400 acres in Washington County on waters of
Little Nolachucky River.  Alexander Martin at Hillsborough, 13 October
1783.


Page 140     No. 831
Joseph Hawkins - 200 acres on headwaters of Horse Stamp Fork of Lick
Creek.  Alexander Martin at Danberry, 13 February 1791.


Page 141     No. 821
Stephen Cotter - 100 acres on Horse Camp Fork of Lick Creek, waters of
Chuckey River, adjoining Robert Wilson, Joseph Hawkins, Samuel Humberd.
Alexander Martin at Danberry, 13 February 1791.


Page 142     No. 881
John Ward - 400 acres on south side French Broad River, adjoining William
Jobb.  Alexander Martin at Fayetteville, 17 November 1790.


Page 143     No. 848
Robert Clark - 200 acres in fork of French Broad and Big Pigeon Rivers,
above first Big Falls, below mouth of Long Creek to spur on Iron Mountain.
Alexander Martin at Fayetteville, 16 November 1790.


Page 144     No. 869
Peter Huff - 300 acres opposite mouth of Big Pigeon River, south side
French Broad River, including Low Grounds and his own improvement, adjoining Benjamin Tipton.  Alexander Martin at Fayetteville, 17 November
1790.


Page 144     No. 1034
Benjamin Lucas - 640 acres on Holston River at mouth of French Broad
River.  Alexander Martin at Newbern, 26 December 1791.


Page 145     No. 917
James Pearce - 640 acres on Little River at Christians War Ford - To be
registered at Richmount.  Alexander Martin at Newbern, 26 December 1791.


Page 146     No. 880
Solomon Cox - 250 acres on Long Creek, south side Holston River, lying on
both sides of Honey Cutts Path, including an improvement, adjoining John
Couch.  Alexander Martin at Fayetteville, 17 November 1790.


Page 147     No. 895
Edward Osburn - 200 acres on north side French Broad River below Big
Falls.  Alexander Martin, 31 October 1791.


Page 148     No. 850
Zopher Johnston - 100 acres adjoining William Hannah, Daniel Brittain.
Alexander Martin at Fayetteville, 17 November 1790.


Page 148     No. 830
George Brown - 100 acres above Sinking Fork of Lick Creek.  Alexander
Martin at Danberry, 13 February 1791.


110

Page 149     No. 878
William Conway - 25 acres on north side Nolachucky River, adjoining himself and Joseph White.  Sealed by Alexander Martin at Fayetteville.

Page 150     No. 884
Joseph Conway - 70 acres on south side Nolachucky River, adjoining himself and Spencer Rice.  Alexander Martin at Fayetteville, 16 November
1790.

Page 151     No. 843
Joseph Conway - 400 acres on Clay Lick Creek on Nolachucky River, adjoining Dixon Edmon, Archibald Blackburn.  Alexander Martin at Fayetteville,
7 November 1790.

Page 151     No. 111
Nathaniel Evens - 600 acres on south side French Broad River below the
mouth of Boyd's Creek, adjoining David Cowan.  Alexander Martin at
Newbern, _____ 1791.

Page 152     No. 872
Hugh Nelson - 66 acres on north side Nolachucky River, corner to Phillip
Hale, Joseph White.  Alexander Martin at Fayetteville, 17 November 1790.

Page 153     No. 912
John Woods - 150 acres on Little Nolachucky River, adjoining Francis
Hamilton, William Lowry.  Alexander Martin at Newbern, 26 December 1791.

Page 154     No. 841
David Ranken - 100 acres in Mitchels survey, adjoining Gilbreath,
Mitchels survey corner.  Alexander Martin at Fayetteville, 17 November
1790.

Page 155     No. 1000
Augustine Brumly - 100 acres on north side Chuckey River, adjoining
Thomas Flippen.  Alexander Martin at Newbern, 26 December 1791.

Page 155     No. 833
Edward Seaburn - 200 acres on Dumplin Creek, including where he now lives,
adjoining William Allen.  Alexander Martin at Danberry, 13 February 1791.

Page 156     No. 1018
Robert Kerr - 200 acres adjoining his old survey, adjoining Copeland.
Alexander Martin at Newbern, 26 December 1791.

Page 157     No. 835
Garret Fitzgerald - 640 acres on French Broad River, adjoining James
Bryant, including head of Copelands Branch.  Alexander Martin at
Fayetteville, 17 November 1790.

Page 158     No. 842
William Headley - 100 acres on Dumplin Creek above Edward Seaburns.
Alexander Martin at Fayetteville, 24 November 1795.

Page 159     No. 836
Garret Fitzgerald - 300 acres on head of Lick Branch including the Flat
Lick on French Broad River, adjoining James Neely.  Alexander Martin at
Fayetteville, 17 November 1790.

Page 159     No. 818
David Brown - 150 acres on Sinking Fork of Long Creek where he now lives.
Alexander Martin at Danberry, 13 February 1791.

Page 160    No. 826
Alexander Montgomery - 450 acres on Long Creek including Days Cabbin.
Alexander Martin at Danberry, 13 February 1791.


Page 161    No. 888
Alexander Wilson - 100 acres on Holleys Creek, adjoining where William
Story formerly lived.  Alexander Martin at Fayetteville, 17 November 1790.


Page 162    No. 871
Alexander Wilson - 100 acres on Franks Creek including an improvement by
William Story.  Alexander Martin at Fayetteville, 17 November 1790.


Page 162    No. 996
John Reaves - 80 acres on the head of a branch of Little Chuckey, adjoin-
ing Samuel Vance, Mark Mitchell.  Alexander Martin at Newbern, 26
December 1791.


Page 163    No. 815
John Carter - 100 acres on a fork of Guests (Gist) Creek of Lick Creek,
adjoining himself.  Samuel Johnston at Fairfield, 6 July 1789.


Page 164    No. 819
Robert Carson - 200 acres on French Broad River, adjoining Robert Gentry,
Michael Coon.  Alexander Martin at Danberry, 13 February 1791.


Page 165    No. 1007
Sparling Bowman - 300 acres on Camp Creek, south side Nolachucky River,
adjoining Thomas Morgan, Francis Hughes, Jacob Vance, Joseph Hickson.
Alexander Martin at Newbern, 26 December 1791.


Page 166    No. 689
William Whitfield - 4oo acres westside of Copper Ridge on a prong of Bull
Run, adjoining Elizabeth Green.  Samuel Johnston at Fairfield, 11 July
1788.


Page 166    No. 700
William Whitfield - 400 acres on north Fork of Bull Run that runs into
Clinch River below his former survey.  Samuel Johnston at Fairfield, 11
July 1788.


Page 167    No. 688
Needham Whitfield - 400 acres on Bull Run.  Samuel Johnston at Fairfield,
11 July 1788.


Page 168    No. 677
Needham Whitfield - 400 acres north fork of Bull Run of Clinch River.
Samuel Johnston at Fairfield, 11 July 1788.


Page 169    No. 683
William Whitfield - 400 acres on both sides of the north of Bull Run that
makes into Clinch River, adjoining Needham Whitfield.  Samuel Johnston at
Fairfield, 11 July 1788.


Page 169    No. 675
Needham Whitfield - 500 acres between Clinch Mountain and Clinch River.
Samuel Johnston at Fairfield, 11 July 1788.


Page 170    No. 847
John Ramsey - 100 acres on north side Nolachucky River including James
Dellards improvement, adjoining David Kerr and Stephen Pate.  Alexander
Martin at Fayetteville, 15 November 1790.

Page 171    No. 995
Hugh Beard - 300 acres on waters of William Emeries River, adjoining
William Blounts south line.  Alexander Martin at Newbern, 26 December
1791.

Page 172    No. 898
Richard Morgan - 100 acres on Dumplin Creek.  Alexander Martin at Newbern,
26 December 1791.

Page 172    No. 913
Nehemiah Pettit - 35 acres on Alexanders Branch of Lick Creek.  Alexander
Martin at Newbern, 26 December 1791.

Page 173    No. 866
Phillip Hale - 100 acres on south side Nolachucky River including an
island lying on the south side of river opposite where Hale now lives,
adjoining Joseph Conway, Spencer Rice.  Alexander Martin at Fayetteville,
17 November 1790.

Page 174    No. 935
Joseph White - 953 acres on Buffalo Ford of Lick Creek, including a big
meadow or Flag Swamp, adjoining Amos Bird, Joseph Conway, William Conway.
Alexander Martin at Newbern, 26 December 1791.

Page 175    No. 1004
Andrew Fox - 300 acres on south side Chuckey River, adjoining Benjamin
Williams, Phillip Sherril.  Alexander Martin at Newbern, 26 December
1791.

Page 176    No. 856
Samuel McCamey - 375 acres on watery fork of Caney Branch, adjoining
John Sherrel.  Alexander Martin at Fayetteville, 17 November 1790.

Page 177    No. 905
Andrew Greer - 640 acres on Four Mile Creek where Indian Pass crosses
creek.  Alexander Martin at Newbern, 26 December 1791.

Page 177    No. 1035
Andrew Greer - 640 acres on Four Mile Creek where Indian Path crosses
creek, on Daniel Shines entry, adjoining Greers Entry No. 120.  Alexander Martin at Newbern, 26 December 1791.

Page 178    No. 1020
William Bryan - 200 acres on a fork of Little Chuckey, adjoining Breed.
Alexander Martin at Newbern, 26 December 1791.

Page 179    No. 846
Abraham McCleary - 100 acres on north side of French Broad River, adjoin-
ing Henry Payne, Jesse Greene.  Alexander Martin at Fayetteville, 17
November 1791.

Page 180    No. 1025
Abraham McCleary - 200 acres on north side of French Broad River includ-
ing first island below the mouth of Dumplin Creek.  Alexander Martin at
Newbern, 26 December 1791.

Page 180    No. 823
James Gibson - 150 acres on French Broad River, adjoining where he now
lives.  Alexander Martin at Danberry, 13 February 1791.

Page 181    No. 1022
Robert Hammel - 200 acres on waters of Little Chucky including where he
now lives.  Alexander Martin at Newbern, 26 December 1791.

Page 182     No. 994
Kezeah Bowers - 100 acres on west side of Lick Creek, on branch running down from Long Lick, adjoining John Newman. Alexander Martin at Newbern, 26 December 1791.

Page 183     No. 886
Sebert Sollars - 200 acres on headwaters of Meadow Creek, northside French Broad River, including an improvement, adjoining James Clement, John Slaughters. Alexander Martin at Fayetteville, 17 November 1790.

Page 184     No. 1049
David Stewart - 500 acres on north side French Broad River below mouth of Clay Creek, adjoining Joseph Hoof, John Campbell, Richard Manning. Alexander Martin at Newbern, 26 December 1791.

Page 185     No. 954
Joseph Vance - 1000 acres on Sinking Branch of Boyd's Creek, adjoining John McCreskey, Samuel Newel, near Great Road, Page Sims, John Ray, James Sims. Alexander Martin at Newbern, 26 December 1791.

Page 186     No. 827
Stephen Cobb - 640 acres at mouth of Lick Creek on Nolachucky River. Alexander Martin at Fayetteville, 17 November 1790.

Page 186     No. 899
Joseph Bird - 300 acres on Nolachucky River including mouth of Oven Creek. Alexander Martin at Newbern, 26 December 1791.

Page 187     No. 923
James Hubbard - 200 acres on Dumplin Creek, adjoining Meek. Alexander Martin at Newbern, 26 December 1791.

Page 188     No. 890
William Tate - 100 acres on north side French Broad River on James Walkers Spring Branch. Alexander Martin at Fayetteville, 17 November 1790.

Page 189     No. 173
Alexander Kelley - 42 acres on an island in Holston River - Hawkins County. Alexander Martin at Newbern, 26 December 1791.

Page 189     No. 830
William Largon - 150 acres on Big Slate Creek, south side Nolachucky River, adjoining line made by John Baskins. Alexander Martin at Fayetteville, 17 November 1790.

Page 190     No. 929
James Hubbert - 300 acres on north side French Broad River, adjoining Catherine Beek, William Goforth. Alexander Martin at Newbern, 26 December 1791.

Page 191     No. 970
Archibald Lackey - 200 acres on waters of Tennessee, adjoining Alexander Mebane. Alexander Martin at Newbern, 26 December 1791.

Page 191     No. 964
James Woods Lackey - 500 acres on south side French Broad River on Nails Creek at foot of Bays Mountain, adjoining Gray, Sherril. Alexander Martin, 26 December 1791.

Page 192     No. 832
Edward George - 200 acres on waters of French Broad River, ease side of where he now lives. Alexander Martin at Danberry, 13 February 1791.

Page 193     No. 977
Alexander Miller, assignee of Edward Williams - 200 acres on Nine Mile
Creek, corner to John Hannah. Alexander Martin at Newbern, 26 December
1791.

Page 194     No. 859
John Gibson - 200 acres on headwaters of the West Fork of Holleys Creek,
adjoining Jacob Smelsor, David Robertson. Alexander Martin at Fayetteville, 17 November 1790.

Page 195     No. 1042
James Moore - 640 acres on waters of French Broad River, head of Limestone Fork of Tuckahoe Creek, adjoining George Tacket. Alexander Martin
at Hillsborough, 14 April 1792.

Page 195     No. 978
Andrew Miller - 300 acres on Nine Mile Creek. Alexander Martin at
Newbern, 16 December 1791.

Page 196     No. 1048
Henry Nave - 200 acres on Little Lick Creek, south of Nolachucky River.
Alexander Martin at Newbern, 26 December 1791.

Page 197     No. 823
Alexander Mebane - 500 acres on west fork of Nine Mile Creek, adjoining
Tedfords Branch, George Tedford. Alexander Martin, (no date) 1791.

Page 197     No. 870
William Hannah - 99 acres on McCartney's Creek, adjoining Joseph Hardin.
Alexander Martin at Fayetteville, 17 November 1791.

Page 198     No. 920
Hugh Kelsey - 100 acres on Kelseys Mill Creek, north side French Broad
River, adjoining Benjamin McFarling. Alexander Martin at Newbern, 26
December 1791.

Page 199     No. 902
Joseph Nation - 113 acres on Little Chuckey Creek at the head of the
Blue Spring, adjoining McBroom. Alexander Martin at Newbern, 26
December 1791.

Page 200     No. 965
James Woods Lackey - 300 acres on the north side of Tennessee River.
Alexander Martin at Newbern, 26 December 1791.

Page 200     No. ___
James Lackey - 1000 acres on south side Holston River, including where he
lives, adjoining John Bird, mouth of Lackeys Creek, Daniel and Alexander
Carmichael. Alexander Martin at Newbern, 26 December 1791.

Page 201     No. ___
David Lyle - 320 acres on north side French Broad River, adjoining Charles
Gentry, William Bryan. Alexander Martin at Newbern, 26 December 1791.

Page 202     No. 894
Andrew Evans - 37 acres on an island in French Broad River that Colonal
William Christian marched through in the night when he marched to the
Cherokee Nation in the year 1776. Alexander Martin at Newbern, 26
December 1791.

Page 203     No. 1010
David Walker - 200 acres on the north fork of Clear Creek, adjoining John
Smith. Alexander Martin at Newbern, 26 December 1791.

Page 204    No. 676
Needham Whitfield - 400 acres on a prong of Bull Run, at the foot of a
copper ridge below Joseph Greenes. Samuel Johnston at Fairfield, 11
July 1788.


Page 205    No. 985
John Reese - 200 acres on Pigeon Creek, adjoining Reese, Frederick Hale,
McMeans. Alexander Martin at Newbern, 26 December 1791.


Page 204    No. 876
Robert Biggs - 200 acres between Cedar Creek and Sinking Fork of Long
Creek, beginning in the Barrens. Alexander Martin at Fayetteville, 17
November 1795.


Page 206    No. 962
Alexander Kelly and Archibald Lackey - 640 acres on north side of
Tennessee River, above mouth of Bakers Creek. Alexander Martin at
Newbern, 26 December 1791.


Page 206    No. 963
Alexander Kelly and Archibald Lackey - 1000 acres on Tennessee River to
lower end of and crossing an island. Alexander Martin at Newbern, 26
December 1791.


Page 207    No. 956
Alexander Kelly, John Cowan, Archibald Lacky and James Woods Lackey - 640
acres on Nine Mile Creek, north side Tennessee River. Alexander Martin
at Newbern, 26 December 1791.


Page 208    No. 281
Nathaniel Evans - 600 acres on Long Creek, north side French Broad River,
adjoining Edwards, Isaac Taylor, Jacob Jackson. Richard Caswell at
Kinston, 20 September 1787.


Page 209    No. 552
James Johnston - 600 acres on south side Nolachucky River, adjoining
Joseph Kyler, John Cunningham. Richard Caswell at Kinston, 20 September
1787.


Page 210    No. 814
James Casey - 300 acres on north side of Lick Creek. Alexander Martin at
Hillsborough, 8 April 1790.


Page 210    No. 908
Alexander McMillan - 200 acres on east fork of Swan Pond Creek, including
William Goldens improvement, adjoining William Parker. Alexander Martin
at Newbern, 26 December 1791.


Page 211    No. 919
John Gillespy - 50 acres on McCartney's Branch, adjoining Isaac Bullard.
Alexander Martin at Newbern, 26 December 1791.


Page 212    No. 1009
John Gillespy - 177 acres on McCartney's Creek. Alexander Martin at
Newbern, 26 December 1791.


Page 213    No. 745
Lon Todd Senr. - 300 acres on south side Nolachucky River, adjoining
James Richards. Samuel Johnston at Fairfield, 11 July 1788.


Page 213    No. 1032
Evin Evans - 200 acres on north side Nolachucky River, adjoining Doherty.
Alexander Martin at Newbern, 26 December 1791.

Page 214    No. 900
Evan Evans - 40 acres on north side Chucky River, adjoining Joseph Posey, said Evans. Alexander Martin at Newbern, 26 December 1791.

Page 215    No. 827
James Hubbard and William Thomas - 600 acres on north side Tennessee River, near Four Mile, below mouth of Holston River. Samuel Johnston at Fayetteville, 27 November 1789.

Page 216    No. 1052
Arthur Moore - 640 acres on Tuckahoe Creek, waters of French Broad River, by virtue of Warrant No. 883, adjoining Fulkerson, Isaac Hammer. Alexander Martin at Hillsborough, 14 April 1790.

Page 217    No. 115
John Cowan - 640 acres on north side Tennessee River, adjoining Alexander Mebane, James Woods Lackey. Alexander Martin at Newbern, 26 December 1791.

Page 218    No. 937
John Miers - 200 acres on Nolachucky River, west fork of Flag Branch, adjoining Joel Matthews. Alexander Martin at Newbern, 26 December 1791.

Page 218    No. 1048
Thomas Rankin - 400 acres on Dumpling Creek on French Broad River, including two Sinking Springs. Alexander Martin at Hillsborough, 14 April 1792.

Page 219    No. 457
Nathaniel Curtis - 150 acres on Little Lick Creek, adjoining a knob. Richard Caswell at Kinston, 20 September 1787.

Page 220    No. 998
Thomas Wilkerson - 100 acres on waters of Nolachucky River, adjoining Henry Willis, Benjamin Totten. Alexander Martin at Newbern, 26 December 1791.

Page 221    No. 926
Thomas Rankin - 150 acres on Dumpling Creek, adjoining said Rankin. Alexander Martin at Newbern, 26 December 1791.

Page 222    No. 939
John Bradshaw - 475 acres on Dumpling Creek, adjoining where he now lives, Bradshaw, Richard Rankin. Alexander Martin at Newbern, 26 December 1791.

Page 222    No. 1064
Anthony Moore - 150 acres on north side Chucky River, adjoining William Morrow, Robert Hood. Alexander Martin at Danberry, 11 May 1792.

Page 223    No. 866
Daniel Rice - 200 acres on Slate Creek or Big Creek, south side Nolachucky River. Alexander Martin at Fayetteville, 17 November 1790.

Page 224    No. 1029
William Davidson - 305 acres on the south side of Holston River, lower end of Painter Bottom to a creek, then along River. Alexander Martin at Newbern, 26 December 1791.

Page 225    No. 991
John Johnston - 120 acres on the head of Collins Creek, northside Nolachucky River. Alexander Martin at Newbern, 26 December 1791.

Page 226     No. 944
Richard Rankin - 300 acres on Dumplin Creek, adjoining John Bradshaw,
where he and I now live, at foot of Knobbs. Alexander Martin at Newbern,
26 December 1791.

Page 226     No. 940
Isaac Taylor - 200 acres on French Broad River, adjoining Joseph Gist,
to mouth of Dumpling Creek then along Taylor's line. Alexander Martin
at Newbern, 26 December 1791.

Page 227     No. 150
Adam Meek - 600 acres on Raspberry Creek, northside Holston River,
beginning at Raspberry's upper line. Richard Caswell at Kinston, 23
April 1787.

Page 228     No. 852
Joseph McMurtrey - 100 acres. Alexander Martin at Fayetteville, 17
November 1790.

Page 229     No. 845
Alexander Moore - 200 acres on Cedar Creek, adjoining James Sherril,
Craig. Alexander Martin at Fayetteville, 17 November 1790.

Page 229     No. 825
William Cox - 140 acres on Sinking Creek, waters of Nolachucky River.
Alexander Martin at Danberry, 13 February 1791.

Page 230     No. 1026
William Nelson - 200 acres on Sinking Creek, northside Chucky River,
adjoining McGill, John Johnston. Alexander Martin at Newbern, 26
December 1791.

Page 231     No. 859
David Russell - 300 acres on Richland Creek, northside Nolachucky River.
Alexander Martin at Danberry, 11 May 1792.

Page 232     No. 833
Joseph Brown - 200 acres on Puncheon Camp Creek on Nolachucky River.
Alexander Martin, 17 November 1790.

Page 233     No. 832
Joseph Brown - 100 acres on French Broad River. Alexander Martin at
Fayetteville, 17 November 1790.

Page 233     No. 986
Hugh Brown Senr. and George House - 200 acres on Grassy Creek, waters of
Lick Creek, adjoining Joseph Brown and Hugh Brown. Alexander Martin at
Newbern, 26 December 1791.

Page 234     No. 867
Joseph Brown and Harry Rowan - 250 acres on Grassy Creek, adjoining Hugh
Brown. Alexander Martin at Fayetteville, 17 November 1790.

Page 235     No. 828
William Hughes - 400 acres on head of Dumpling Creek, adjoining Bradshaw.
Alexander Martin at Danberry, 13 February 1791.

Page 236     No. 415
James Short - 150 acres below Poor Valley Creek, northside Holston River,
adjoining Bunches entry. Richard Caswell at Kinston, 20 September 1787.

Page 237     No. 947
John Bennet - 300 acres on Branch of Richland Creek, northside Nolachucky

River, adjoining Benjamin Ray, Fishback, edge of Barrens. Alexander Martin at Newbern, 26 December 1791.

Page 237      No. 1069
James Richardson - 300 acres adjoining Hood, Beards, Thompson. Alexander Martin at Danberry, 20 July 1792.

Page 238      No. 974
John Ish - 200 acres southside Holston River at head of Blacks Branch. Alexander Martin at Newbern, 26 December 1791.

Page 239      No. 955
Thomas Buckingham - 600 acres on south side French Broad River, adjoining Shields Branch, Buckinghams Island. Alexander Martin at Newbern, 26 December 1791.

Page 240      No. 892
Michael Woods - 300 acres on Meadow Creek, adjoining Nolachucky River, crossing Meadow Creek, Samuel Sherril. Alexander Martin at Newbern, 26 December 1791.

Page 241      No. 980
Michael Woods - 200 acres on south side Tennessee River in 3rd large bottom below mouth of Holston River. Alexander Martin at Newbern, 26 December 1791.

Page 242      No. 896
Alexander McCleneghan - 475 acres on north side French Broad River at the Bent of said river, below mouth of Nolachucky River, adjoining Robert Lamb and Alexander Morrow. Alexander Martin at ____, 31 October 1791.

Page 243      No. 973
John Ish - 640 acres on south side Holston River, adjoining Peter Bowerman, an Indian grave. Alexander Martin at Newbern, 26 December 1791.

Page 244      No. 961
James Gallagher - 800 acres on Gallaghers Creek, south side Holston River, adjoining John McCulley, Robert Gillespie. Alexander Martin at Newbern, 26 December 1791.

Page 245      No. 981
John Hannah - on Nine Mile Creek. Alexander Martin at NewBern, 26 December 1791.

Page 245      No. 976
Tarrance Conner - 300 acres on south side Holston River. Alexander Martin at Newbern, 26 December 1791.

Page 246      No. 851
Christopher Myers - 100 acres on both sides Long Creek, beginning at mouth of Sinking Fork, adjoining Jacob Jackson, Dittes, Nathaniel Evans. Alexander Martin at Fayetteville, 17 November 1790.

Page 247      No. 956
Hugh Wear - 640 acres on Pistol Creek. Alexander Martin at Newbern, 26 December 1791.

Page 247      No. 981
Lawrence Glaze - 247 acres on south side Chuckey River, adjoining his old survey, Henry Earnest. Alexander Martin at Newbern, 26 December 1791.

Page 248    No. 997
Lawrence Glaze - 150 acres on south side Nolachucky River, adjoining
Alexander Evins called Walnut Bottom, Jeremiah Jack, Charles Deaveny.
Alexander Martin at Newbern, 26 December 1791.


Page 249    No. 982
Lawrence Glaze - 250 acres on south side Nolachucky River, adjoining
Henry Earnest. Alexander Martin at Newbern, 26 December 1791.


Page 250    No. 1024
Henry Peaton - 300 acres on Clear Creek near Mill Shoal, adjoining
Benjamin Holland. Alexander Martin at Newbern, 26 December 1791.


Page 250    No. 883
Flighman Smith - 164 acres adjoining Peter King. Alexander Martin at
Fayetteville, 17 November 1790.


Page 251    No. 844
Isaac Davis - 100 acres on the Double Lick Fork of Lick Creek. Alexander
Martin at Fayetteville, 17 November 1790.


Page 252    No. 109
Joseph Bird - 500 acres on bank of Little Pigeon, adjoining John Rentfroe
near an old Indian Town House marked B. Alexander Martin at Newbern, 26
December 1791.


Page 253    No. 826
William Elliot - 100 acres. Alexander Martin at Fayetteville, 17
November 1790.


Page 254    No. 989
Absalom Hayworth - 50 acres on Nolachucky River below mouth of Sinking
Creek, adjoining John Lovelady. Alexander Martin at Newbern, 26 December
1791.


Page 254    No. 1002
John Brumly - 40 acres on south side Nolachucky River, adjoining Mr.
Armstrong. Alexander Martin at Newbern, 26 December 1791.


Page 255    No. 32
John Webb - 100 acres on the southside of Nolachucky River, on river
bank, adjoining William Nelson. Richard Caswell at Kinston, 1 November
1786.


Page 256    No. 49
Michael Hatter - 200 acres on waters of Nolachucky River. Samuel Johnston at Edenton, 11 August 1789.


Page 257    No. 859
Robert McTear - 800 acres on Ellijoy Creek, adjoining Benjamin Tipton,
McKair, Samuel Bogle, Williams. Alexander Martin at Newbern, 26 December
1791.


Page 257    No. 1041
Garret Fitzgerald, Michael and John Swingle - 400 acres on northside of
French Broad River. Alexander Martin at Hillsborough, 14 April 1792.


Page 258    No. 1004
James Pierce - 300 acres northside of Nolachucky River at mouth of
Richland Creek, running along river and including an island, adjoining
Dunham. Alexander Martin at Newbern, 26 December 1791.

Page 259    No. 824
Alexander Mebane, assignee of Isaac Taylor - 2000 acres in Greene County
on Tennessee River at mouth of Tellico River. Alexander Martin at ____,
__ April 1791.

Page 260    No. 949
William Hutchison - 150 acres on waters of Cove Creek, southside Nola-
chucky River, adjoining Acquilla Sherrill, Houston, Samuel Wilson.
Alexander Martin at Newbern, 26 December 1791.

Page 260    No. 77
Matthew Willeba - 640 acres on south side Holston River on the head of
Painter Creek. Alexander Martin at Danberry, 13 February 1791.

Page 261    No. 979
William Hutton - 1200 acres on Bakers Creek, adjoining Robert Wilson,
John Jackson, Samuel Henry. Alexander Martin at Newbern, 26 December
1791.

Page 262    No. 1038
Garret Fitzgerald - 400 acres on bank of Lick Creek, adjoining Moore
(formerly Waits) including an improvement. Alexander Martin at Hillsborough, 14 April 1792.

Page 262    No. 1005
Joseph Lovelady - 200 acres on Sinking Fork of Oven Creek, south side
Nolachucky River, including Joseph Birds improvement, adjoining Nelson.
Alexander Martin at Newbern, 26 December 1791.

Page 263    No. 901
George Hopkin - 200 acres on northside French Broad River on the Sinking
Cain, adjoining David Brown. Alexander Martin at Newbern, 26 December
1791.

Page 264    No. 1039
Garret Fitzgerald, Michael and John Swingle - 1000 acres on northside
French Broad River, including Benjamin Wilcox improvement, adjoining
James Kennedy. Alexander Martin at Hillsborough, 14 April 1790.

Page 265    No. 40
Thomas and Alexander Greer - 5000 acres on south side Duck River, Middle
District. Samuel Johnston at Fairfield, 10 July 1788.

Page 266    No. 866
John Ryan - 150 acres on Clear Fork of Lick Creek in Washington County,
including spring where Edered Erbry is on. Samuel Johnston at Fayetteville, 26 November 1789.

Page 266    No. 993
James Pierce - 150 acres on Moses Moore's line, adjoining Benjamin Ray,
William Glass. Alexander Martin at Newbern, 26 December 1791.

Page 267    No. 894
Samuel Montgomery - 220 acres on waters of Long Creek, northside French
Broad River, adjoining George Hopkins, William Lemmons. Alexander Martin
at ____, 1 October 1791.

Page 268    No. 960
David Rankin - 100 acres on head branch of Moors Creek in Washington
County, adjoining David Campbell, Delany. Alexander Martin at Danberry,
11 May 1792.

Page 269     No. 51
David Johnston - 200 acres on north side French Broad River, near mouth
of Little Laurel Creek. Alexander Martin at Newbern, 26 December 1791.

Page 269     No. 941
John Loyd - 150 acres on Meadow Creek on waters of Nolachucky River,
adjoining Hugh Heir, John Grant, Samuel Gregg, Richard Gullet. Alexander
Martin at Newbern, 26 December 1791.

Page 270     No. 885
David Johnston - 44 acres in the Forks of Long Creek between French
Broad and Nolachucky Rivers, including the Punching Camp. Alexander
Martin at Fayetteville, 17 November 1790.

Page 271     No. 1008
David Johnston - 100 acres on Matthews Branch, south side Nolachucky
River, adjoining Jervis. Alexander Martin at Newbern, 26 December 1791.

Page 272     No. 1044
Samuel Hill - 375 acres below fork of Nolachucky and French Broad Rivers,
adjoining Gideon Richey. Alexander Martin at Hillsborough, 14 April 1792.

Page 272     No. 1046
John Swingle - 200 acres on the north side of French Broad River, on
road that goes to Copeland Mill, adjoining James Bryant. Alexander
Martin at Hillsborough, 14 April 1792.

Page 273     No. 1040
Garret Fitzgerald, Michael and John Swingle - northside French Broad
River, adjoining Stephen Copeland and Fitzgeralds own line. Alexander
Martin at Hillsborough, 14 April 1792.

Page 274     No. 567
Jacob McConnel - 200 acres on Clear Creek, waters of French Broad River,
adjoining James Anderson, Nicholas Neal and Frederick Swaggerty. 20
September 1787.

Page 275     No. 823
Alexander Mebane - 500 acres on a Fork of Nine Mile Creek, south side
Tedford's Branch, adjoining George Tedford. Alexander Martin at Hills-
borough, 14 April 1791.

Page 276     No. 957
Samuel Wear - 700 acres on Crooked Creek. Alexander Martin at Newbern,
26 December 1791.

Page 276     No. 909
John Fien - 200 acres on north side French Broad River, on a branch of
Clear Creek, adjoining Swaggerty. Alexander Martin at Newbern, 26
December 1791.

Page 277     No. 952
Samuel McGahey, William McGahey and John McCroskey - 3000 acres on Loyd's
Creek. Alexander Martin at Newbern, 26 December 1791.

Page 278     No. 822
Alexander Mebane - 250 acres on Tennessee River, opposite John Cowans.
Alexander Martin, April 1791.

Page 279     No. 907
Henry Cross - 100 acres on Long Fork of Lick Creek. Alexander Martin at
Newbern, 26 December 1791.

Page 280    No. 960
Archibald Sloan - 640 acres in Washington County.  Alexander Martin at Newbern, 26 December 1791.

Page 280    No. 907
Daniel Rawlings - 300 acres on Lick Creek at mouth of Long Fork of Lick Creek, adjoining Patrick Morris.  Alexander Martin at Fayetteville, 17 November 1790.

Page 281    No. 999
David Johnston Senr. - 200 acres on north side French Broad River on Long Creek.  Alexander Martin at Newbern, 26 December 1791.

Page 282    No. 859
Adam Wilhite - 200 acres in Washington County on Camp Creek, adjoining Thomas Morgan, Caldwell and Hughes.  Samuel Johnston at Edenton, 18 May 1789.

Page 283    No. 874
James Paul - 640 acres on north side of Holston River, opposite to the mouth of Little River.  Alexander Martin at Fayetteville, 17 November 1791.

Page 284    No. 928
James Johnston - 150 acres on south side Nolachucky River, adjoining himself.  Alexander Martin at Newbern, 26 December 1791.

Page 284    No. 738
John Cunningham - 100 acres on south side Nolachucky River on both sides of Cove Creek, adjoining Wall, Charles Robertson, Ryters.  Samuel Johnston at Fairfield, 11 July 1788.

Page 284    No. 953
Samuel McGaughey, John McCroskey and William McGaughey - 300 acres on south side French Broad River on west fork of Knobb Creek.  Alexander Martin at Newbern, 26 December 1791.

Page 286    No. 959
David Rankin - 100 acres on head of Moores Creek, adjoining David Campbell, Washington County.  Alexander Martin at Danberry, 11 May 1792.

Page 287    No. 1015
John Jones - 200 acres on the east side of Lick Creek on the Dividing Ridge between Lick Creek and Grassy Creek, adjoining William Frances.  Alexander Martin at Newbern, 26 December 1791.

Page 288    No. 313
George Halmark - 350 acres on both sides of Lick Creek, including his improvement, adjoining James Armstrong.  Richard Caswell at Kinston, 20 September 1787.

Page 289    No. 968
David Scott - 400 acres on a branch of Crooked Creek.  Alexander Martin at Newbern, 26 December 1791.

Page 290    No. 1050
John Crockett - 300 acres southside of the main Holston Road within a few miles of Perkins Iron Works on Mossy Creek, waters of Holston River, adjoining Grills.  Alexander Martin at Hillsborough, 14 April 1792.

Page 290    No. 948
Joseph Pryar - 200 acres on Cove Creek, adjoining Sherril.  Alexander Martin at Newbern, 26 December 1791.

Page 291     No. 893
Thomas Morgan - 50 acres on south side Nolachucky River on Camp Creek, at
mouth of watery fork of Camp Creek, adjoining Francis Hughes, Bowman.
26 December 1791.

Page 292     No. ___
Benjamin Gist, assignee of C. Lowry - 395 acres on south side Little
Chuckey, adjoining Stewarts. Richard Dobbs Spraight at Newbern, 12
January 1793.

Page 293     No. 109
John Thompson - 150 acres adjoining Seven Island Tract. Richard Dobbs
Spraight at Newbern, 12 January 1793.

Page 293     No. 914
Daniel Reed - 250 acres on north side Nolachucky River on Pidgeons Creek,
adjoining William Brumley. Alexander Martin at Newbern, 26 December 1791.

Page 294     No. 719
James Cameron - 200 acres on south side Nolachucky River and east side of
Cove Creek, adjoining Ephraim Wilson. Samuel Johnston at Fairfield, 11
July 1788.

Page 295     No. 660
John Gibson - 100 acres on Pidgeon Creek, north side Nolachucky River,
adjoining Daniel Reed, John Gass. Alexander Martin at Danberry, 17 May
1792.

Page 296     No. 911
Thomas Love - 80 acres on south side Nolachucky River, including a bent
in river, adjoining Joseph Epperson. Alexander Martin at Newbern, 26
December 1791.

Page 297     No. 1055
John Shields - 153 acres on a Draft of Long Creek of Nolachucky River.
Alexander Martin at Danberry, 11 May 1792.

Page 297     No. 1130
Amos Bird - 300 acres on the northside of Nolachucky River. Richard
Dobbs Spraight, 12 January 1793.

Page 298     No. 817
Isaac Taylor - 500 acres on north side Nolachucky River. Alexander
Martin at Fayetteville, 27 November 1789.

Page 299     No. 1023
Andrew Martin - 100 acres on the head of the second creek, including
Robert Herald's improvement, adjoining Moore, John Patterson. Alexander
Martin at Newbern, 26 December 1791.

Page 300     No. 341
Michael Barnet - 200 acres on South Fork of Clear Creek, adjoining Jacob
Borden. Richard Dobbs Spraight at Newbern, 8 March 1793.

Page 300     No. 972
Benjamin Crow - 200 acres. _____ at NewBern, 26 December 1792.

Page 301     No. 1056
John Liggett, Joseph Dobson and Frances Brotherson - 300 acres on Big
Gap Creek, adjoining Joseph Self. Alexander Martin at Danberry, 11
May 1792.

124

Page 302    No. 945
Thomas Tadlock - 100 acres on Clear Creek in Washington County, adjoining
James Hust.  Alexander Martin at Fayetteville, 17 November 1790.


Page 303    No. 988
Benjamin Rector - 200 acres on the west side of Lick Creek, a place
called Cane Camp, adjoining Lemuel Hebbert and James Manghen.  26
December 1791.


Page 304    No. 1089
John Smith - 500 acres nigh Camp Creek, adjoining Donahue.  Richard Dobbs
Spraight at Newbern, 12 January 1793.


Page 305    No. 1256
George Gillespy - 100 acres on the head of McCartneys Branch, south side
McCartney's Mountain, adjoining John Denton.  Alexander Martin at Newbern,
27 November 1792.


Page 306    No. 1245
Joseph Kerns - 400 acres by the head of a creek that runs into Holston
River, adjoining Lyons, Brown.  Alexander Martin at Newbern, 27 November
1792.


Page 306    No. 1249
Hugh Beard - 100 acres on Deep Creek, northside French Broad River,
adjoining himself.  Richard Dobbs Spraight at Newbern, 29 July 1793.


Page 307    No. 1215
John Byrd - 100 acres northside French Broad River.  Richard Dobbs
Spraight at Newbern, 24 July 1793.


Page 307    No. 1248
Joseph Dameron - 200 acres adjoining Hoggs.  Richard Dobbs Spraight at
Newbern, 29 July 1793.


Page 308    No. 1262
William Morrow - 100 acres northside French Broad River, adjoining himself.  Richard Dobbs Spraight at Newbern, 29 July 1793.


Page 309    No. 1251
Joshua Gist - 150 acres northside French Broad River on Dumpling Creek.
Richard Dobbs Spraight at Newbern, 29 July 1793.


Page 309    No. 1246
William Hadley - 150 acres on Drafts of Tuckahoe Creek, north side French
Broad River.  Richard Dobbs Spraight at Newbern, 29 July 1793.


Page 310    No. 1205
Jonathan Langdon - 640 acres on Grassy Creek, waters of Beaver Dam Creek,
adjoining John Blair.  Alexander Martin at NewBern, 17 November 1792.


Page 310    No. 1226
William Wallace - 200 acres on north side French Broad River.  Richard
Dobbs Spraight at Newbern, 29 July 1793.


Page 311    No. 1242
John Kerns - 400 acres on waters of Tuckahoe Creek, on French Broad
River, adjoining James Moore.  Alexander Martin at Newbern, 27 November
1792.


Page 311    No. 1269
Martin Prewitt - 100 acres on Lick Creek, adjoining Nathaniel Davis,
John Howard, James English.  29 July 1793.

Page 312      No. 132
Michael Woods - 400 acres on south side Tennessee River, third large
bottom below mouth of Holston River, adjoining himself.  Richard Dobbs
Spraight at Newbern, 14 January 1792.

Page 312      No. 1266
John Baggs - 100 acres on waters of Little Chuckey.  Richard Dobbs
Spraight at Newbern, 20 July 1793.

Page 313      No. 1075
Samuel Atherton - 100 acres on Clay Lick Creek, south side Nolachucky
River, adjoining himself.  Richard Dobbs Spraight at Newbern, 12 January
1793.

Page 314      No. 1218
Thomas Lee - 100 acres south side Holston River at mouth of Medavns?
Branch.  Alexander Martin at Newbern, 27 November 1792.

Page 314      No. 1268
Thomas Gragg and Thomas Potter - 600 acres adjoining John Slawter, Henry
Gragg.  Richard Dobbs Spraight at Newbern, 29 July 1793.

Page 316      No. 1263
James Jones - 100 acres on Clear Branch of Lick Creek, adjoining Joseph
Henderson.  Alexander Martin at Newbern, 27 November 1792.

Page 316      No. 1217
Hugh Brown - 100 acres on north side French Broad River, including a
sinking spring, adjoining James White.  Richard Dobbs Spraight at
Newbern, 29 July 1793.

Page 317      No. 1100
Andrew Belfour - 300 acres on Swan Pond, adjoining 640 acres of David
Campbell, known as Swan Ponds.  Richard Dobbs Spraight at Newbern, 12
January 1792.

Page 318      No. 1217
Frederick Whittenberger - 300 acres on a Draft of Richland Creek.
Alexander Martin at Newbern, 27 November 1792.

Page 319      No. 1105
John Bird - 200 acres adjoining Phillip Bird.  Richard Dobbs Spraight at
Newbern, 12 January 1792.

Page 319      No. 1260
John Glass - 100 acres on the waters of Pigeon Creek, adjoining Samuel
McGill, William Wyatt, William Logan.  Alexander Martin at Newbern, 27
November 1792.

Page 320      No. 1243
John Crockett - 197 acres on waters of Lick Creek, Stocktons Fork.
Alexander Martin at Newbern, 27 November 1792.

Page 321      No. 1115
Francis Hughes - 640 acres on south side Nolachucky River, adjoining
English.  Richard Dobbs Spraight at Newbern, 12 July 1793.

Page 322      No. 1204
Frederick Swaggerty - 100 acres on Clear Creek, adjoining himself and
Parrott.  Richard Dobbs Spraight at Newbern, 8 March 1793.

Page 322      No. 1202
Frederick Swaggerty - 200 acres on Clear Creek.  Richard Dobbs Spraight

at Newbern, 8 March 1793.


Page 323    No. 1262
George Gillespy - 100 acres on McCartney's Creek.  Alexander Martin at
Newbern, 27 November 1792.


Page 324    No. 1255
George Gillespy - 50 acres on McCartney's Creek, north side Nolachucky
River.  Alexander Martin at Newbern, 27 November 1792.


Page 325    No. 1227
George Gillaspy - 100 acres on McCartney's Creek.  Alexander Martin at
Newbern, 27 November 1792.


Page 325    No. 1206
Samuel Frazier - 300 acres on Sinking Creek, adjoining Ellis, William
Reese, Jones.  Alexander Martin at Newbern, 27 November 1792.


Page 326    No. ___
Guilford Dudley - 5000 acres on Duck River.  Alexander Martin at Hillsborough, 3 August 1792.


Page 327    No. 1223
John Williby - 100 acres on Stony Creek, waters of Lick Creek, adjoining
James Pickens.  Richard Dobbs Spraight at Newbern, 29 July 1793.


Page 328    No. 1215
Samuel Frazier - 100 acres on head of Little Sinking Creek, adjoining
William Reese.  Alexander Martin at Newbern, 27 November 1792.


Page 328    No. 1242
John Stone - 200 acres north side Nolachucky River, adjoining McCroskey,
Buckingham, Robert Campbell.  Richard Dobbs Spraight at Newbern, 29 July
1793.


Page 329    No. 1220
Henry Cross - 200 acres on Sinking Fork of Lick Creek, adjoining Drew
Morris, Shadrach Morris.  Richard Dobbs Spraight at Newbern, 29 July
1793.


Page 330    No. 1210
William Reese - 500 acres on Little Sinking Creek, adjoining Samuel
Frazier, E. Jone, Stanbrough, E. Ellis, J. Ellis, R. Paris.  Alexander
Martin at Newbern, 27 November 1792.


Page 331    No. 1221
Isaac Davis - 100 acres on waters of Lick Creek.  Richard Dobbs Spraight
at Newbern, 29 July 1793.


Page 332    No. 1273
John Shields - 200 acres on Vinnett Fines line, adjoining himself and
Fine.  Richard Dobbs Spraight at Newbern, 29 July 1793.


Page 333    No. 1211
James Woods Lackey and John Shields - 53 acres on north side of French
Broad River, corner to Francis Dean, adjoining Dean and Kelsey.  Richard
Dobbs Spraight at Newbern, 29 July 1793.


Page 334    No. 1207
John Shields and James Woods Lackey - 640 acres on northside French Broad
River, adjoining Francis Dean, Kelso, on Great Road, Charles Tully.
Richard Dobbs Spraight at Newbern, 29 July 1793.

Page 335     No. 1216
Andrew Simpson - 200 acres on Dry Fork of Lick Creek, adjoining Casteel.
Alexander Martin at Newbern, 27 November 1792.

Page 335     No. 1651
James Woods Lackey, for officers and soldiers in the Continental,
assignee of John Wood, Private in said Continental line - at the head
of McClouds Branch.  Richard Dobbs Spraight at Newbern, 29 July 1793.

Page 336     No. 1248
James Robenson - 50 acres on the line of Anthony Kelly and himself.
Alexander Martin at Newbern, 27 November 1792.

Page 337     No. 1235
Samuel Robbins - 100 acres on north side Nolachucky River on French Creek,
adjoining Edward Crump.  Alexander Martin at Newbern, 27 November 1792.

Page 338     No. 1232
John Wear - 200 acres on north side Nolachucky River, 3rd bottom below
mouth of Richland Creek, crossing into an island, adjoining Jacob Bean.
Alexander Martin at Newbern, 27 November 1792.

Page 338     No. 1240
Samuel Baker - 100 acres on Horse Creek, south side Nolachucky River,
adjoining John Byrd, George Baker.  Richard Dobbs Spraight at Newbern,
29 July 1793.

Page 339     No. 1222
Joseph Williams - 200 acres on Dry Fork of Clear Creek, adjoining Jacob
Borden, Bigam, Williams other land.  Alexander Martin at Newbern, 27
November 1792.

Page 340     No. 1214
Anthony Bewley - 100 acres on north side Nolachucky River, adjoining John
Bewley.  Alexander Martin at Newbern, 27 November 1792.

Page 341     No. 1231
Solomon Hoggett - 100 acres on Sinking Creek, branch of Lick Creek.
Alexander Martin at Newbern, 27 November 1792.

Page 341     No. 1207
John McCroskey - 100 acres on Holleys Creek, adjoining Hughes, Holley.
Richard Dobbs Spraight at Newbern, 29 July 1793.

Page 342     No. 1261
John White - 100 acres on Dividing Ridge between Sinking Creek and Lick
Creek, adjoining Thomas Rease.  Alexander Martin at Newbern, 27 November
1792.

Page 343     No. 1233
John Reed - 150 acres on Harmon Kings line.  Richard Dobbs Spraight at
Newbern, 29 July 1793.

Page 344     No. 1229
Benjamin Iddins - 70 acres on head of Sinking Creek.  Alexander Martin
at Newbern, 27 November 1792.

Page 344     No. 863
James Hutcheson - 100 acres at mouth of Oven Creek, south side Nolachucky
River, adjoining Joseph Berd, David Russell.  Alexander Martin at Newbern,
17 November 1792.

Page 345     No. 1199
John Borden - 250 acres on south side Nolachucky River on Sinking Creek,
adjoining Henry Roads, Thomas Gilbreath.  Richard Dobbs Spraight at
Newbern, 29 July 1793.


Page 346     No. 1219
Samuel Lewis - 100 acres on the head of McCartney's Branch, adjoining
William Liggett.  Richard Dobbs Spraight at Newbern, 29 July 1793.


Page 347     No. 1244
Joshua Low - 100 acres north side Nolachucky River, adjoining Joshua
Whittenberger, Baker, Woods.  Alexander Martin at Newbern, 27 November
1792.


Page 347     No. 1260
Richard Morgan - 300 acres on Dumplin Creek.  Richard Dobbs Spraight at
Newbern, 27 July 1792.


Page 348     No. 1247
Benjamin McFarland - 200 acres on north side French Broad River, adjoin-
ing Charles Gentry, Hugh Kelsey.  Richard Dobbs Spraight at Newbern, 29
July 1793.


Page 349     No. 1253
Jonathan Tribut - 100 acres on waters of Meadow Creek, north side Nolachucky River.  Richard Dobbs Spraight at Newbern, 29 July 1793.


Page 350     No. 1257
John McAlister, Thomas Hart, William Duglas and John Sharp - 1000 acres
on Cumberland River, on Spring Creek.  Richard Dobbs Spraight at Newbern,
30 July 1793.


Page 350     No. 1209
John Jackson - 300 acres on Limestone Creek, adjoining Andrew Jackson,
Davis, Delaney.  Alexander Martin at Newbern, 7 November 1792.


Page 351     No. 1254
Daniel Harrison - 300 acres on south side Nolachucky River at the mouth
of Cove Creek.  Richard Dobbs Spraight at Newbern, 29 July 1793.


Page 352     No. 1256
Archibald McSpadden - 400 acres on Doaks and Dry Creek, waters of Holston
River.  Richard Dobbs Spraight at Newbern, 29 July 1793.


Page 353     No. 1218
Phillip Babb - 100 acres on the waters of Stockton Creek, adjoining Babb.
Richard Dobbs Spraight at Newbern, 29 July 1793.


Page 353     No. 1247
Barnet Brumley - 200 acres on south side Nolachucky River, adjoining
Shadrach McNew, Johnson.  Alexander Martin at Newbern, 27 November 1792.


Page 354     No. 1003
Moses Moore - 200 acres in Washington County on Big Limestone and Browns
Creeks, adjoining J. Gillihan and Thomas Brown, including Moses Moore
Junr. improvement.  Alexander Martin at Newbern, 27 November 1792.


Page 355     No. 1234
George Smith - 250 acres on Panther Creek, adjoining David Southerland.
Richard Dobbs Spraight at Newbern, 29 July 1793.


Page 356     No. 1231
Benjamin Merrot - 300 acres on south side Clinch River on Sycamore Creek,

adjoining Thomas King.  Richard Dobbs Spraight at Newbern, 29 July 1793.

Page 356      No. 1012
Jasper Miller - 200 acres on Lanty Armstrong's line and Stone line.
Alexander Martin at Newbern, 26 December 1791.

Page 357      No. 362
James Millaken - 150 acres on the South Fork of Cedar Branch of Lick
Creek, adjoining Joseph Henderson, John Odle, Permenas Taylor.  Richard
Caswell at Kingston, 20 September 1787.

Page 358      No. 1244
James Gilbreath - 640 acres on Drafts of Richland Creek, adjoining John
Gibson.  Richard Dobbs Spraight at Newbern, 29 July 1793.

Page 359      No. 1264
Samuel Robinson - 100 acres on north side Nolachucky River on French
Creek.  Alexander Martin at Newbern, 27 November 1792.

Page 360      No. 1065
Francis Alexander Ramsey - 150 acres on north side Nolachucky River and
west side of Sinking Creek, adjoining Joseph Whittenberg.  Alexander
Martin at Danberry, 11 May 1792.

Page 361      No. 891
Robert Kirkpatrick - 300 acres on Plumb Creek, including the War Path,
adjoining David Linsey, John Blare.  Alexander Martin at Fayetteville,
17 November 1790.

Page 361      No. 984
John Wilson - 100 acres adjoining Samuel Wilson.  Alexander Martin at
Newbern, 26 December 1791.

Page 362      No. 865
Isaiah Vinsandtt - 356 acres in Greene County, adjoining Hutchison, John
Wilson.  Alexander Martin at Fayetteville, 17 November 1790.

Page 363      No. 933
Isaac Vinsant - 585 acres on Cove Creek, south side Nolachucky River,
adjoining John Lescollet, Huston, mountain side.  Alexander Martin at
Newbern, 26 December 1791.

Page 364      No. 932
Isaac Vinzant and James Pierce - 200 acres on south side Nolachucky River
on Cove Creek, adjoining Andrew Miller, foot of mountain along Cove Mt.,
Charles Robenson, Hackett.  Alexander Martin at Newbern, 26 December
1791.

Page 365      No. 1122
Sparling Bowman - 100 acres on watery fork of Camp Creek, adjoining
McDonald, Hopsons line.  Richard Dobbs Spraight at Newbern, 12 January
1793.

Page 366      No. 1230
John Bull - 55 acres on Bulls Gap of Bays Mountain.  Alexander Martin at
Newbern, 27 November 1792.

Page 366      No. 976
Thomas Gillespy - 200 acres on west side Nolachucky River - Washington
County.  Alexander Martin at Newbern, 26 December 1791.

Page 367      No. 925
Samuel Lewis - 100 acres on the head of McCartney's Branch, adjoining an

entry 7, Hannah. Alexander Martin at Newbern, 26 December 1791.

Page 368     No. 887
Thomas Johnston - 640 acres on Bent Creek, including the Crab Orchard,
beginning at Blue Spring west side Bent Creek, adjoining James Roddy,
Haines Branch. Alexander Martin at Fayetteville, 17 November 1790.

Page 369     No. 1255
Henry Willis - 400 acres on south side Nolachucky River, including his
improvement, adjoining Corin, Oarrs. Richard Dobbs Spraight at Newbern,
29 July 1793.

Page 370     No. 282
James Woods Lackey - 640 acres on the Swan Pond Creek, south side Holston
River. Richard Dobbs Spraight at Newbern, 14 January 1793.

Page 371     No. 828
Thomas Blackburn - 200 acres on Camp Creek, waters of Nolachucky River.
Alexander Martin at Fayetteville, 17 November 1790.

Page 371     No. 1241
Joseph Brown - 200 acres on north side French Broad River, on Cabbin
Branch. Alexander Martin at Newbern, 27 November 1792.

Page 372     No. 1238
David Allison - 260 acres on north side Nolachucky River on Richland
Creek, adjoining David Russell. Alexander Martin at Newbern, 27 November
1792.

Page 373     No. 1238
David Rankin - 100 acres on Head Drafts of Stories Creek, north side
Nolachucky River. Richard Dobbs Spraight at Newbern, 29 July 1793.

Page 374     No. 1263
Isaac Thomas - 100 acres on Starktons Mill Creek, a branch of Lick Creek,
adjoining Dutton Lain, John Morris. Richard Dobbs Spraight at Newbern,
29 July 1793.

Page 374     No. 1258
John Reed - 150 acres on north side Nolachucky River at mouth of Meadow
Creek, adjoining Alexander McFarland, including an island. Alexander
Martin at Newbern, 27 November 1792.

Page 375     No. 450
William Ritchey - 299 acres in Washington County on Sinking Fork of Lick
Creek. Alexander Martin at Hillsborough, 13 October 1783.

Page 376     No. 440
Henry Cross - 100 acres on Cedar Fork of Lick Creek in Washington County,
including a large spring above the Horse Camp. Alexander Martin at
Hillsborough, 13 October 1783.

Page 377     No. 1011
Benjamin Carter - 100 acres on Roaring Fork of Lick Creek, adjoining John
Carter, Stanfield. Alexander Martin at Newbern, 26 December 1791.

Page 378     No. 1240
Thomas Jonokin - 3960 acres on north side of Holston River on Richland
Creek. Richard Dobbs Spraight at Newbern, 29 July 1793.

Page 379     No. 910
Samuel Humber - 50 acres on waters of Lick Creek, adjoining his land,
Samuel Cotter, Thomas Ray. Martin at Newbern, 26 December 1791.

Page 380     No. 1245
Daniel Anderson - 100 acres on the waters of Edwards Branch, adjoining
Patrick Kirkpatrick. Alexander Martin at Newbern, 27 November 1792.

Page 380     No. 1127
Isaac Collet - 640 acres on south side Nolachucky River, including bottom
with Indian Cabbin. Richard Dobbs Spraight at Newbern, 12 January 1793.

Page 381     No. 1274
James Dunlap - 500 acres on west side French Broad River, adjoining Jane
Calvert, Millerans? Creek, Robert Calvert and Cantry. Richard Dobbs
Spraight at Newbern, 29 July 1793.

Page 382     No. 1133
James Johnston - 300 acres on south side Nolachucky River on Flat Rock
Branch, adjoining Robert Oneal, Thomas Johnston. Richard Dobbs Spraight
at Newbern, 12 January 1793.

Page 382     No. 1236
David Johnston - 300 acres on north side French Broad River. Richard
Dobbs Spraight at Newbern, 29 July 1793.

Page 383     No. 1259
Britten Smith - 200 acres on the head of Bent Creek, adjoining James Lee,
Jesse Cheek. Alexander Martin at Newbern, 27 November 1792.

Page 384     No. 1223
David Taylor - 100 acres adjoining Moore. Alexander Martin at Newbern,
27 November 1792.

Page 385     No. 853
Lewis Christian - 250 acres on Lick Fork of Bent Creek. Alexander Martin
at Fayetteville, 17 November 1790.

Page 385     No. 818
Isaac Bullard - 100 acres on north side Lick and Swan Pond Creek.
Alexander Martin at Fayetteville, 19 November 1790.

Page 386     No. 1226
John Savage - 200 acres on Nolachucky River, adjoining Joseph Lovelady.
Alexander Martin at Newbern, 27 November 1792.

Page 387     No. 1230
Isaiah Harrison - 200 acres on south side Chuckey River, adjoining Henry
Willis. Richard Dobbs Spraight at Newbern, 29 July 1793.

Page 388     No. 1264
Joseph Lusk - 350 acres on waters of Little Chuckey, adjoining James
Swan, Thompson, Davis. Richard Dobbs Spraight at Newbern, 29 July 1793.

Page 388     No. 127
James Woods Lackey - 400 acres in our Eastern District on the northside
Holston River and south side Sinking Creek. Richard Dobbs Spraight at
Newbern, 14 January 1793.

Page 389     No. 1072
Seth Smith - 200 acres on Stones Creek, adjoining John Delaney, David
Campbell. Smith is assignee of Joseph Whittenberger. Richard Dobbs
Spraight at Newbern, 26 December 1792.

Page 390     No. 1071
Michael Bacon - 200 acres on French Broad River. Richard Dobbs Spraight
at Newbern, 24 December 1792.

Page 391      No. 717
Jordon Roach - 640 acres on Holston River, including Rock House on Cove
Spring. Samuel Johnston at Fairfield, 11 July 1788.

Page 391      No. 305
Michael Reed - 132 acres on the Buffaloe Branch of Pigeon Creek, adjoining James Boxs, John Chambliss. Richard Caswell at Kinston, 20 September
1787.

Page 392      No. 1112
George Gillaspie - 300 acres on the Cedar Branch. Richard Dobbs Spraight
at Newbern, 12 January 1793.

Page 393      No. 1074
George Gillaspie Junr. - 310 acres on north side Nolachucky River on
McCartney's Branch, adjoining Drain, Reese, McCartneys Mountain and
Stanfield. Richard Dobbs Spraight at Newbern, 12 January 1793.

Page 394      No. 1174
Elisha Baker - 200 acres on north side French Broad River on both sides
Long Creek, adjoining himself, William Bigham. Richard Dobbs Spraight
at Newbern, 12 January 1793.

Page 395      No. 1170
Elisha Baker - 300 acres on Long Creek down Walnut Valley, including
Baker's improvement, adjoining William Boyd, Andrew Bigham. Richard
Dobbs Spraight at Newbern, 12 January 1793.

Page 395      No. 1031
William Boilston - 200 acres on north side French Broad River on Sinking
Creek, adjoining David Brown. Alexander Martin at Newbern, 26 December
1791.

Page 396      No. 1128
William Ranken - 100 acres on Little Chuckey Creek, including his improve-
ment, adjoining Nicholas Davis. Richard Dobbs Spraight at Newbern, 12
January 1793.

Page 397      No. 1124
James Milliken - 200 acres on north side Nolachucky River, adjoining
Thomas Ray. Richard Dobbs Spraight at Newbern, 12 January 1793.

Page 398      No. 1082
Adonijah Morgan - 200 acres on Camp Creek, adjoining Thomas Davis, east
side of Camp Creek. Richard Dobbs Spraight at Newbern, 12 January 1793.

Page 399      No. 1104
Thomas Davis - 200 acres adjoining his former survey on Camp Creek.
Richard Dobbs Spraight at Newbern, 12 January 1793.

Page 400      No. 1172
Samuel Ellis - 200 acres on Long Fork of Sinking Creek, north side Nolachucky River, adjoining John Ellis, David Rankin. Spraight at Newbern,
12 January 1793.

Page 401      No. 1171
James Wright - 100 acres on north side Nolachucky River on Little Sinking
Creek, adjoining Owen Owens and spur of McCartney's Mountain. Richard
Dobbs Spraight at Newbern, 12 January 1793.

Page 402      No. 1161
Joseph Posey - 150 acres on south side Richland Creek, adjoining David
Allison. Richard Dobbs Spraight at Newbern, 12 January 1793.

Page 402     No. 57
Lanty Armstrong - 300 acres on Big Limestone in Washington County, adjoining John Williams, Lanthys Knobs. Alexander Martin at Fairfield, 23 October 1782.

Page 403     No. 1247
William Handley - 200 acres on north side Nolachucky River on a branch of Sinking Creek. 27 November 1792.

Page 404     No. 1228
John Delaney - 100 acres on north side Nolachucky River on Sinking Creek. Alexander Martin at Newbern, 27 November 1792.

Page 405     No. 989
James Rodger - 600 acres on Little Sinking Creek at foot of McCartney Mountain, adjoining Joseph Bullard. Richard Dobbs Spraight at Newbern, 14 January 1793.

Page 406     No. 1140
Alexander McFarlin - 200 acres on north side Nolachucky River. Sealed by Richard Dobbs Spraight at Newbern, 12 January 1793.

Page 407     No. 1176
John Shields - 400 acres on north side Dumplin Creek, adjoining Isaac Taylor, Thomas Rankin Senr., Richard Rankin. Richard Dobbs Spraight at Newbern, 12 January 1793.

Page 408     No. 1142
Robert Stephenson - 300 acres on Lick Creek, adjoining Charles Haus, James Ashmore, Lick Creek. Richard Dobbs Spraight at Newbern, 12 January 1793.

Page 409     No. 1152
Ewen Allison - 200 acres on north side French Broad River, northside Dumplin Creek, adjoining Nicolas Davis. Richard Dobbs Spraight at Newbern, 12 January 1793.

Page 409     No. 983
Daniel Rawlings - 440 acres adjoining Lick Creek Knobs in Washington County. Richard Dobbs Spraight at Newbern, 14 January 1793.

Page 410     No. 1237
James Swan - 100 acres on Little Chuckey in Greene County. Alexander Martin at Newbern, 27 November 1792.

Page 411     No. 1108
James McPheran - 350 acres southside Lick Creek, adjoining Hugh Cavender, Thomas Russell. Richard Dobbs Spraight at Newbern, 12 January 1793.

Page 412     No. 1249
Tilman Smith - 50 acres on a branch of Lick Creek. Alexander Martin at Newbern, 27 November 1792.

Page 413     No. 181
John Waddle - 600 acres westside of the mouth of McCall's Creek, adjoining Benjamin Holland. Richard Caswell at Kinston, 20 September 1787.

Page 414     No. 1162
John Waddle - 200 acres on McCalls Creek. Richard Dobbs Spraight at Newbern, 27 January 1793.

Page 415     No. 1267
John Murphey - 100 acres on Wolf Creek, adjoining his old entry. Richard

Dobbs Spraight at Newbern, 12 July 1793.


Page 415     No. 1221
John Woolsey - 100 acres between Pyburns and Pruet's land.  Richard Dobbs
Spraight at Newbern, 12 January 1793.


Page 416     No. 353
Claudius Bailey - 320 acres on south branch of Lick Creek.  Richard
Caswell at Kinston, 20 September 1787.


Page 417     No. 1237
Christopher Houts - 275 acres on Little Gap Creek and Big Lick Creek,
adjoining Benjamin Stewart and John Francisco.  Richard Dobbs Spraight
at Newbern, 12 July 1794.


Page 418     No. 1163
Thomas Whittaker - 200 acres on Blacks Creek running to Lick Creek,
adjoining John and James Gillaspy.  Richard Dobbs Spraight at Newbern,
12 January 1793.


Page 418     No. 1241
Leonard and Phillip Simmons - 100 acres on Little Chuckey, adjoining Boyd
and David Reed.  Richard Dobbs Spraight at Newbern, 12 January 1793.


Page 419     No. 1123
Frederick Whittenberg - 200 acres.  Richard Dobbs Spraight at Newbern,
12 January 1793.


Page 420     No. 1277
Jesse Bounds - 640 acres on the Roaring Fork and Dunhams Fork of Lick
Creek, adjoining Hankens and John Gist.  Spraight at Newbern, 12 July
1794.


Page 421     No. 1290
William Nelson - 100 acres on south side Nolachucky River, adjoining
Henry Kees.  Spraight at Newbern, 17 July 1794.


Page 422     No. 1294
Joseph Hickson - 60 acres on Middle Creek, south side Nolachucky River,
adjoining Gillespie.  Richard Dobbs Spraight at Newbern, 17 July 1794.


Page 423     No. ___
William Terrel - 300 acres on north side Nolachucky River on Long Creek,
adjoining Capt. James Hill's Mill Pond, crossing road to a Smith Shop.
Richard Dobbs Spraight at Newbern, 12 July 1794.


Page 423     No. 1251
Coonrod Barnhart - 200 acres on south side Nolachucky River, adjoining
Broyles, Hoover.  Richard Dobbs Spraight at Newbern, 12 July 1794.


Page 424     No. 1085
Samuel Henderson - 100 acres on headwaters of Long Creek, north side
French Broad River, including where he lives, adjoining Clements.
Richard Dobbs Spraight at Newbern, 12 January 1793.


Page 425     No. 1138
Samuel Henderson - 100 acres on south side Nolachucky River.  Richard
Dobbs Spraight at Newbern, 12 January 1794.


Page 426     No. 979
James English - 280 acres on both sides of Limestone Fork of Lick Creek
where he now lives.  Richard Dobbs Spraight at Newbern, 17 January 1793.

Page 427    No. 683
James English - 100 acres between his settlement and a survey that lies
on the War Path.  26 October 1786.


Page 428    No. 1279
David Rankin - 200 acres on Stories Creek, adjoining Herrolds land.
Spraight at Newbern, 12 July 1794.


Page 429    No. 749
James English - 100 acres on both sides Limestone Fork of Lick Creek.
Sealed 26 October 1786.


Page 430    No. 1218
Henry Newby - 150 acres on Lick Creek including Gasses Lick.  Richard
Dobbs Spraight at Newbern, 7 January 1793.


Page 430    No. 1218
Robert Henderson - 51 acres land adjoining Robert Greentree.  Richard
Dobbs Spraight at Newbern, 27 November 1793.


Page 431    No. 1242
Joseph Carter Junr. - 200 acres in Greene County adjoining Joseph Carter
Senr.  Richard Dobbs Spraight at Newbern, 12 January 1793.


Page 431    No. 1265
Michael Bryle - 100 acres in Greene County.  Richard Dobbs Spraight at
Newbern, 12 July 1794.


Page 432    No. 1236
Michael Broyles - 100 acres in Greene County adjoining Miller - watery
fork of Horse Creek.  Spraight in Newbern, 12 July 1794.


Page 433    No. 1243
William Hannah - 200 acres on Roaring Fork of Lick Creek, adjoining
William Britten.  Richard Dobbs Spraight at Newbern, 12 July 1794.


Page 433    No. 1154
Thomas Williamson - 100 acres in Greene County.  Richard Dobbs Spraight
at Newbern, 12 January 1793.


Page 434    No. 1245
Isaac Bullard - 340 acres on Lick Creek.  Richard Dobbs Spraight at
Newbern, 12 July 1794.


Page 435    No. 1297
James Ranken - 100 acres on Swan Pon Creek.  Richard Dobbs Spraight at
Newbern, 17 July 1794.


Page 436    No. 1266
James Davis - 50 acres on north side Nolachucky River.  Richard Dobbs
Spraight at Newbern, 12 July 1794.


Page 436    No. 1159
James Broyles - 200 acres west side Horse Creek, adjoining Emanuel
Sedusky, deceased.  Richard Dobbs Spraight at Newbern, 12 January 1793.


Page 437    No. 684
James English - 150 acres in Washington County on Limestone Fork of Lick
Creek.  Richard Dobbs Spraight at Newbern, 12 January 1793.


Page 438    No. 1167
James Broyles - 200 acres westside Horse Creek in Greene County, adjoin-

ing Jacob Broyles, John Waddle. Richard Dobbs Spraight at Newbern, 12 January 1793.

Page 439      No. 1222
Nathan Carter - 200 acres on Nolachucky River on Puncheon Camp Creek. Sealed by Richard Dobbs Spraight at Newbern, 12 January 1793.

Page 439      No. 1270
William Carr - 89 acres on south side Holston River, adjoining Robert Brown, McCulley. Richard Dobbs Spraight at Newbern, 12 July 1794.

Page 440      No. 1293
William Wilson and Phillip Fann - 100 acres on south side Nolachucky River on bank of river. Richard Dobbs Spraight at Newbern, 17 July 1794.

Page 441      No. 1234
Thomas Wyatt - 328 acres on a branch of Lick Creek called Alexander's Creek, beginning at head spring of creek. Richard Dobbs Spraight at Newbern, 12 July 1794.

Page 442      No. 1250
David Russell - 200 acres on Richland Creek, north side Nolachucky River, adjoining Hood, David Allison. Alexander Martin at Newbern, 27 November 1792.

Page 442      No. 1275
John Harris - 200 acres on south side Nolachucky River, corner to Robert Arawood. Richard Dobbs Spraight at Newbern, 12 July 1794.

Page 443      No. 1254
Guion Leeper - 400 acres on south side Tennessee River on a creek of the same. Richard Dobbs Spraight at Newbern, 12 July 1790.

Page 444      No. 1219
Jane Calvert - 300 acres on south bank of French Broad River below Hubbards Flat Landing, then to bank of Little Pigeon River. Richard Dobbs Spraight at Newbern, 27 November 1793.

Page 445      No. 1249
William Wyatt - 200 acres on Buffalo Branch of Pigeon Creek near John Glasses, adjoining John Bennet. Richard Dobbs Spraight at Newbern, 12 July 1794.

Page 445      No. 1271
Samuel Smith - 400 acres on north side of Tennessee River and branch of same name. Richard Dobbs Spraight at Newbern, 1794.

Page 446      No. 1299
Richard Nikelson - 200 acres on waters of Swan Pon Creek, adjoining Ashmores. Richard Dobbs Spraight at Newbern, 17 July 1784.

Page 447      No. 1305
Thomas Williamson - for 50 shillings per 100 acres - 640 acres on south side Nolachucky River on waters of Horse Creek. Richard Dobbs Spraight at Newbern, 17 July 1794.

Page 448      No. 1253
Phillip Hale - for 10 pounds per 100 acres - 200 acres on north side Nolachucky River on Grassy Creek, adjoining James Shore. Richard Dobbs Spraight at Newbern, 12 July 1794.

Page 449      No. 1227
Joseph Self - 100 acres on Big Gap Creek. Richard Dobbs Spraight at

Newbern, 12 January 1793.

Page 449     No. 1242
William Brylston - 200 acres adjoining William Leymonds.  Richard Dobbs
Spraight at Newbern, 12 July 1794.

Page 450     No. ___
James Delany - on Delanys Branch of Little Chucky.  Richard Dobbs
Spraight at Newbern, 17 July 1794.

Page 451     No. 1217
Jacob Gass - for 50 shillings per 100 acres - 50 acres on Clay Branch of
Lick Creek.  Richard Dobbs Spraight at Newbern, 12 January 1793.

Page 452     No. 1260
Joseph Ramsey - 100 acres on Nolachucky River, waters of Stony Creek.
Richard Dobbs Spraight at Newbern, 12 June 1794.

Page 452     No. 1071
Henry Shields - 100 acres on headwaters of Bans? Creek, north side Rich
Mountain.  Richard Dobbs Spraight at Newbern, 27 November 1793.

Page 453     No. 1053
Ruben Darring - 200 acres on south side Nolachucky River on Providence
Creek, adjoining David Wagers.  Alexander Martin at Danberry, 11 May
1792.

Page 454     No. 1238
Levi Carter - 175 acres on both sides Lick Creek.  Richard Dobbs Spraight
at Newbern, 12 January 1793.

Page 454     No. 1234
Adam Guthrie - 123 acres on north bank of French Broad River, adjoining
James Hubbard.  Richard Dobbs Spraight at Newbern, 12 January 1793.

Page 455     No. 1281
Nicholas Long - 200 acres in Greene County.  Sealed 12 July 1794.

Page 456     No. 1073
John McCallister and John Shields - 640 acres adjoining Emanuel Sinduskie,
James Byles, Stephen Hathers.  Richard Dobbs Spraight at Newbern, 27
November 1793.

Page 457     No. 1230
Thomas Gragg - 200 acres on Dry Fork of Meadow Creek.  Richard Dobbs
Spraight at Newbern, 12 January 1793.

Page 458     No. 1243
William Cate - 250 acres in Greene County, adjoining Trout, John Parks.
Richard Dobbs Spraight at Newbern, 12 January 1793.

Page 459     No. 1216
Henry Netherton - 100 acres on the fork of French Broad and Big Pigeon
Rivers, including part of an island.  Sealed 7 January 1793.

Page 459     No. 1286
Isaac Hammer - 200 acres on north side French Broad River on Tuckahoe
Creek.  Spraight at Newbern, 12 July 1794.

Page 460     No. 1220
Frederick Hail - 200 acres on north side Nolachucky River on Limestone
fork of Little Chucky.  Spraight at Newbern, 12 January 1793.

Page 461     No. 1221
John Shields - 400 acres on north bank of French Broad River.  Richard
Dobbs Spraight at Newbern, 27 November 1793.


Page 462     No. 1259
Dutton Lane - 100 acres on first branch of Cedar Creek, adjoining Fowler,
Claudius Bailey.  Sealed by Richard Dobbs Spraight at Newbern, 12 July
1794.


Page 463     No. 1258
Daniel Robinson - 200 acres at Mulberry Bottom.


Page 463     No. 1239
Francis Brown - 200 acres on Caly Creek, adjoining Francis Rowan.
Richard Dobbs Spraight at Newbern, 1790.


Page 464     No. 1306
James Feirs - 200 acres on south side Holston River on Bark Bottom.
Sealed 12 July 1794.


Page 465     No. 1220
John Shields - 640 acres on the Sinking Cane Valley, adjoining George
Hopkins, Vinett Fine.  Sealed 12 November 1793.


Page 466     No. 1278
John Thompson - 300 acres on north side Nolachucky River on Pigeon Creek,
adjoining Charles Kilgore, Samuel McGill.  Sealed 12 July 1794.


Page 467     No. 1280
William Mays - 400 acres on head of Clear Branch of Long Creek, waters
of Chuckey River, adjoining Benjamin McFarland, Elisha Witt.  Sealed 12
July 1794.


Page 467     No. 1239
Ann Mitts - 100 acres in Greene County.  Sealed 12 July 1794.


Page 468     No. 1228
William Tipton - 200 acres on Lick Creek.  Sealed 12 June 1794.


Page 469     No. 1287
Daniel Pearce - 600 acres on north side Nolachucky River.  Sealed 12
July 1794.


Page 470     No. 124
John Jones - 300 acres on south side Nolachucky River on Little Lick
Creek, adjoining Peter Cain, Wins.  Sealed 12 July 1794.


Page 470     No. 1217
John Shields - 500 acres at foot of Bays Mountain, adjoining Isaac
Taylor, James Hubbard, Seaburn.  Sealed 27 November 1793.


Page 471     No. 1155
Edmond Stevens - 100 acres on Lick Creek, adjoining Robert Davis.  Sealed
12 January 1793.


Page 472     No. 1086
Edmond Stevens - 100 acres on Lick Creek at a sugar tree marked by Pruet.
Sealed 12 January 1793.


Page 473     No. 1272
George Jameson - 200 acres on Burneys Branch, waters of Little Chuckey,
adjoining Richard Woods.  Sealed 12 July 1794.

Page 474     No. 1107
George House - 100 acres, corner to Elijah Payton and Nolichucky River
on Long Creek.  Sealed 12 January 1793.

Page 475     No. 1157
George House - 100 acres on Nolichucky River, adjoining another 100 acres
of said Houses.  Sealed 11 January 1793.

Page 476     No. 83
Thomas Isbel - 200 acres on north side of Long Creek.  Sealed 1 November
1786.

Page 477     No. 1156
Thomas McMeans - 200 acres on Limestone Fork of Little Nolachucky, adjoin-
ing Nathaniel McMeans, John Jackson, including improvement.  Sealed 12
January 1793.

Page 477     No. 1302
Lewis Broyles - 450 acres on the waters of Horse Creek, south side of
Nolachucky River, adjoining himself, Hughes, Williamson and Baker.
Sealed 17 July 1794.

Page 478     No. 1262
Jacob Broyles - 200 acres westside of Horse Creek, adjoining Emanuel
Sindusky in T.S.O. (Territory of United States, south of river Ohio),
Wagners Branch and Birds line.  Sealed 12 July 1794.

Page 479     No. 1166
Nehemiah Pettit - 200 acres on Alexander Creek.  Sealed 12 January 1793.

Page 480     No. 1102
Thomas McMahan - 100 acres on Mill Creek, a fork of Big Limestone,
adjoining James Roberts, Robert Campbell.  Sealed 12 January 1793.

Page 481     No. 1221
Jacob Hise - 200 acres on the northside of Nolachucky River.  Sealed 27
November 1792.

Page 481     No. 1114
Jacob Hise - 100 acres on northside Nolachucky River on Muddy or Cedar
Creek, adjoining himself.  Sealed 12 January 1793.

Page 482     No. 1097
William Black - 150 acres on south side Nolachucky River.  Sealed 12
January 1793.

Page 483     No. 1212
Avery Breed - 100 acres on both sides Little Chucky, adjoining Richard
Woods, Job Baker.  Sealed 29 July 1793.

Page 484     No. 1238
John Bowman - 200 acres on south side Nolachucky River on the west fork
of Camp Creek.  Sealed 12 July 1794.

Page 484     No. 1289
Andrew Smiley - 100 acres on waters of Lick Creek.  Sealed 17 July 1794.

Page 485     No. 1608
John Bond - 640 acres on the head branch of Stones Creek.  Bond, assignee
of Edward Sharwood, a private in the Continental line of said state - 640
acres in our County of Davidson on the head branches of Stones Creek and
Sugs Creek, adjoining Harris.  Sealed 27 April 1793.

Page 485     No. 2153
John Bond, assignee of Sanson Sikes, a private in the Continental line of
this state - 640 acres in Sumner County on Pond Lick Creek, waters of
Stones River.   Sealed 20 May 1793.


Page 486     No. 1320
Lawrence O'Bryan, assignee for heirs of William Buckingham, a private in
Continental line - 640 acres in Tennessee County on Brush Creek of Yellow
Creek, adjoining Daniel Anderson.   Sealed November 16, 1790.


Page 487     No. 1291
Laurence O'Bryan, assignee of Henry Robinson, a private in Continental
line - 640 acres on the north side of Cumberland River in Tennessee
County on a small drain that empties into the west fork of Red River.
Sealed 1790.


Page 487     No. 1295
Lawrence O'Bryan, assignee for John Masons heirs, he being a private in
Continental line - 640 acres on south side Cumberland River on east side
of East Fork of Blooming Grove Creek - Tennessee County.   Sealed 16
November 1797.


Page 488     No. 2562
Stockley Donaldson and William Terrel - 640 acres in Sumner County on a
large fork of the Caney Fork, a branch of Cumberland River - for the
heirs of Pvt. James Chisolm.   Sealed 7 March 1796.


Page 489     No. 2559
Stockley Donelson and William Terrel - 640 acres in County of Sumner -
assignee of Miles Claton, a private in Continental line, to his heirs,
adjoining Donaldsons and Terrels survey as assignee of Jedekiah Brooks.
Sealed 7 March 1796.


Page 490     No. 2558
Stockley Donaldson and William Terrel - 640 acres in Sumner County for
heirs of Richard McCormich, a private in Continental line, adjoining
their grant for services of David Davis.   Sealed 7 March 1796.


Page 490     No. 2549
Stockley Donaldson and William Terrel - 640 acres on head branches of
Carrs Creek and the Sulphur Fork of Red River - for heirs of William
Love, deceased, a private in Continental line of said State.   Sealed
7 March 1796.


Page 491     No. 2552
Stockley Donaldson and William Terrel, assignee for William Perry, a
private in Continental line - 640 acres in Sumner County on a branch
of Pond Lick Creek, one mile east of Pond Lick Road, adjoining William
Nash.   Sealed 7 March 1796.


Page 492     No. 2563
Stockley Donaldson and William Terrel, assignee for heirs of David Davis,
private in Continental line - land adjoining their survey for heirs of
Miles Clayton.   Sealed 7 March 1796.


Page 493     No. 2554
Stockley Donaldson and William Terrel, assignees for heirs of Arthur
McKurry - land adjoining their grant for heirs of James Chisolm.   Sealed
7 March 1796.


Page 493     No. 2551
Stockley Donaldson and William Terrel, assignees for heirs of Ruben
McCormick - 640 acres.   Sealed 7 March 1796.

Page 494     No. 2579
Stockley Donaldson, William Terrel and Robert King - 1000 acres on waters
of Cany Fork, called King and Company's Little Creek - for heirs of
Zachariah Durham, a Sgt. in Continental line.  Sealed 7 March 1796.

Page 494     No. 2573
Stockley Donaldson and William Terrel - 640 acres in Tennessee County on
the branch of Kerrs Creek, a branch of Cumberland River - for William
Newberry, a private in Continental line.  Sealed 7 March 1796.

Page 495     No. 2556
Stockley Donaldson and William Terrel, assignees of Josiah Rinehart, a
private in Continental line of this state - land in Tennessee County on
a branch of Sulphur Fork of Red River.  Sealed 7 March 1796.

Page 495     No. 2560
Stockley Donaldson and William Terrel, assignees of Zedekiah Brock, Pvt.
in Continental line - 640 acres in Sumner County, adjoining the tract as
assignees of heirs of Arthur McKory.

Page 496     No. 2576
Stockley Donaldson and William Terrel, assignees of James Marderd, Pvt.
in Continental line - land in Tennessee County on a west branch of
Sulphur Fork of Red River.  Sealed 17 March 1796.

Page 497     No. 2557
Stockley Donaldson and William Terrel, assignees of Isaac Jessap, Pvt. in
Continental line of this state - 640 acres in Davidson County on waters
of Stones River.  Sealed 7 March 1796.

Page 497     No. 2228
Anthony Hart, assignee of heirs of William Wright, Pvt. in Continental
line of this state - 640 acres in Sumner County on the Cany Fork.  Sealed
28 May 1796.

Page 498     No. 2415
John Shepperd, assignee of William Hicks, a private in Continental line -
640 acres on Obeys River, a fork of Cumberland River.  Sealed 12 December
1794.

Page 499     No. 2458
Martin Armstrong and Stockley Donaldson, assignees for Solomon Williams,
a Sgt. in Continental line - 640 acres on a south branch of Cumberland
River.  Sealed 21 February 1795.

Page 499     No. 2426
Martin Armstrong and Stockley Donaldson, assignees for Marmaduke Brantly,
private in Continental line - 640 acres on a fork of Obeys River, a south
branch of Cumberland River.  Sealed 21 February 1795.

Page 500     No. 2468
Martin Armstrong and Stockley Donaldson, assignees of heirs of Josiah
Whittaker, Sgt. in North Carolina line - 640 acres on a south branch of
Cumberland River in Sumner County.

Page 501     No. 2449
Martin Armstrong and Stockley Donaldson, assignees for heirs of Jockhe
Jefferson, Private in Continental line - 640 acres on south branch of
Cumberland River on west fork of Obey's River.  Sealed 2 February 1795.

Page 502     No. 2712
Stockley Donaldson, assignee of James Daget, Private in said line - 640
acres on waters of Stones River, adjoining Jason Thompson, Daniel McGooden
and John Thompson.  Sealed by Samuel Ashe at Raliegh, 20 July 1796.

Page 503     No. 2728
Stockley Donaldson and William Tyrrell, assignees for Thomas Smith, a
private in said line - 465 acres in Davidson County on the waters of
Leepers and fork of Harpeth Creeks.  Sealed by Samuel Ashe, Commissioner
in Chief at Raleigh, 20 July 1796.

Page 504     No. 2732
Stockley Donaldson, assignee for heirs of Jeremiah Shelway, private in
the line of this state - 640 acres in Sumner County on west side of west
fork of Obeys River.

Page 505     No. 2733
Stockley Donaldson, assignee for heirs of William Whitlock, a private in
Continental line - 640 acres on west side of West Fork of Obeys River,
adjoining Col. Glasgows survey.

Page 506     No. 2735
Stockley Donaldson, assignee for heirs of Thomas Wear, private in
Continental line of this state - 640 acres in Sumner County westside of
West Fork of Obeys River.  Samuel Ashe at Raleigh, 21 July 1796.

Page 507     No. 2725
Stockley Donaldson, assignee for Jesse Donaldson, Pvt. in said line -
640 acres in Davidson County on waters of Stones River, adjoining Phillip
Phillips, John Buchanan, Benjamin Flood.  Samuel Ashe at Raleigh, 20 July
1796.

Page 507     No. 2718
Stockley Donaldson, assignee for Jesse Nelson, private in said line - 640
acres in Davidson County on Mill Creek and Stones River, adjoining Richard
Cross.  Samuel Ashe at Raleigh, 20 July 1796.

Page 508     No. 2416
John Sheppard, assignee of John Harris, a private in Continental line -
640 acres on Obeys River, a fork of Cumberland River, adjoining Sheppard.
Sealed 12 December 1794.

Page 509     No. 2698
James Easton, assignee for Watson Andrews, Pvt. in Continental line - 640
acres in Sumner County on Caney Fork of Cumberland River.  Samuel Ashe at
Raleigh, 27 March 1796.

Page 510     No. 2699
James Easton, assignee for Grishom Tyson, Private - 640 acres in Sumner
County on Caney Fork of Cumberland River, adjoining Easton, Watson Andrews
heirs.  Samuel Ashe at Raleigh, 27 March 1796.

Page 511     No. 2700
James Easton, assignee of A. J. Delany, Pvt. in said line - 640 acres in
Sumner County on Cany Fork of Cumberland River, adjoining Easton and heirs
of Grishom Tyson.  Samuel Ashe at Raleigh, 27 March 1796.

Page 512     No. 2707
James Easton, assignee for John Winoak - land in Sumner County on Caney
Fork of Cumberland River.  Samuel Ashe at Raleigh, 27 March 1796.

Page 512     No. 2706
James Easton, assignee for heirs of Dugold McCoy, Pvt. - 640 acres in
Sumner County adjoining his survey as assignee of heirs of Matthias
Dudley.  Samuel Ashe at Raleigh, 27 March 1796.

Page 513     No. 2704
James Easton, assignee for William Goodwins heirs, private in Continental
line - 640 acres on Cany Fork of Cumberland River, adjoining heirs of

David Moore. Sealed by Samuel Ashe at Raleigh, 27 March 1796.

Page 514    No. 2705
James Easton, assignee for heirs of Matthias Dudley, private in said line
- 640 acres in Sumner County on Cany Fork of Cumberland River, adjoining
heirs of William Goodwin. Samuel Ashe at Raleigh, 27 March 1796.

Page 515    No. 2703
James Easton, assignee for heirs of John Davis Moore, Pvt. - 640 acres in
Sumner County, adjoining his survey for heirs of Watson Reed. Samuel Ashe
at Raleigh, 27 March 1796.

Page 515    No. 2702
James Easton, assignee for heirs of Watson Reed - 640 acres in Sumner
County, adjoining his survey for heirs of James Madoc. Samuel Ashe at
Rocky Point, 27 March 1796.

Page 516    No. 2585
James Easton, assignee for heirs of Joshua Parnal - land adjoining grant
for heirs of David Cannody. Samuel Ashe at Raleigh, 7 March 1796.

Page 517    No. 2586
James Easton, assignee for heirs of Edward Etheridge - land adjoining
Joshua Parnal heirs grant. Samuel Ashe at Raleigh, 7 March 1796.

Page 517    No. 258
James Easton, assignee for the heirs of John Calvin, Pvt. - land adjoining survey for heirs of Edmond Bebby. Samuel Ashe at Raleigh, 7 March
1796.

Page 518    No. 2701
James Easton, assignee for heirs of James McAdoo, Pvt. - land adjoining
his survey for A. J. Delany. Samuel Ashe at Rocky Point, 27 March 1796.

Page 519    No. 2531
James Easton, assignee for heirs of Henry Hicks, Pvt. - 640 acres.
Samuel Ashe at Raleigh, 7 March 1796.

Page 520    No. 2589
James Easton, assignee for heirs of David Canady - 640 acres adjoining
survey for heirs of James Cram. Samuel Ashe at Raleigh, 7 March 1796.

Page 520    No. 287
James Easton, assignee for heirs of Edmond Bebby, Pvt. - 640 acres.
Samuel Ashe at Raleigh, 7 March 1796.

Page 521    No. 2503
James Easton, assignee for heirs of James Cram - 640 acres adjoining
survey for heirs of David Canady. Samuel Ashe at Raleigh, 7 March 1796.

Page 522    No. 2584
James Easton, assignee for heirs of William Carry - 640 acres land.
Samuel Ashe at Raleigh, 7 March 1796.

Page 522    No. 1427
To James and Andrew Luckey - for 50 shillings per 100 acres - 150 acres
in Greene County on Little Chuckey, adjoining McCall, John Thompson.
Samuel Ashe at Raleigh, 18 January 1796.

Page 523    No. 1372
Joseph Brown - for 50 shillings per 100 acres - 200 acres in Greene
County, adjoining Thomas Harmon. Sealed 27 February 1796.

Page 524     No. 1343
Henry Patton - 200 acres on northside French Broad River, adjoining John
Parrott, south side Clear Creek.  Sealed by Richard Dobbs Spraight at
Newbern, 27 February 1795.

Page 525     No. 365
William Morrow - 200 acres for services of assignee of Martin Armstrong -
Greene County - adjoining Morrows 300 acre survey.  Sealed 4 July 1797.

Page 526     No. 528
William Morrow - 327 acres on Richland Creek.  Richard Caswell at Kinston,
20 December 1797.

Page 527     No. 1222
Isaac Taylor - for 50 shillings per 100 acres - 100 acres in Greene
County.  Sealed by Richard Caswell at Kinston, 20 December 1797.

Page 527     No. 128
Robert Warren - 40 acres in Greene County on Little Chucky Creek -
assignee of Martin Armstrong, surveyor of lands for officers and soldiers
in this state.  Sealed 4 February 1797.

Page 528     No. 129
Robert Warren - 80 acres on Little Chucky Creek - for services of Martin
Armstrong.  Sealed 4 February 1797.

Page 529     No. 1416
Matthew Leeper - for 10 shillings per 100 acres - 640 acres on Richland
Creek, adjoining Jamison, Bennet.  Samuel Ashe at Raleigh, 19 February
1797.

Page 530     No. 1057
Jacob Bowman - for 10 shillings per 100 acres - 100 acres on head of
North Branch of Roaring Fork, adjoining David Rankin, William McAmish.
Alexander Martin at Danberry, 11 May 1792.

Page 531     No. 1436
John McNutty - 182 acres on Pigeon Creek.  Samuel Ashe at Raleigh, 17
November 1797.

Page 532     No. 15
Drury Morris - for 50 shillings per 100 acres - 199 acres in Washington
County on Cedar Fork of Lick Creek.  Alexander Martin at Fairfield, 23
October 1782.

Page 532     No. 1170?
Elizabeth Crowley - for 10 pounds per 100 acres - 100 acres on Little
Chuckey on Delaneys Branch.  Alexander Martin at Fairfield, 23 October
1782.

Page 533     No. 1147
Henry Gregg - for 50 shillings per 100 acres - 200 acres in Greene County,
adjoining John Baskim.  Sealed by Richard Dobbs Spraight at Newbern, 12
January 1793.

Page 534     No. 882
Henry Gregg - for 10 pounds per 100 acres - 400 acres on northside French
Broad River on head branches of Clear Creek, adjoining Joseph Williams.
Alexander Martin at Fayetteville, 17 November 17__, 15th year of our
independence.

## BOOK V

Page 1        No. 1295
State of North Carolina - for 50 shillings per 100 acres - to Johnston
Wilson, 200 acres on Little Lick Creek, south side Nolachucky River.
Sealed by Richard Dobbs Spraight at Newbern, 13 July 1794. This grant
recorded in Greene County, Tennessee for Johnston Nelson, 17 February
1795.

Page 2        No. 1273
James Wicker - 100 acres on Nolachucky River opposite Major Conway's.
Richard Dobbs Spraight at Newbern, 12 July 1794.

Page 4        No. 1240
Thomas Goble - 150 acres on north side Nolachucky River.  Richard Dobbs
Spraight at Newbern, 12 July 1794.

Page 6        No. 1096
William Dun - 100 acres on north side Nolachucky River at Seven Islands.
Spraight at Newbern, 12 January 1793.

Page 7        No. 1235
John Shields - 1000 acres - 500 acres on Clear Creek crossing Long Creek,
adjoining William Bigham, Williams, Baker, Andrew Bigham.  Sealed 12
July 1794.

Page 11       No. 1215
Corbon Sane - 46 acres adjoining his other lands and Robert Steel.
Sealed 12 January 1793.

Page 13       No. 1225
John Hackett - 100 acres on the head of Little Chuckey, including the
head spring.  Sealed 27 November 1792.

Page 15       No. 1229
Jacob Smelcer - 400 acres on the head of Holleys Creek, adjoining Smelcer,
McClung, McGaughey, William Henderson and John Patterson.  Sealed 12 June
1794.

Page 17       No. 1268
Andrew Smiley - 100 acres at the head of the Blue Spring Branch, waters
of Little Nolachuckey.  Sealed 12 July 1794.

Page 19       No. 1223
Gabril McCool - 200 acres on the head of McCartney Creek, adjoining
Samuel Moore, John Oliphant, Gillespie, Taylors.  Sealed 12 January
1793.

Page 21       No. 1288
John Sanders - 200 acres.  Sealed 17 July 1794.

Page 23       No. 1244
Jacob Myre - tract of land south side Nolachuckey River.  Sealed 12 July
1794.

Page 25       No. 1235
Andrew English - 25 acres on Pyburns Fork of Lick Creek, adjoining James
English, including mouth of Limestone Fork of said creek.  Sealed 12
January 1793.

Page 27       No. 1230
Andrew English - 25 acres on the watters of Lick Creek, adjoining James

English, including mouth of Limestone Fork on both sides Christiana War Path. Sealed 12 January 1793.

Page 29    No. 1228
James English - 300 acres on Limestone Fork of Lick Creek between Henry Monteeth and Charles Hayse, including Waddles Spring. Sealed 12 January 1793.

Page 31    No. 1291
Samuel McCamy - 150 acres in our County of Greene. Sealed 17 July 1794.

Page 32    No. 1226
Daniel Nelson - 200 acres on Lick Creek Branch of Nolachucky River, on the south side, adjoining Johnson Nelson. Sealed 12 January 1793.

Page 34    No. 1244
Joseph Richardson - 40 acres on Nolachucky River on the head of Dry Creek. Sealed 12 January 1793.

Page 36    No. 399
John Gass - 300 acres on Lick Creek including the improvement, adjoining John Waggoner. Sealed 19 September 1787.

Page 38    No. 1348
Thomas Jonagan (Journagan) - 100 acres on north side Nolachucky River on Long Creek. Sealed 17 July 1794.

Page 40    No. 1213
David Robinson - 300 acres on both sides Little Chuckey, adjoining Wilson, Nathan Breed. Sealed 29 July 1793.

Page 42    No. 1319
John Reives - 100 acres on the head branch of Little Chuckey, adjoining John Jackson. Sealed 4 January 1795.

Page 44    No. 1325
Agnes Hopkins - 300 acres on south side Nolachucky River on Cain Branch, adjoining Joseph Williams, Gragg, McMurtrie. Sealed 4 January 1795.

Page 46    No. 692
William Shores - 200 acres on Grassy Creek. Sealed 11 July 1788.

Page 48    No. 371
Permenas Taylor - 200 acres on Lick Creek. Sealed 20 September 1787.

Page 49    No. 1328
John Rhea - 100 acres on north side Nolachucky River on waters of Lick Creek, adjoining Hugh Cavender. Sealed 5 January 1795.

Page 51    No. 132
Thomas Love - 80 acres on south side Nolachucky River - for relief of officers and soldiers in the Continental line - Love an assignee of Martin Armstrong, surveyor of lands in this state - adjoining former survey. Sealed 4 February 1795.

Page 52    No. 1322
John Harmon - 150 acres on Delaneys Creek, adjoining William Dunwoody. Sealed 4 January 1795.

Page 54    No. 1326
John Goar - 300 acres on the waters of Lick and Bent Creeks, adjoining where he now lives, Joseph Stewart. Sealed 4 February 1794.

147

Page 56     No. 1329
Leonard Simons - 150 acres on Little Chuckey River.   Sealed 4 February
1795.

Page 57     No. 980
James Grimes - 100 acres on Little Limestone in Washington County, adjoining Broyles and McColester.   Sealed 14 January 1793.

Page 59     No. 1160
John Denton - 600 acres on Lick Creek, corner to James Ashmores, Frazier,
F. A. Ramsey.   Sealed 17 January 1793.

Page 60     No. 1328
Jacob Dyer - 150 acres on the watters of Lick Creek and Little Chuckey,
including dwelling house said Dyer bought of John Smith, to a sugar tree
on Bacon Branch below the spring.   Sealed 4 February 1795.

Page 61     No. 827
John Milliken - 100 acres on the south fork of the Horse Camp Fork of
Lick Creek, adjoining Azariah Doty.   Sealed 13 February 1791.

Page 63     No. 575
Jeremiah Jack - 50 acres on the south side Nolachucky River in Washington
County.   Sealed 10 November 1784.

Page 64     No. 133
Nehemiah Pettitt - 40 acres on south side French Broad River, adjoining
a tract granted to Robert Clark - by Martin Armstrong, surveyor of land
allotted soldiers and officers of the Continental line of this state.
Pettitt, a friend of said Armstrong.   Sealed 4 February 1795.

Page 66     No. 1233
Nicholas Hays - 300 acres on the Lick Fork of Lick Creek.   Sealed 17
November 1792.

Page 67     No. 428
Robert Bay - 300 acres on Medow Creek, the north side of Nolachucky
River, adjoining John Fillips, George Howard.   Sealed 20 September 1787.

Page 68     No. 1175
Samuel Moore - 200 acres on Little Sinking Creek, waters of Little
Chuckey River, adjoining where he now lives, James Wright, Charles
Hutchison, Phillip Miller.   Sealed 12 January 1793.

Page 70     No. 1220
John Bowers - 200 acres on a branch of Lick Creek, adjoining Newman.
Sealed 27 November 1792.

Page 72     No. 1327
George Gordon - 200 acres on north side Nolachucky River on a branch of
Lick Creek, adjoining Daniel Slaver? (Shaver).   Sealed 4 February 1795.

Page 73     No. 1207
James McPheron - 300 acres on the Roran (Roaring) Fork of Lick Creek,
adjoining Moses Poor, William Robison, John McPherron.   Sealed 27
November 1792.

Page 75     No. 1070
Andrew Fox - 92 acres south of Nolachucky River, adjoining himself and
Francis Hughes.   Sealed 3 December 1792.

Page 77     No. 299
Stokely Donnelson - 5000 acres in Eastern District on Crow Creek, waters

of Tennessee River. Sealed 27 August 1795.

Page 78      No. 233
Stokely Donelson - 5000 acres on Crow Creek, waters of Tennessee River -
Eastern District - Survey No. II adjoining above survey. Sealed 27
August 1795.

Page 80      No. 230
Stokely Donelson - 5000 acres in Eastern District on Crow Creek of
Tennessee River. Sealed by Richard Dobbs Spraight at Newbern, 27 August
1795.

Page 81      No. 236
Stokely Donelson and Martin Armstrong - 5000 acres on Crow Creek, waters
of Tennessee River. Registered 15 October 1795.

Page 83      No. 235
Stokely Donelson - 5000 acres. Registered 27 August 1795.

Page 84      No. 232
Stokely Donelson - 5000 acres. Registered 27 August 1795.

Page 86      No. 231
Stokely Donelson - 5000 acres. Registered 27 August 1795.

Page 87      No. 237
Stokely Donelson and Martin Armstrong - 5000 acres. Registered 27 August
1795.

Page 89      No. 228
Stokely Donelson - 5000 acres. Registered 27 August 1795.

Page 90      No. 234
Stokely Donelson - 5000 acres. Registered 16 October 1795.

Page 92      No. 238
Stokely Donelson and Martin Armstrong - 5000 acres. Registered 27 August
1795.

Page 93      No. 220
Stokely Donelson - 5000 acres. Registered 16 October 1795.

Page 94      No. 223
Stokely Donelson - 5000 acres. Registered 16 October 1795.

Page 95      No. 222
Stokely Donelson - 5000 acres. Registered 16 October 1795.

Page 97      No. 221
Stokely Donelson - 5000 acres. Registered 16 October 1795.

Page 98      No. 224
Stokely Donelson - 5000 acres. Registered 16 October 1795.

Page 100      No. 136?
Stokeley Donelson - 5000 acres on north side Nolachucky River, adjoining
David Wilson, Joseph Wilson, William Rankin. Sealed 28 August 1795.

Page 101      No. 1356
Stokeley Donelson - 5000 acres north side Nolachucky River, adjoining
Thomas Keeps, Donelson and Girdner 840 acre tract, Philip Hail, Georgia

Leeper, Warrens, Leonard Simons. Sealed 28 August 1795.

Page 104    No. 1357
Stokeley Donelson - 60,400 acres on south side French Broad River, east
of Big Pigeon River, east of Indian Boundary on Spring Creek near Rey-
nold's Camp called by same, the Punchun Camp. Sealed 28 August 1795.

Page 105    No. 1358
Stokeley Donelson - 5000 acres on north side Nolachuckee Creek, adjoining
William Lovelady, George Gordon, Robert Smith, Frederick Whittenberger
opposite Matthew Pate's island, John Lewis, Darby Ragon, Col. Henry
Conway, Charles Smith. Sealed 20 August 1795.

Page 108    No. 1339
Stokeley Donelson - 5000 acres on Nolachucky River, adjoining Donelsons
and George Gordons 840 acre survey, Robert Warren, Isaac Maden, Thomas
Keeps. Sealed 28 August 1795.

Page 110    No. 1358
John Sulivan - 200 acres on north side Chuckey River, south fork of
Pigeon Creek, adjoining Thomas Graham. Sealed 28 August 1780.

Page 111    No. 1354
William Logan - 200 acres on north side Nolachucky River on a branch of
Pigeon Creek. Sealed 28 August 1794.

Page 113    No. 230
Stokeley Donelson - 60,400 acres on south side Cumberland River in Sumner
County, where Virginia Line crosses Cumberland River. Sealed 28 August
1795.

Page 114    No. 1334
Stokeley Donelson and George Gordon - 1000 acres on south side Nolachucky
River opposite mouth of Meadow Creek, near John Hendersons survey, includ-
ing McCartneys and Armstrongs branches. Sealed 22 February 1794.

Page 116    No. 1353
Hugh Neilson - 550 acres in Greene County on north side Nolachucky River,
near Old Improvement, corner to William Conway, adjoining Joseph White.
Sealed 28 August 1795.

Page 118    No. 1076
John Hopton - 200 acres on south side Nolachucky River on Middle Creek.
Sealed 12 January 1793.

Page 119    No. 1438
William Wilson - 50 acres on both sides Delaney's Branch, adjoining
Wilson. Sealed 19 January 1795.

Page 121    No. 1253
Robert Young Junr. - 400 acres west side Boyd's Creek, crossing Great
Road, running east to bank of French Broad River, including the bottom
that Col. Christian marched his army through in the night up to mouth
of said creek. Sealed 27 November 1792.

Page 122    No. 131
John Sears - 120 acres on north side Nolachuckey River joining his former
survey - for relief of officers and soldiers of the Continental Line and
consideration of the services of Martin Armstrong, surveyor of lands for
officers and soldiers of this state - give and grant to Sears, assignee
of said Armstrong, adjoining Matthew Pates. Sealed 4 February 1795.

Page 124     No. 1326
Thomas West – 117 acres, part of a plantation where he once lived.
Sealed 5 December 1794.


Page 125     No. 1336
Zopher Johnston Senr. – 100 acres on Little Chuckey and Pigeon Creeks,
adjoining Frederick Hale, Henry Dunham.  Sealed 18 August 1795.


Page 127     No. 1334
Andrew Lewis Junr., assignee of Alexander Brown – 300 acres on French
Broad River opposite his former survey.  Sealed 21 July 1795.


Page 129     No. 2486
William Neilson, assignee of Thomas Modlin – 365 acres north side French
Broad River, adjoining Henry Conway, now the property of Neilson.  Thomas
Modlin, a private in Continental Line.  Sealed 28 August 1795.


Page 131     No. 2487
William Neilson, assignee of James Avery, a Pvt. in Continental Line –
228 acres on south side French Broad River, adjoining grant to Grasor
Dugglass, now property of Neilson.  Sealed 28 August 1795.


Page 133     No. 1338
John Thompson – 168½ acres north side Nolachucky River where he now lives,
adjoining James Lacky, James Richardson.  Sealed 18 August 1795.


Page 134     No. 1208
John Ellis – 400 acres on the Long Fork of Sinking Creek, north side
Nolachucky River, adjoining Samuel Ellis, Robert Parress, Samuel Gibson.
Sealed 27 November 1795.


Page 137     No. 1315
Laurence Glaize – 300 acres south side Nolachucky River, known by name
of Walnut Bottom, including his own improvement and what is called Oak
Patete?  Sealed 6 January 1795.


Page 139     No. 1335
Thomas Gragg – 500 acres adjoining Thomas Paters (Peters?), Robert Gragg.
Sealed 18 August 1795.


Page 141     No. 1224
Adam Starnes – 150 acres on Lick Creek, adjoining Starnes, Holets.
Sealed 27 July 1793.


Page 142     No. 1059
George Couch – 100 acres in the gap of Bays Mountain on Big Gap Creek.
Sealed 11 May 1792.


Page 144     No. 511
John Tigh – 200 acres in Hawkins County on the head of Muddy Fork of
Lick Creek, adjoining Jones, Bous.  Sealed 7 January 1793.


Page 146     No. 1330
Stoneley Donelson and George Gordon – 840 acres on Peters Creek, a fork
of Lick Creek, adjoining Benjamin Robertson, a leaning post oak in the
Hericain, Potters Creek.  Sealed 19 February 1795.


Page 148     No. 160
William Terrell and George Gordon, assignees of Col. Martin Armstrong of
the Continental Line – 250 acres north side Nolachucky River, adjoining
William Mill Survey.  Sealed 22 February 1795.

Page 150    No. 1231
George Taylor - 200 acres land.   Sealed 11 July 1794.


Page 151    No. 1364
George Alexander - 100 acres north side Nolachucky River, adjoining his
former survey.   Sealed 27 November 1795.


Page 153    No. 1323
George Farnsworth - 56 acres south side Nolachucky River, adjoining his
other survey.   Sealed 14 January 1795.


Page 155    No. 1343
John Rhea and George Gordon - 1920 acres on the waters of Spring and
Wolf Creek.   Sealed 27 August 1795.


Page 156    No. 330
Robert Greene - 200 acres north side Nolachucky River near his improvement, adjoining Doherty, Robert Greer.   Sealed 20 September 1787.


Page 157    No. 1269
Elizabeth Lowry - 150 acres adjoining Edwards Old Place.   Sealed 14 July
1794.


Page 159    No. 1216
Matthew Cox - 100 acres on the Roaring Fork of Lick Creek, adjoining
Harmon.   Sealed 18 December 1793.


Page 160    No. 881
Patrick Morrison - 200 acres in Washington County on Lick Creek above the
mouth of Cedar Creek.   Sealed 17 November 1790.


Page 162    No. 1240
Samuel Wear - 100 acres on a branch of Lick Creek, adjoining Daniel
Kennedy's old corner, James Wilson.   Sealed 12 July 1794.


Page 164    No. 499
Robert King - 300 acres on the north of Bent Creek on White Horn Creek,
waters of Nolichucky River, in Hawkins County?   Sealed 27 January 1793.


Page 165    No. 1360
Joseph Tipton - 400 acres on White Horn Creek, waters of Bent Creek.
Sealed 4 November 1795.


Page 167    No. 1341
Solomon Reed - 100 acres on Wolf Creek.   Sealed 27 August 1795.


Page 168    No. 1349
George Leeper - 168 acres on north side Nolachucky River, joining his
former survey.   Sealed 28 August 1795.


Page 170    No. 1363
Elizabeth Telfaer - 100 acres north side Nolachucky River, adjoining
George Crump, James Laws.   Sealed 27 November 1795.


Page 172    No. 1153
George House - 150 acres on Lick Creek, crossing Long Fork of Lick Creek.
Sealed 12 January 1793.


Page 173    No. 1377
William Wilson - 200 acres adjoining John Wilson.   Sealed 20 July 17__.

Page 175    No. 1113
James Black - 200 acres on a branch of Lick Creek. Sealed 12 January 1793.

Page 177    No. 1340
Phillip Love - 400 acres on the Cany Fork of Spring Creek. Sealed 27 _____ 1795.

Page 178    No. 1117
James Craig - for 10 pounds per 100 acres - 437 acres north side Nolachucky River, adjoining Hutcheson. Sealed 12 January 1793.

Page 180    No. 1365
John Wilson, assignee of James Ruddle - 300 acres on Little Chuckey Creek, including where Wilson now lives and others, adjoining David Wilson. Sealed 8 December 1795.

Page 182    No. 1132
Joseph Loveletty - 100 acres on south side Nolachucky River, adjoining John Savage. Sealed 12 January 1793.

Page 183    No. 1333
Frederick Whittenberger - 200 acres north side of Nolachucky River. Sealed 27 April 1795.

Page 185    No. 849
John Shields - 200 acres south side Nolachucky River below Sherrill's Entry, Joseph Williams. Sealed 17 November 1790.

Page 187    No. 465
John Lester - 280 acres south side Nolachucky River above Great Bent of said river, including his improvement. Sealed 20 September 1787.

Page 189    No. 1166
Jacob Hise - 50 acres north side Nolachucky River. Sealed 12 January 1793.

Page 190    No. 53
Joseph Fowler - 150 acres south side Lick Creek in Washington County, adjoining Brown, Drury Morrison. Sealed 23 October 1782.

Page 192    No. 1368
Nathan Veach - 100 acres south side Nolachucky River on Oven Creek, adjoining Birds. Sealed 27 November 1795.

Page 193    No. 1428
John Wilson - 100 acres land. Sealed 26 January 1797.

Page 195    No. 635
Thomas Stanfield - 606 acres in Washington County on Roaring Fork of Lick Creek, including Old Indian Camp , adjoining James Robertson, Hugh. Sealed 10 November 1784.

Page 197    No. 1429
Robert Gamble Senr. - 100 acres on Little Chuckey, adjoining William Willison Esq., Charles Lowery. Sealed 8 June 1797.

Page 199    No. ___
Samuel Lyle - 50 acres in Washington County on Lick Creek, adjoining Joseph Fowler. Sealed 24 October 1782.

Page 201    No. 363
John Meriott, assignee of Martin Armstrong - for services of Martin
Armstrong in Continental Line - 154 acres on Little Chuckey, adjoining
Joseph Lusk, James Stinson, said Merriott, Thompson, Thomas Mitchell.
Sealed 4 July 1797.


Page 203    No. 1365
John Sevier Senr. - 3000 acres on Camp Creek, south side Nolachucky River,
adjoining James McMurtrey, Henry Reynolds. Sealed 27 November 1795.


Page 205    No. 1435
Thomas Pritchett - 271 acres in Greene County, adjoining James Stinson,
Joseph Lusk, Newley. Sealed 12 November 1779.


Page 207    No. 1346
George Gordon - 100 acres north side Nolachucky River.   Sealed 27 August
1794.


Page 209    No. 577
James Henry - 100 acres in Greene County eastside of Clinch River,
including mouth of Buffaloe Creek.   Sealed 3 August 1788.


Page 211    No. 1081
Alexander Prethero - 400 acres in Greene County, adjoining Adonijah
Morgan - line with Camp Creek, Thomas Morgan crossing the watery fork,
Sperling Boman.  Sealed 12 January 1793.


Page 214    No. 345
Joseph Hardin - 200 acres in Washington County on Roaring Fork of Lick
Creek, called South Fork of Roaring Fork, adjoining Jessus?  Sealed 24
October 1782.


Page 216    No. 347
Abraham Carter - 275 acres on Main Lick Creek, adjoining Daniel Carter,
John Melones, formerly John Carters, surveyed by Joseph Brown 20 Sept-
ember 1787.


Page 218    No. 1384
Henry Cross - 50 acres south of Howard's Branch on Lick Creek, adjoining
John Howard.  Sealed 20 July 1796.


Page 220    No. 287
Robert McCall, assignee of Martin Armstrong for Continental Line Service
- 124 acres adjoining Joseph Lusk, Ramsey.  Sealed 6 June 1796.


Page 222    No. 1339
Stokeley Donelson and George Gordon - 500 acres on Lick Creek, adjoining
Joseph White survey, Buffaloe Ford.  Sealed 7 August 1795.


Page 225    No. 1373
Thomas Harmon - 200 acres on Lick Creek, adjoining John Richardson, John
Carter, Zachariah Casteel, John Goodman, Charles Harmon, Edward Tate.
Sealed 27 February 1796.


Page 227    No. 1374
Whaley Newby - 150 acres on Lick Creek, adjoining a tract in Elizabeth
Akers name.  Sealed 27 November 1796.


Page 229    No. 1345
James Woods Lackey and George Gordon - 1000 acres north side Lick Creek,
adjoining William Conway, Stokeley Donelson, George Gordon and Joseph
White's survey.  Sealed 27 August 1796.

Page 231     No. 1331
William Terrill and George Gordon - 480 acres north side French Broad
River in fork of Kelleys Mill Creek, including the high rock spring,
adjoining Kelley.  Sealed 21 February 1795.

Page 233     No. 1245
William Davidson - 300 acres on north side Nolachuckey River on the head
of Delaney's Creek, adjoining Andrew Jackson Delaney.  Sealed 7 November
1792.

Page 235     No. 310
John Rhea and William Terrel - 5000 acres of a fork of the Cany Fork,
called by King and Company, McClures River and on both sides of an
Indian Path leading to Chicomoga in our Middle District.  Granted by
virtue of a warrant entered in John Armstrong's office, No. 2345.
Sealed 6 March 1796.

Page 237     No. 309
John Rhea and William Terrel - 200 acres in Middle District on Little
Lick Creek, on waters of Caney Fork, adjoining Stockley Donelsons and
William Terrells lines near a Lick.  Sealed 7 March 1796.

Page 239     No. 311
John Rhea and William Terrell - 640 acres in Middle District on waters of
Cany Fork of Cumberland River, including a remarkable Lick found by Robert
King and Company in the year 1795.  Sealed 7 March 1796.

Page 242     No. 284
Stokeley Donelson, assignee of Martin Armstrong - for relief of officers
and soldiers in the Continental Line and for and in consideration of the
services of Martin Armstrong, surveyor of the lands allotted officers and
soldiers - 200 acres in Greene County, adjoining David Frames, Samuel
Jack, William Morrow.  Sealed 6 June 1796.

Page 243     No. 1410
Stokeley Donelson - 640 acres on Butch Creek.  Sealed 21 January 1797.

Page 245     No. 1367
Joseph McMullen - 200 acres on the waters of Lick Creek, north side Nolachucky River, on road leading from Greeneville to Bulls Gap, including
his improvement, on line made by McMullin and Samuel Dutton.  Sealed 7
December 1795.

Page 246     No. 2937
William Asken, assignee for the heirs of Jesse Biggot, Pvt. in Continental
Line - 640 acres in Sumner County on the waters of the Fifth Creek that
the Virginia Line crosses to the east of Red River, it being waters of
Big Banon River, beginning on Virginia Line.  Sealed 1 March 1797.

Page 248     No. 211
John Rhea, Ananias McCoy and James W. Lackey - 3000 acres in the Eastern
District, in the bent of Tennessee River opposite the mouth of Clinch
River.  Sealed 4 February 1795.

Page 259     No. 201
John Hackett and Stokeley Donelson - 5000 acres in Eastern District, at
mouth of High Wassee River on Tennessee River, including an island opposite the mouth of High Wassee.  Sealed 17 July 1794.

Page 252     No. 55
John Sevier - 1000 acres in Middle District on the north side of
Tennessee River, on the east side of John Hardins survey of No. 2127,
adjoining Isaac Taylor.  Sealed 10 July 1788.

Page 254     No. 140
Peter Kirkendall - 900 acres in Greene County on Sinking Creek - Warrant
No. 2327, entered 4 December 1779 and No. 2526, entered 8 April 1780.
Sealed 13 December 1798.


Page 257     No. 1371
Westen Williams - 100 acres on Nolichucky River on Puncheon Camp Creek,
adjoining Nathan Carter - for 50 shillings per 100 acres.  Sealed 9
December 1795.


Page 259     No. 1252
James Robinson - 200 acres in Greene County on Ainton's Fork of Lick
Creek, adjoining David Hughes.  Sealed 29 July 1793.


Page 260     No. 1229
Richard David - 200 acres on Lick Creek, adjoining George Martin, Cox,
James Wheeler.  Sealed 12 January 1793.


Page 263     No. 1424
Robert Gamble - 640 acres on Nolachucky River, adjoining Campbell, Robert
Carson, Thomas Temple, Widow Morrow, Andrew Russell, Frederick Whitten-
berger, George Crump, Alexander.  Entered 26 February 1778.  Sealed 8
June 1797.


Page 266     No. 850
Asahel Rawlings - 150 acres in Washington County between William Ritchies
land and Robert Stevensons and Elisha Haddons, James Robinsons, Parkins.
Sealed 18 May 1789.


Page 268     No. 848
Asahel Rawlings - 200 acres in Washington County on Limestone Fork of
Lick Creek, adjoining Elisha Haddon.  Sealed 18 May 1789.


Page 270     No. 849
Asahel Rawlings - land in Washington County on waters of Lick Creek,
including a spring at the east corner of Haddons land.  Sealed 18 May
1789.


Page 272     No. 1234
Thomas Wyatt - 328 acres in Greene County on Lick Creek, known by the
name of Alexanders Creek.  Sealed 12 July 1794.


Page 275     No. 1324
Robert Gordon - 25 acres on north side Nolachucky River, a branch of
Lick Creek, adjoining John Gilespie.  Sealed 4 February 1795.


Page 277     No. 1245
William Milbourn - 100 acres north side Nolachucky River on the head of
the Cedar Branch, adjoining James Delaney, George Gilespie, Reese.
Sealed 12 January 1793.


Page 278     No. 1332
William Galbreath - 400 acres on Tilmans Creek, adjoining John Malone,
Thomas Smith and Jacob Gist.  Sealed 27 April 1795.


Page 280     No. 1380
John Pearce - land in Greene County, adjoining Ephraim Wilson.  Sealed
20 July 1796.


Page 282     No. 922
Daniel Briton - 200 acres on Roaring Fork of Lick Creek.  Sealed 26
December 1791.

Page 284     No. 1375
Phillip Waggoner - 150 acres in Greene County, adjoining Matthias Hoover.
Sealed 20 July 1796.

Page 286     No. 1443
William Henderson - 150 acres in Greene County on Holley's Creek, adjoining David Robison. Entered 4 January 1781. Sealed 17 March 1801.

Page 287     No. 1442
William Henderson - 200 acres on Hendersons Creek on Holleys Creek,
adjoining David Robertson. Sealed 31 March 1801.

Page 289     No. 1438
John Allen - 200 acres on both sides Lick Creek, waters of Nolachucky
River. Sealed 2 December 1797.

Page 292     No. 1292
William Wilson - 200 acres on waters of Nolachucky River, adjoining Elias
Mackey. Sealed 17 July 1794.

Page 294     No. 493
Henry Reynolds - 300 acres in Washington County, adjoining Thomas Davis,
James McMurtrey. Sealed 10 November 1784.

Page 296     No. 1139
John Bowers - 200 acres on a branch of Lick Creek, known by the name of
Cedar Lick Branch, adjoining John Newman. Sealed 12 January 1793.

Page 298     No. 417
Curtis Williams - 98 acres in Washington County on Lick Creek, adjoining
Aaron Burleson Junr., John Guest, Fleming. Sealed 13 October 1783.

Page 300     No. 433
John Tinn - 150 acres on John Prises Branch of Lick Creek. Sealed 20
September 1787.

Page 302     No. 267
Robert Blackburn - 200 acres on Richland Creek, north side Nolachucky
River, adjoining Henry Farnsworth, Leeper, McKeehan. Sealed 20 September
1787.

Page 303     No. 261
George Brock - 211 acres north side Nolachucky River. Sealed 20
September 1787. Transcribed from Hardins Book.

Page 305     No. 161
John Loyd - 200 acres on a branch of Nolachucky River, adjoining Potters.
Sealed 20 September 1787. Transcribed from Hardins Book.

Page 307     No. 234
John Newman - 50 acres on Lick Creek, adjoining his former survey,
Francis Johnston. Sealed 20 September 1787. Transcribed from Hardins
Book.

Page 308     No. 253
John Newman - 100 acres on Lick Creek, adjoining his former survey,
Francis Johnstons and Tighs line. Sealed 20 September 1787. Tran-
scribed from Hardins Book.

Page 310     No. 229
John Newman - 640 acres on Lick Creek, adjoining Adam Starns, John Equrs.
Sealed 20 September 1787. Transcribed from Hardins Book.

Page 312    No. 159
Joseph Bullard - 3000 acres south side Holston River, opposite Loss Creek,
adjoining William Robison. Sealed 20 September 1787. Transcribed from
Hardins Book.

Page 313    No. 806
Joseph Bullard - 150 acres in Washington County on a branch near McCartneys
Mountain. Sealed 20 September 1787. Transcribed from Hardins Book.

Page 315    No. 160
Joseph Bullard - 1000 acres in Greene County on Beaver Dam Creek. Sealed
20 September 1787. Transcribed from Hardins Book.

Page 316    No. 171
Joseph Bullard - 100 acres south side Holston River. Sealed 20 September
1797. Transcribed from Hardins Book.

Page 318    No. 214
Joseph Bullard - 140 acres north side Lick Creek, adjoining Daniel Carter.
Sealed 20 September 1787. Transcribed from Hardins Book.

Page 320    No. 226
Joseph Bullard - 400 acres in Greene County on Beaver Dam Creek, adjoining his 1000 acre tract. Sealed 20 September 1787. From Hardins Book.

Page 321    No. 206
Joseph Bullard - 400 acres south side Holston River in Greene County,
including an island. Sealed 20 September 1787. From Hardins Book.

Page 323    No. 158
Joseph Bullard - 400 acres on a branch of Lick Creek, adjoining Daniel
Carter, Abraham Carter, Philiman Higgins, John Kees (McKees?), Jacob
Carter. Sealed 20 September 1787. Transcribed from Hardins Book.

Page 325    No. 11
James Lee - 218 acres in Greene County on Bent Creek near the creeks
head, south side Holston River in the Cany Valley, adjoining Brelam
Smith, George Evans, John Smith, William Horner. Sealed 17 November
1786. From Hardins Book.

Page 327    No. 197
David Rankin - 200 acres at the head of Stories Creek, adjoining Herralds.
Sealed 20 September 1787. From Hardins Book.

Page 329    No. 224
John McDonald - 400 acres north side Holston River on Richland Creek,
adjoining James McDonald. Sealed 20 September 1787. From Hardins Book.

Page 330    No. 46
Alexander McFarland - 200 acres known by the Meadows, adjoining Richard
Higgins. Sealed 1 September 1786. From Hardins Book.

Page 332    No. 190
Robert McNutt - 200 acres north side Holston River between mouth of
Richland Creek and Spring Creek, adjoining Robert Young. Sealed 20
September 1787. From Hardins Book.

Page 334    No. 265
John Blackburn - 400 acres on Long Creek, adjoining Andrew McPheron.
Sealed 20 September 1788. From Hardins Book.

Page 336    No. 49
Joseph Hardin - 400 acres on Big Gap Creek about 2 miles below his upper

entry of 600 acres, adjoining Benjamin Goodin, Ninian Steel, Jacob Carter and foot of Bays Mountain. Sealed 1 November 1786. Transcribed from Hardins Book.

Page 337      No. 131
Joseph Hardin - 600 acres on both sides Big Gap Creek, beginning on a spur of Bays Mountain. Sealed 1 November 1786. From Hardins Book.

Page 339      No. 417
Joseph Hardin - 200 acres on Loss Creek, south side Holston River. Sealed 20 September 1787. From Hardins Book.

Page 340      No. 194
John and Joseph Hardin Junr. - 300 acres on Flat Creek, north side Holston River. Sealed 20 September 1787. From Hardins Book.

Page 342      No. 186
John Hardin - 200 acres south side Holston River below Turleys survey. Sealed 20 September 1787. From Hardins Book.

Page 343      No. 814
Joseph Hardin - 200 acres on Roaring Fork of Lick Creek, adjoining himself, Dean. Sealed 10 December 1789. From Hardins Book.

Page 345      No. 58
Joseph Hardin - 3000 acres north side Tennessee River, Middle District, adjoining Swift Creek, Isaac Taylor. Sealed 10 July 1788. From Hardins Book.

Page 347      No. 4
John Harden - 1000 acres east side Tennessee River on Swift Creek, Middle District, between Samuel Sample and Joseph Hardin, adjoining Isaac Taylor. Sealed 10 July 1788. From Hardins Book.

Page 349      No. 164
John Hardin - 100 acres on Roseberry Creek, north side Holston River. Sealed 20 September 1787. From Hardins Book.

Page 350      No. 163
John Harden - 400 acres on a ridge that divides Holston and French Broad Waters, adjoining John Finton. Sealed 20 September 1787. From Hardins Book.

Page 352      No. 1363
James Pickens - 200 acres on Stony Creek, viz Lick Creek. Sealed 2 December 1795.

Page 354      No. 456
Nathaniel Davis - 200 acres on Lick Creek between Pytoms and Pruith, adjoining John Woolsey, William Pruith, Martin Pruith. Sealed 20 September 1787.

Page 356      No. 1376
John Allison - 100 acres on waters of Nolachucky River, to (James Allison ? in description), adjoining Joseph Brown. Sealed 20 September 1796.

Page 358      No. 1370
James Pickens - 200 acres on Lick Creek, adjoining Daniel Slavens. Sealed 9 December 1795.

Page 359      No. 1383
William McAmish - 200 acres on head of Roaring Fork of Lick Creek, adjoining Dunn. Sealed 20 July 1796.

Page 361    No. 1392
Abraham Hines - 100 acres adjoining Drury Morrison.  Sealed 2 December
1796.

Page 363    No. 1361
John Mallon and Zachariah Casteel - 200 acres on the waters of Lick Creek,
adjoining Daniel Carter.  Sealed 12 November 1795.

Page 365    No. 1433
Elizabeth Cameron - 260 acres in Greene County, adjoining Andrew English,
Alexander Beatty.  Sealed 11 April 1780.

Page 367    No. 1434
Alexander Beatty - 80 acres on the waters of Lick Creek, adjoining James
McBay, James Condry.  Entered 6 March 1780.  Sealed 12 April 1797.

Page 369    No. 1090
Alexander Galbreath - 400 acres on Sinking Creek, adjoining Nicholas
Hayse.  Sealed 1790.

Page 371    No. 1431
Thomas Stanfield - 150 acres in Greene County, adjoining James McFeran,
George Harmon.  Sealed 30 June 1797.

Page 373    No. 41
Thomas Isbell - 100 acres on waters of Lick Creek.  Sealed 1 November
1786.

Page 374    No. 1253
Jonathan Trebit - 100 acres on Meadow Creek, now called Sinking Creek,
northside Nolachucky River - adjoining Jonathan Evans, William McGill.
Sealed 29 July 1793.  This grant was altered by an order of Greene
County, 27 March 1801.

Page 376    No. 1226
Daniel Nelson - 200 acres on south side Nolachucky River, adjoining
Jonathan Nelson, George Wells.  Sealed 12 January 1793.

Page 379    No. 143
Daniel Nelson - 200 acres - 18 February 1795 - Certificate of Alteration
of the courses of this grant at Raleigh, North Carolina, by order of
Greene County Court, 30 July 1805.


Last two grants:

No. 491
State of North Carolina - Andrew Simpson - 20 September 1787; Book 24;
Page 38 - 240 acres land south side Lick Creek, adjoining John Gass,
Andrew Mitchell, Alexander Williams, Claudius Bailey.  Registered 2
January 1802.

No. 1093
State of North Carolina - Phillip Babb - 19 July 1793; Book 20; Page 744
- 100 acres on a branch of Lick Creek.  Registered 3 October 1842.

INDEX

ABSTRACTS OF NORTH CAROLINA LAND GRANTS
Compiled by
Sandy Hodges
Ft. Worth, Tex.

#